It
Might
As Well
Be Spring

It Might As Well Be Spring

A Musical Autobiography

*Margaret Whiting
and Will Holt*

WILLIAM MORROW AND COMPANY, INC.
New York

Copyright © 1987 by Margaret Whiting

Permissions, constituting a continuation of the copyright
page, are listed on pages 379–380.

Library of Congress Cataloging-in-Publication Data

Whiting, Margaret.
It might as well be spring.

Includes index.
1. Whiting, Margaret.   2. Singers—United States—
Biography.   I. Holt, Will.   II. Title.
ML420.W49A3   1987   784.5′0092′4   [B]   86-18163
ISBN 0-688-06406-X

Printed in the United States of America

First Edition

1 2 3 4 5 6 7 8 9 10

BOOK DESIGN BY RICHARD ORIOLO

I dedicate this book to the people who have
touched my life and hopefully made it better:

My father, Richard, who showed me the rules of the
game, taught me all the words and music,
and guided my way.

My mother, Eleanore, with her great sense of humor
and her most marvelous way of facing life. I thank
her for teaching me how to become a survivor.

My Aunt Margaret, who showed me all the tricks of
the trade. I wish every singer could have a
teacher like her.

Barbara, my funny, talented, and bright little
sister, who's just as charming as the day we met!

My daughter, Debbie, who turned out to be a perfect
daughter—and the best friend that anyone
could want.

To all the songwriters in my life: Jule Styne,
Frank Loesser, Uncle Jerry, Harry Warren, Harold Arlen,
Johnny Meyer, and dear Uncle Leo Robin. I thank
them all for their guidance and support.

To Ginger and Johnny Mercer: Ginger for her loyalty
and great friendship to me always—and Johnny, for being
my mentor.

To Lou Busch, Debbie's father, for his impeccable taste in
music, and from whom I learned so much.

To Tex Arnold, my wonderful conductor-pianist-arranger, thanks for
all the beautiful music you've given me.

To Jack Wrangler, who gave me such encouragement with this book
and who lived through a great deal of it with me.
My best friend, my love.

Thank you all . . .

ACKNOWLEDGMENTS

To Jay Garon, my agent, who said to me one day, "You have a book in you, and I know just the person to write it with you—Will Holt." I thank him for his wisdom and help and understanding.

To Will Holt. No book has ever been in better hands. I thank him for his patience, humor, his gentle guidance—and for getting me through the tough parts. I couldn't have done it without him.

To Lisa Drew, my editor, who wanted this book for seventeen years and kept after me until the manuscript was in her hands. I thank her for her dedication, her friendship, and all her help in bringing this about.

To David Means, her associate, who was so helpful in every way.

To Michael Kirker of ASCAP, for his friendship and assistance in research for the book.

To Ruth Mackin, for her marvelous typing, the Bill Evans music, and the terrific coffee.

To Photosphere, for all their photocopying.

To Robert Nikora, for his discography.

To Eric Steven Jacobs, for the wonderful jacket photograph.

Without them, and many others, this book never could have happened.

Contents

1

Welcome

My nervous breakdown lasted exactly one hour (which was all my mother, Eleanore, would have allowed), and it started with seven producers, a surplus of cleaning help, and a bunny.

First, the cleaning crisis. I have a cleaning lady, Elizabeth, who keeps my apartment as spotless as any in a commercial. But she does have a problem. She is allergic to dust and to cleaning products, which makes her job a little difficult since she has to wear a mask at all times. And also gloves. To watch Elizabeth at work is a bit like watching Trapper John bearing down on an appendectomy. But Elizabeth is good and she is thorough—and, unfortunately, at the time, she was in need of a two-week vacation. So she had sent me Olga, a huge, strapping woman whom I immediately thought of as Big-Foot. Big-Foot was also thorough, but she, too, had a problem. She needed constant instruction. She had this unnerving habit of entering a room every ten minutes and booming out, *"Now* what?"

I had a *third* cleaner. Don. He was a very nice guy who was being thrown out of his apartment, who had been robbed and needed money, who was having problems with his family in Virginia. I felt sorry for him, and so I said, "Oh, come, clean. Clean anything." So he was. He was cleaning the bathroom.

At this time I was also preparing to go to Washington for a singing engagement. I don't rehearse like other people. I tend to walk around the room, straightening flowers and moving ashtrays—and also cleaning. I have a very clean apartment. Sometimes while rehearsing, I go into the library to take a phone call—or answer the doorbell. But I will come back in at the end of a phrase, without missing a beat, which never ceases to astound Tex Arnold, who has been my musical director for nine years.

The man I am living with—and have been for the past nine years—is a charming man twenty years my junior, who is enormously talented as an actor. He is also a former porn star. Yes, you heard it right. Jack Wrangler is his name, and he has been Jack in *Jack and Jill* and the devil in *The Devil and Miss Jones: Part II*, and he is also very gifted as a writer and director—which brings us to the second crisis.

He had written and directed several acts for me—one, a tribute to Ethel Merman, who liked it so much she came four times. The others were ones I had played all over the country. Now, we had put together a show featuring the songs of Johnny Mercer entitled *I Remember Johnny*, and with Julius La Rosa, Marlene VerPlanck, and a newcomer named Carol Woods, we had tried it out at the 92nd Street Y Lyrics and Lyricists series in New York City. It had been, as they say, boffo, and now seven producers were after the property, and it was up to me to decide which producer would be the right one.

And then there was Bunny. Or, more formally, Eddie Rabbit. Bunny is Jack's rabbit, and we have had rabbits ever since the first one, who was named Jump-Jump. Bunny is wonderful, and he has the run of our apartment, and he gets in no one's way, and it would be a terrible thing for me to blame a nervous breakdown on a rabbit. But that's how it goes.

Tex was playing the piano and I was singing:

"Will I ever find the boy in my mind
The one who is my ideal . . ."

The vacuum cleaner was humming along in B-flat, when the doorbell rang C-natural and I strolled to the door, still singing, to be greeted by a registered letter from one of the producers, who would like an answer. I thanked the messenger, signed his sheet, closed the door, and returned to the living room.

". . . just around the corner waiting for me—
Will I recognize . . ."

The phone rang a blurry F-sharp and Jack called to me, "It's Alvin on the phone and he must talk to you." Alvin Deutsch is my lawyer who was handling negotiations on the Mercer show.

". . . That no other eyes reveal?
Or will I pass him by and never even know that he is—"

"Hello, Alvin. . . ."
"Margaret, you have got to make up your mind."
This was all very new to me. I had to make the right move. Get the right producer. It was important. I didn't want to hurt anyone. I never wanted to hurt anyone. I didn't want to hurt Hubbell Robinson, my first husband. That's why I married him. I didn't want to say no.
"Alvin, I am trying to make up my mind, but I can't be sure. They are all so nice."
"Margaret, you are going to have to say no to six of them, and yes to one of them."
I repeated that, as though repeating it made me efficient. "Yes— no to six and yes to one."
"What?" Alvin's voice was justifiably perplexed.
"I'm just reminding myself to make a note," I said vaguely.
"Oh," he said. "Well, Margaret, six people are going to be disappointed. But think of it this way. One person is going to be ecstatic."
He rang off. I started back to the living room and the piano.

"*Now* what?" Big-Foot accosted me.

"Oh . . . clean the bathroom."

"Someone *is* cleaning the bathroom," Big-Foot said.

"Yes, that's right. Well, how about the kitchen? Is anybody cleaning the kitchen?"

"I'll need some Pledge," Big-Foot said.

"Uh-huh," I mumbled, and went in to meet Tex at bar twenty-four, second chorus of "My Ideal." We were rehearsing a medley of songs by my father, Richard Whiting. It was at this point that I realized Bunny didn't have any paper in his litter basket, so I began tearing up the *New York Post. Shred-shred-shred.*

> *"Every morning, every evening,*
> *Ain't we got fun . . ."*

Shred-shred-shred. I went into the study. What was the note I was supposed to be writing myself? I couldn't remember.

Don, the cleaning man, found me in the den.

"Margaret, I called my family in Virginia. . . ."

"Mmm, that's nice. . . ."

"And they don't want me."

"Mmm, that's too bad." Where was some notepaper? What was the note I was supposed to be writing myself?

"But the real reason is—I am involved in a religion down there where you sit on top of a mountain and think."

That sounded good to me.

"But then I'd think about how my family doesn't want me," Don continued.

Jack saved me. "I'm going to the bank," he announced from the corridor.

> *". . . The rent's unpaid, dear.*
> *We haven't a car.*
> *But anyway, dear,*
> *We'll stay as we are . . ."*

"I want *my* money in cash," Big-Foot bellowed from the kitchen. Jack looked at me. "Who's *that?*"

"That's Big—" I stopped myself. "That is . . . she is . . . a big help. She is cleaning. Elizabeth sent her."

"I thought Don was cleaning."

"He is. She is helping him clean. Oh, I need to give Bunny some more paper." I started shredding again.

"You just gave him paper," Jack reminded me.

"Not enough." *Shred-shred-shred.* "I have to make up my mind. I don't know. Fran and Barry? They seemed to change concept." *Shred-shred-shred.*

". . . *Even if we owe the grocer,*
Ain't we got fun.
Tax collector getting closer . . .

"Dick and Maurice? I don't know. And Lester?" *Shred-shred-shred.* "I don't know. Alvin says I've got to make up my mind."

"Not before I get back from the bank."

"Oh, are you going to the bank?" *Shred-shred-shred.*

"Margaret, stop shredding the paper."

"I don't know what else to do. I can't make up my mind. I've got to go over the lyrics. There are four new songs. . . ."

"*Now* what?" Big-Foot had finished the kitchen.

"I don't know '*now* what,' " I said, my voice starting to rise. "Go find something to clean. Clean Jack's room. He's out of it now."

"I was just asking," Big-Foot said, hurt.

"Don't ask. Just clean. Please don't anybody ask me anything!

". . . *In the meantime,*
In between time,
Ain't we got fun."

Jack disappeared out the door. Big-Foot went into Jack's room. Tex . . . into the piano, maybe. Suddenly I was all alone. I felt like a little girl. I didn't want to make any of these grown-up decisions. When I was a kid, my mother, Eleanore, had made all the moves. And my father. When my father died, Johnny Mercer had taken over his role. "Here, kid, sing this." And I sang. And I became a star. I sold millions of records. And then there were plenty of people to make decisions for me. Agents and managers. And husbands.

And always Eleanore.

Here I was, sixty, and I did not want to grow up. I did not want to make decisions. I did not want to say no to anyone. I wanted everyone to love me. Everyone *did* love me. I had worked very hard getting everyone to love me.

That's when the doorbell rang.

"I've come about the eviction," the man at the door said.

"What eviction!" I gasped. What had happened? Had I forgotten to pay the rent? I could hear Eleanore saying to me, "You see how easily people can lose their minds? . . ."

"The lady in 4-C. She's being evicted and wants to know if you'd like to buy her sable cape."

"If she's got a sable cape, how come she's being evicted?" I wanted to know.

He shrugged. "Beats me. She just asked me to ask you."

"Well, thank you, but no," I said, already feeling guilty because I hadn't helped the woman out. Maybe I should buy a sable cape I don't need. Oh come on, Margaret, I thought. Enough is enough. Eleanore would not have approved of this behavior. It's time to get out. Time to get on that train and go to Washington, read a book, hole up, get ready for the opening. Everything will work out. But just leave—now.

And I did. And, of course, it all became very clear. I knew exactly whom I wanted to produce the Mercer show. I rang up Alvin from Washington and told him. And I learned my lyrics. And the opening went fine.

After all that, I started to laugh. Laughter had gotten me through a lot. Right from the very beginning. The Whiting house had always been a little crazy. What was it Frank Loesser had said as Johnny Mercer walked in one door and Jerome Kern out the other? Ah yes:

"The Whiting household is a series of exits and entrances."

So, welcome to it.

2

That's Entertainment: A Real-Life Backstage Musical

My parents' love story reads like a script from a 20th Century-Fox musical—the kind Tyrone Power, Alice Faye, and Betty Grable made back in the thirties and forties. In fact, when I first saw one of those movies, I thought, Hey, wait a minute, I've been here before! However, in the case of Richard and Eleanore Whiting there are a few differences. No one would ever have mistaken my father for Tyrone Power! Tyrone Power couldn't play the piano.

Daddy started out as a song plugger in Detroit. He had grown up in Peoria, Illinois, a typical Middle American town where there was a piano in every parlor. In my father's family, everyone played. His mother was an accomplished musician, and his father, a real-estate broker, tinkered around with every kind of musical instrument he could find. At night, they all gathered around the piano and sang the songs of the day, the Victorian ditties that were so popular then. My father, who was born in 1891, learned to play solely by ear,

without ever having a music lesson. As a school kid he would perform for an admiring group of school chums who included Charles
Correll (of *Amos 'n' Andy* fame), Fulton Sheen, and Fibber McGee.
My father played all the tunes everyone hummed on verandas and
sang to the stars. It was a very nice existence. Middle-class, Middle
West. Absolutely American apple-pie normal. Except for the fact
that Daddy was stagestruck. Somehow, when he reached high-school
age, he persuaded his family to let him attend Harvard Military
School in Los Angeles, where his whole family *moved* until he finished.

When Daddy first went to Hollywood, in 1905, it was no more
than a village. Six years before, the Hollywood Board of Trustees
had felt the need to pass municipal ordinances. Among its prohibi-
tions were:

   –the sale of liquor except by pharmacists on prescription.
   –the riding of bicycles, tricycles, or velocipedes on sidewalks—
    particularly Mr. Whitley's and Mr. Beveridge's sidewalks [which
    were the only ones in town at the time].
   –the driving of horses, cattle, or mules through the streets of
    Hollywood in bands or herds of more than two hundred, or
    more than two thousand sheep, goats, or hogs, unless accom-
    panied by competent men in charge.
   –the operation or maintenance of slot machines, card machines,
    or other mechanical devices in the city of Hollywood, for money
    or other articles of value, depending on chance or hazard.

After Daddy finished with high school, he started to haunt the
theaters. In 1910, southern California didn't have any movie studios,
but there were theaters—Oliver Morosco's Burbank Theater and the
old Los Angeles Orpheum. Daddy found himself a "partner," a kid
named Mickey Neilan, and they put together an act of songs and
patter—the patter courtesy of *Joe Miller's Joke Book*, the songs courtesy of my father and Neilan. Their only problem was that neither
one of them had a voice that would carry beyond the third row.
(Later, when Daddy was working with Ethel Merman in a Broadway
show called *Take a Chance*, he told my mother in tones of awe, "You

should hear Merman's voice. It carries to the very last row in the balcony. And that's before she starts singing!")

In traditional theatrical fashion, Whiting and Neilan persisted. The manager of the Orpheum let them rehearse on his bare stage, where they practiced projecting. Daily, the manager would cry, "Louder!" and daily, Daddy and Mickey would valiantly attempt to increase their volume, but, frankly, both had voices only mice could appreciate. However, Daddy was nothing if not a realist. He was aware that Whiting and Neilan were not going to make the big time. (Actually, they *did*. Daddy as a composer, and Mickey as Marshall Neilan, a distinguished motion-picture director.)

My father just missed the first influx of movie studios. In 1911, David Horsley of the Nestor Film Company of Bayonne, New Jersey, was shown the former Blondeay Tavern on the northwest corner of Sunset and Gower. The small roadhouse, suffering from Hollywood's recent liquor prohibition ordinance, had a barn, corral, twelve small single-room structures built along a fence, and a five-room bungalow. Horsley leased the tavern for thirty dollars a month and used the corral for horses that appeared in westerns, the barn for props, the small rooms for dressing areas, and the bungalow for his executive offices. A baggage car carrying three cameras, chemicals, and some props arrived in Hollywood the following Monday, was unloaded overnight, and the company was ready to shoot. Three complete pictures were supposed to be filmed each week.

By that time, Daddy had returned with the family to Peoria, where he started to watch the rejection slips pile up. But he was a very determined man. I can still see him—short, mild-looking, gentle, wearing glasses. But he had a strength in his face, especially around the mouth. There was a determination in that mouth. That mouth was determined to be a songwriter! Somehow, he persuaded his parents to finance the publication of some of his songs just to see what they would look like in print. Apparently they looked just fine, because they brought him to the attention of Jerome Remick, the veteran music publisher, who lived in Detroit. (He lived in Detroit so he could keep track of his cows, since he also kept a dairy farm.) Daddy journeyed to Detroit for an interview with Mr. Remick, who bought three of his songs for fifty dollars apiece and then offered him a job as professional manager of his office at fifteen dollars a week. Daddy returned to Peoria to think it over. There he found three telegrams from Remick, the last one raising the offer to twenty-five dollars a week. Daddy accepted, on the condition that he could write songs on the side. Before his first year in Detroit was up, he not only had his name on several pop songs but was earning an extra fifty dollars a week as a pianist with six native Hawaiians in a hotel orchestra. However, this was not all clear profit. He had to spend a dollar a week on brown makeup in order to try to look like a real islander.

In the years before World War I, vaudeville was king—New York was its center—the movies were some little upstart—but vaudeville was Theater. And Theater was heaven on earth. Grand. Sumptuous. Glamorous. Even in Detroit. The stars came to Detroit. Nora Bayes and Marian Harris sang ballads there. Sophie Tucker and Belle Baker sang "character songs," which were faintly racy and daring numbers. Al Jolson and Eddie Cantor worked in blackface, as did Bert Williams (who was black to begin with). And they sang "Mammy" and "When the Midnight Choo-Choo Leaves for Alabam."

Novelty songs. "Mammy" songs. Character songs. It was a very naïve period in American life when my father appeared on the pop music scene. He surveyed this scene and proceeded to write songs he hoped would fit the stars' personalities. As Remick's professional manager he was in a wonderful position to meet all these performers. While performing the latest songs from the Remick catalogue, he would let them hear some of his own songs. He played "I Wonder Where My Loving Man Has Gone" for Sophie Tucker and she grabbed it. This was his first big song, and he had the thrill of hearing her perform it at our local vaudeville house.

Flower songs came in. So Daddy and Ray Egan wrote "When It's Tulip Time in Holland," and with the royalty check from that, he bought the Steinway grand on which he wrote so many of his big songs in the years to come. The same Steinway sits in my living room now—continuing the tradition of the piano in the parlor, you might say.

Enter my mother, Eleanore.

And her sister Margaret.

These two young girls were ready to crash through the gates of show business. My Aunt Margaret had already been performing at charity and church affairs around Detroit. Al Green, the leader of the Temple Theater orchestra, suggested she think seriously about going on the stage and advised her to look up Dick Whiting, manager of Remick Music Publishers, who might have the right kind of songs for Margaret to sing, might even help her get her act together. At seventeen, Eleanore was already managing eighteen-year-old Margaret's career.

The first meeting between my father and mother occurred at the Temple Theater. The stage show was devoted to promoting his new song, "Tulip Time in Holland." Following the presentation, Daddy walked up the aisle to the rear of the theater. And there was Eleanore. They met. Seventeen-year-old Eleanore, twenty-four-year-old Richard, and eighteen-year-old Margaret. It was love at first sight.

But not between my mother and father. It was Richard and Margaret who fell for each other. And Richard agreed to write some special material for her. Margaret Youngblood (soon to be shortened to Young) had a fine single vaudeville turn that Richard Whiting had fashioned, and it was Christmastime when she stepped out for her first real stage appearance. Eleanore was standing in the wings holding a glass of water and *managing* things.

The appearance was a solid success, and after the first week, the Temple Theater owners offered to book Margaret in their Rochester, New York, theater. But the girls wanted to be home with their family for Christmas. The following year, Margaret did make it to Rochester, and then on to New York City. The three of them—Richard, Eleanore, and Margaret—were always together. Eleanore was in awe of Richard, hardly aware that she was also in love with him. There was no jealousy. Eleanore thought it only natural that Dick had fallen in love with her wonderful big sister. Dick was continuing to write successful songs. For Jolson he wrote "Mammy's Little Coal Black Rose," "Where the Black-Eyed Susans Grow," and a lovely little knockout entitled "They Made It Twice As Nice As Paradise—and They Called It Dixieland," which wasn't about the South at all, but rather about a sedate tearoom in Detroit, run by two lovely ladies who catered parties for Daddy's friends when they played Detroit. (Daddy was so fond of Dixieland, when I came along he almost named me Dixie. Fortunately, Eleanore interceded.)

Along came World War I. America entered the war in 1917, inspiring a rash of patriotic songs. Daddy was right in there with "So Dress Up Your Dollars in Khaki and Help Win Democracy's Fight." And then he wrote, with Ray Egan, "Till We Meet Again."

When Daddy and Ray wrote that song, neither one liked it much. They crumpled up the paper and threw it in the wastebasket, where a secretary fished the song out, played a few bars on the piano, and then handed it to Mr. Remick, who hummed a few more bars (I can see the film now) and then pressed a buzzer, summoning my father:

REMICK: Dick, what is this song?

WHITING: That—oh, sir, that is nothing.

REMICK: On the contrary, that song is very good. Sit down. Play it through.
    (WHITING does)

REMICK: I have it! We'll enter it in the war-song contest next week at the Michigan Theater. What is the title?

WHITING: *"Auf Wiedersehen."*

REMICK: Hmmm. That's German. Not a popular title for a war-song contest. What does it mean in English?

WHITING: Till we meet again.
    (MUSIC up)

REMICK: That's it! That's it! We'll call it "Till We Meet Again."

The reaction to the song was fit for any backstage musical. Introduced at the Michigan Theater in Detroit, the song was a sensation. People stood up and shouted. It had to be repeated. Within the next week there were five thousand requests for copies and within a month, the entire nation was singing it. Today, the song has sold over seventeen million copies, more than any other popular song.

And that brings me to a point about pop music. Songs tend to define an era. When you hear eight bars of "Alexander's Ragtime Band," you get the flavor of an entire period. "Till We Meet Again" still conjures up a time of heartfelt leave-taking, hasty romances, the enormous promise of an America developing into a world power.

The songs really do delineate the popular culture of the time. "Till We Meet Again" was such a song for the First World War.

At the end of that war, Daddy was in an enviable position. He was the top man in his business—age twenty-eight. In 1920, Nora Bayes came to Detroit. Mr. Remick instructed my father to sell her a song. Around 5:00 P.M., after the matinee, Daddy arrived at the theater where she was performing and was ushered into her dressing room.

Miss Bayes was resting. "Richard, darling." She held out her hand and he took it. "I understand from Jerome you have written a song for me."

"Yes, Miss Bayes."

"Call me Nora. And please sit down and play it for me."

Dressing rooms—like parlors—always had a piano in those days. (Nowadays you're lucky not to be dressing in the kitchen.) Daddy played a couple of bars and Miss Bayes said, "How exquisite!" She picked up the music and started to sing along. "A great song, Richard. We'll put it in the act tonight. I'll introduce it and you can play for me!"

My father—after those abortive efforts in Los Angeles—had a horror of performing; it always made him terribly nervous. But if Nora Bayes wanted him to play, Jerome Remick would insist he play. Daddy smiled very weakly and consented. I imagine he took a couple of belts before showtime and then stood there in the wings, shaking, while Nora Bayes (on next to closing, as befitted a great star) made her introduction.

"Ladies and gentlemen, tonight you are going to have the extraordinary privilege of hearing for the first time the most glorious song in the world—with the added attraction of hearing its composer at the piano. May I introduce—Detroit's own Richard Whiting!" *Tremble, tremble, tremble.* My father crept to the keyboard, sat down, and began to play. There was no reason to be afraid: The song was immediately successful. In those days, audiences in vaudeville houses loved to discover new material. That night there were cries of "Sing it again!," which Miss Bayes graciously did. Later, back in the dressing room, she said to Daddy, "Have Jerome print up the sheet music. I'll record it as soon as I can."

And she did. Which was how "Japanese Sandman" came into the world. You see how easy it is to get a hit song—in a backstage musical?

Following the script, my father and Margaret Young grew apart. She was more concerned with her career, which took her all over the country, and my father began to concentrate on a serious career as a popular composer. He had a wonderful reputation as a song-writer. George Gershwin, who was just starting out, came to my father and sang him some of his early creations. My father, realizing he was in the presence of genius, encouraged Gershwin, and even gave him a job at Remick to help him get started.

My father went to New York two or three times a year, which was where Eleanore and Margaret were based. During this period, my mother, who was used to *managing* things, thought that Richard Whiting's career would soar if only he wasn't so far away. There were any number of lyric writers who were dying to work with him. She began focusing on *his* career, and soon he began focusing on *her*. To end this backstage musical happily, they were married in 1923.

And that's when I came on the scene.

Music up.

3

Hooray for Hollywood

Eleanore wanted to get my father out of Detroit. But he loved it there. He could write songs, and he could play golf. Eleanore looked at him, and saw that he had plans to be a serious *golfer*. (He won every tournament he entered.) She felt he was too talented a composer for that. Ray Egan, his collaborator in Detroit, was a serious *dreamer*. From time to time, Daddy would go to Chicago to write with Gus Kahn. Eleanore wanted more than that. If only Daddy would leave Detroit. But he was very comfortable. Detroit was like a piece of Grand Rapids furniture. So comfortable to sink into. And so hard to get out of! My father had bought a new house so that his mother, Blossom, could move in with us. The two women got along very well, but Blossom could not understand Eleanore's drive. Eleanore, the businesswoman, was well aware that all that golf and no productive song writing had almost used up Daddy's savings. Finally, she persuaded him to give New York a whirl. Daddy was a terribly shy man.

Thank God he had somebody like my mother to help him, or I might have ended up taking in washing in Flint, Michigan. She had heard that the lyricist Buddy DeSylva needed a melody writer because his former collaborator, George Gershwin, had decided to team up with brother Ira. She kept urging my father to get in touch with DeSylva, but he was too nervous to make the call. Her big mistake, she always felt, was not calling up DeSylva herself. DeSylva began a collaboration with Lew Brown and Ray Henderson. Under his guidance, the team made millions, and my father's shyness caused him to lose out on one of the greatest chances of his life.

Not that Daddy was such a slouch. In the next couple of years, he wrote a big hit with Gus Kahn, "Ukelele Lady" (Hawaiian songs were still very big) and a little number with Ray Egan called "Sleepy Time Gal." Oh, yes, and "Honey." *And* "Horses, Horses, Horses," beloved by all racetrack devotees. *And* "Breezin' Along with the Breeze." But in Eleanore's opinion, that was all Daddy was doing —just breezing along with the breeze. So, when talking pictures came out with Jolson in *The Jazz Singer* the call went out to songwriters everywhere: "Go West, Young Man" to the West Coast. And go they did. There was such a demand for product at the studios, my mother said, with perhaps just a touch of exasperation, "Richard, go east—or go west, but just *go!*" Daddy got an offer from Paramount to write with a young lyricist, Leo Robin, who had collaborated with Vincent Youmans on the Broadway show *Hit the Deck*. He would have to leave immediately for the Coast. Needless to say, he had my mother's blessing. My grandmother, Blossom, my mother, and I would stay in Detroit until summoned.

Leo Robin and my father had never met. Leo was a Jewish boy from Pittsburgh who had graduated from Carnegie Tech, come to New York, and auditioned for music publishers until he had landed the job writing with Youmans. He was a painfully shy man—like my father. They were supposed to travel to Los Angeles together, my father coming from Detroit, Leo from New York. It was arranged that they meet in Chicago. Neither had the temerity to approach the other. Both sat in the lobby of the Sherman Hotel, eyeing strangers nervously, until Leo had the bright idea of paging my father. When my father got up to answer the page, Leo followed him.

"Excuse me," Leo said, writhing with embarrassment, "but, by any chance, do you *happen* to be Richard Whiting?"

"Oh," said my father, nervously, "*you* must be Leo Robin."

"I am, I am," Leo answered happily. And thus a collaboration was born. They boarded the *Super Chief* together, stayed at the Roosevelt Hotel together, and were inseparable friends for the rest of my father's life.

Their first assignment was to write for Maurice Chevalier's American picture debut *Innocents of Paris*. While they were collaborating, they both discovered they had a fondness for smelly cheese and crunchy apples. It helped them think. One morning, as they were working and munching away, the telephone rang. It was the desk downstairs, announcing that M. Chevalier was on his way up. The two shy men, never having met the star, were in a panic and hurriedly tidied up the room, stuffing the cheese into a drawer. The buzzer sounded. My father nervously opened the door. And there he was, Chevalier, with that cheery smile and twinkle in the eye. Whiting and Robin introduced themselves, and Chevalier entered the room. The two writers offered him a chair, offered him a drink. He sat. He drank. Conversation immediately palled. Then Chevalier started sniffing the air. Leo and my father looked at each other uncomfortably. The Gallic nose wrinkled, and then Chevalier cried out triumphantly, "Camembert! I smell some wonderful Camembert." Sheepishly, my father took out the cheese from its hiding place, offered some to Chevalier, who accepted it happily, and that broke the ice. Then they played him the song they had been working on, one that forever became identified with Chevalier.

Every little breeze
Seems to whisper "Louise" . . .

And nobody else ever sang it with that incredible Chevalier swagger.

My father loved California. And why not? He got up every morning to a golf game in the sparkling California weather, then on to the studio, where he worked on one musical assignment after another. My mother sold the house in Detroit, and early in February 1929, the furniture was put in storage and the family joined my father. We lived in the Roosevelt hotel for a few weeks and then moved into a home in Hollywood. And just to show how good a golfer Daddy was—one morning, the doorbell rang. My father answered the door and there stood his caddy, who had hitchhiked all the way from Detroit to be with him!

The only blight on this rosy scene occurred that fall when the crash of 1929 wiped out some of my father's investments. Aunt Mag came to the rescue and contributed money to the family. But the wolf was not at the door. I had to laugh when I saw the movie based on Gus Kahn's life, *I'll See You in My Dreams*, and it showed Danny Thomas, as Gus, driving a milk wagon down the street during the Depression. Milk wagon! Gus Kahn was earning a thousand dollars a week at the time, and that was just what the music publishers paid him. All these songwriters had not only their royalties that accrued from their song hits, but they had their studio jobs besides. Rest assured, none of these men ever stood in breadlines.

What did happen was that my father got an offer to write with Oscar Hammerstein in New York. And my mother got pregnant. The show, *Free for All* was a flop, but my sister, Barbara, was a big hit. Daddy returned to Hollywood, vowing never to leave again. But in 1932, Buddy DeSylva lured him east to write the tunes for a show he was producing called *Humpty Dumpty*.

Well, *Humpty Dumpty* had a great fall. In Pittsburgh. The sound of that flop could be heard all the way to California, where Daddy fled. His nerves were not able to deal with the rigors of the Broadway musical. Only with a great deal of pleading from the very persuasive DeSylva did he return.

DeSylva knew he had a good show there, somewhere. Perhaps a little rewriting, a little more savvy in the musical numbers, a little more daring.

"Come on, kids," he exhorted his troops. "Take a chance!" Of course, that became the new title of the show. The revitalized *Take a Chance* became a big hit, and Ethel Merman, who had been in the hapless *Humpty Dumpty*, wowed 'em with the song "Eadie Was a

Lady" and "You're an Old Smoothie," which she sang with Jack Haley.

But Daddy had had it. He returned to Los Angeles, where he didn't have to go so far for a good game of golf.

L.A. was paradise in those days.

Bread was a nickel a loaf. Cigarettes eleven cents a pack, eggs twenty-six cents a dozen, the round-trip railroad fare to San Francisco fourteen dollars. A trip to Hawaii on the Matson Line cost seventy-five dollars, a 1935 Nash cost just six hundred dollars more than that. A nine-room Italian mansion on Larchmont was being offered for $7,500. The first drive-in opened on Pico and Westwood, its billboard promising customers they could sit in their car, see and hear TALKING PICTURES on the world's largest screen. Hamburger stands opened with all the flair of a Hollywood premiere, and on August 21 Benny Goodman brought his orchestra to the Palomar Ballroom at Vermont and Second. The admission was forty cents, and cocktails were a quarter.

It was an historic evening. The band, discouraged by their cross-country reception, played a couple of apathetic sets to a listless crowd. Sensing that his band-leading days were over, Benny decided to go out with a bang, and led the band into those big swinging Fletcher Henderson arrangements. The crowd responded with a roar. Later, Goodman discovered that most of the crowd had been University of Southern California students who tuned in regularly to his radio show, *Let's Dance*, and they were just waiting for swing to come their way. That night it did, and the Swing Era was born.

A couple of years later, my father collaborated with a young lyricist named Johnny Mercer on a song for Dick Powell to sing in the film *Hollywood Hotel*. It just *happened* that this same Benny Goodman band was going along to see him off at the airport. The exuberant little musical celebration that resulted was called "Hooray for Hollywood!" I think that's how they all felt about that town. I know I still feel that way with every lovely royalty check that comes in four times a year from ASCAP.

My father was already teaching me about listening. "You know, Margaret," he told me, "there's a whole world of music out there. And you may not like it all." He had good friends, Rachmaninoff and Stravinsky as well as Harry Warren and George Gershwin. My father had studied it all—classical, Tin Pan Alley. He was open to everything.

"You may not like it all," he continued, "but listen to it all. Like life, there's a whole spectrum of people and colors and ideas out there. At the very least, expose yourself to them."

And I have.

4

The
Good Ship
Lollipop

Growing up, I never knew anyone who wasn't famous.

The town I lived in was small. Everyone talked to everyone else. My father and his friends worked in factories and played golf on weekends. Neighbors dropped in unannounced, the way neighbors do in small towns. My gang of kids rode around in convertibles, talked endlessly about dates, and danced close on Saturday nights.

But there was a difference. My town was Beverly Hills, and the neighbors—all America knew our neighbors—they were Bing Crosby and Shirley Temple, Jack Warner and George Gershwin. Since Daddy was Richard Whiting, his friends were Gus Kahn, Harry Warren, and Leo Robin. To me, Leo was Uncle Leo. Jerome Kern was Uncle Jerry. Harold Arlen was Harold. And Johnny Mercer—he was Johnny and he was special.

The factories were called Paramount, MGM, 20th Century-Fox, and Warner Brothers. These men worked on an assembly line (before such a term had come into popular usage), putting together words and music and manufacturing a product that went all over the world, changing the way others behaved—from the way they smoked cigarettes to the way they made love. These people were friends, neighbors, and my father's contemporaries. But they were also immensely popular idols, which made them very powerful.

I took all this for granted. The line between make-believe and reality was blurred. Judy Garland played the Girl Next Door, but she *was* the girl next door—or actually, just a few blocks away. We used to have girl lunches and talk about boyfriends. And Mickey Rooney played the Brash Young Man who was girl crazy. Well, Mickey *was* girl crazy.

And what was I? Johnny Mercer called me The Kid. I was like his kid sister who wanted to sing. Both Richard and Eleanore encouraged me. Every night, if I finished all the food on my plate, my treat was to go to the piano with Daddy and run through songs he had written, or songs he had just heard from writer friends he admired. I'll never forget the night he first played Rodgers and Hart's "My Funny Valentine."

"Now, *that's* a verse," he said appreciatively when he finished. Daddy always played the verses, too, and by the time I was five or six, I knew practically every song that had been published. One evening, he seemed particularly anxious to play one of his songs. I sat and listened to a very wistful melody.

"Are there words?" I asked.

He sang them in that halting half-spoken way that songwriters have.

"Will I ever find the boy in my mind
The one who is my ideal."

When he had finished, I said, with a five-year-old's enthusiasm, "Oh, Daddy. That's the best thing you've ever written!" A half-century later, I have no reason to differ with the five-year-old's opinion. Constantly, during his career, he would refer to "My Ideal," play it, compare it with the latest song he had just composed, and I would hear him mutter. "Jesus Christ, will I ever write another one like that?"

Daddy took me to the theater. My first experience was a show of Kern's called *The Cat and the Fiddle*. Before the overture, the conductor waved at my father.

I said, "Daddy, who is that?"

My father said, "That's Max Steiner. This is his last show here. He's going to Warner Brothers to write movie scores." The producers had brought over a French singing actress, Odette Myrtil. In the second act, she appeared dressed as Pierrot and sang "Poor Pierrette." When she was through with the song, I grabbed my father's arm and said, "Oh, Daddy, I know what I want to be when I grow up. I want to be an actress and go on the stage and sing!" And more credit to Daddy. He didn't scoff. He merely said, "We'll see."

Well, I *did* see. I would prevail upon Grace Kahn (Gus Kahn's wife) to play for me when Daddy wasn't available. She had been a song plugger in Chicago before she married Gus, and she could play any song in any key. No importance to me that her husband had written "Ain't We Got Fun" with my father, and "It Had to Be You," "Memories," and "My Buddy" as well. No, Grace was put on this earth to be my piano player. I probably pestered her the way kids do, but she was wonderful and helpful and encouraging. So The Kid hung around her house waiting for a chance to sing. I remember one day while I was rehearsing, a man with a funny European accent walked through the room, nodding approval. "Verrry gut, Marrgarett," he said. "Keep vorrrkink!" Grace asked me if I knew who he was.

I said, "No, but he's cute. Who is he?"

"Sigmund Romberg," she said.

"That's nice," I replied and went right back to the second chorus.

Grace just smiled and said, "It may not mean anything to you now, but someday you'll appreciate his remark."

I'm trying to put this in perspective because, if nothing else, I have been called an encyclopedia of the American popular song. My mother, and her sister, Margaret Young, had sprung from the vaudeville years and toured with Jolson and Sophie Tucker (who was my god-mother). And in the Whiting residence, that house of "exits and entrances," as Loesser had termed it, everyone was onstage. It may have caused me some problems in my life, but it was enormously stimulating just to *be* there as Loesser, Jule Styne, Jimmy Van Heusen, Sammy Cahn, Johnny Mercer, Gershwin, Arlen, Kern, *and* Kahn wandered through, chatted in the kitchen, diving into my mother's chocolate cake (she was the best cook I have ever known), joking with my father or working with him.

Someone once asked me if I wasn't terrified singing before the exacting Jerome Kern, whose temper was well known. I looked at him in disbelief. Scared of Uncle Jerry? I had never gotten anything but love and encouragement from him. And, oh yes, he did happen to write "Smoke Gets in Your Eyes" and "All the Things You Are." And "Ol' Man River." (No, I stand corrected. As Mrs. Oscar Hammerstein so neatly put it, "Kern wrote '*dah-dah-dum-dum.* . . .' Oscar wrote "Ol' man river. . . .")

The point is, I just happened to be around when so many of these men wrote their songs, argued over them, tossed them away, retrieved them, and turned them into hits. Daddy was working with Johnny Mercer on a movie, *Ready, Willing and Able.* In the script, the star, Ross Alexander, was supposed to be dictating to his secretary, but it was actually a love letter to Ruby Keeler, and the whole reason for the dictation was that, later on, the Busby Berkeley girls would form a human typewriter, those glorious legs acting as keys. Johnny got stuck and said, "Dick, I'm going to the dictionary to look for words like *glamorous,*" and then they started coming. *Amorous* and the rest. The result:

> *You're much too much,*
> *And just too very, very!*
> *To ever be in Webster's Dictionary . . .*

"Too Marvelous for Words." And it all came from the fact that Johnny was stuck for a word.

Speaking of being stuck, while my father was working at the factory (20th Century-Fox at the time), he also had his own studio over the garage, and every day after school I always wandered in to see what he was doing. One day, I found him sweating over a song for Shirley Temple, who was the hottest property in Hollywood. I happened to be sucking a lollipop and went up to give him a kiss.

"Get that lollipop out of the way. You're going to get the piano sticky."

"Sure thing, Daddy," I said. He was never really cross with me.

"Wait a minute!" he shouted. "Lollipops. Candy store. Kids. Bonbons. That's it! That's it!"

If I am credited with nothing more in my life, I may modestly claim that I, personally, was the sticky inspiration for "On the Good Ship Lollipop."

The line between make-believe and reality was thin, but a great deal of hard calculation went into creating that make-believe. Ernst Lubitsch, for instance, knew exactly what he was doing. Lubitsch was famous for his directorial touch. He loved to mix up innocent Americans like Jeanette MacDonald with continental sophisticates like Maurice Chevalier. Chevalier would parade up and down grand staircases a thousand times in Lubitsch films, which were populated with madcap heiresses and conniving barons. American audiences ate it up. The result was sparkling champagne, but the effects had been planned down to the last detail. My father, Leo Robin and W. Franke Haring collaborated with Lubitsch on *Monte Carlo*, in which Jeanette MacDonald played a princess running away from her kingdom in order not to marry the man her father wants her to. Jeanette runs away in her underwear and a mink coat, and with barely enough money to book a compartment on a train. She is wearing only a chemise, because that is what Lubitsch wanted. And so there she is, sitting in her compartment while southern France goes whizzing by. The train passes fields where peasants are picking grapes. The train goes *doodle, doodle*, the sound only a train can make. Jeanette looks out. A peasant waves to her and then goes back to his grape picking. Jeanette waves back. Now, more peasants wave, and pick more grapes. Everyone is picking and waving and smiling—we're in the heart of the wine country. Suddenly, Jeanette stands up, throws off her mink, opens her mouth, making a sound only *Jeanette* can make, and sings:

"Blow whistle, blow away,
Blow away the past
Go engine, anywhere,
I don't care how fast . . ."

then launches into the chorus of "Beyond the Blue Horizon." Lubitsch had emphasized to my father, "Richard, I must hear a train —the sound of a train—during the verse." Lubitsch knew he was going to have the peasants wave, have Jeanette wave, have everybody wave—and then Jeanette (with peasant chorus behind her) would sing this wonderful song, and the effect would be terrific. Who cared if this was not quite reality? This was that Dream World—a princess in her underwear, getting the hell out of a kingdom in order to avoid marrying the second lead, and there was a great song. Who cared about being literal? Certainly not the public. Of course, this inspired silliness infused most of the great musicals, but it was also the spirit of the times. "It sounds like fun." "Anything is possible." "Let's do it."

The point is: I was surrounded by talented people doing wonderful things, and I took it for granted. I expected everyone to do just that: create wonderful things. But then, life was rather lighthearted in those days—in spite of the Depression. You might say that neither America nor I grew up until the Second World War.

Safe. Everything was safe and comfortable and beautiful to look at. I was sailing on the Good Ship Lollipop, on a swell trip that would last forever. Far away, in some distant land, there was the Dust Bowl. I knew this from the John Ford film *The Grapes of Wrath.* Most of my information about the country, I got from the movies. But criminals growing up in Warner Brothers slums, the poor suffering through MGM close-ups: *that* was fantasy. Reality was Beverly Hills, twenty-room houses, chauffeurs, immaculately manicured country clubs. (These included the Rancho near 20th Century-Fox, a public course where my father played when we first came out; Hillcrest, the Jewish club right down the street from the Rancho; the Bel-Air Country Club, where Daddy, Fred Astaire, and Robert Montgomery were the only three theatrical members for a long time; the Los Angeles Country Club, right on Wilshire Boulevard, five blocks from my home on Beverly Glen; and Lakeside, in the Valley, which did not allow Jews.)

Reality consisted of the souvenir dolls, table decorations, of Norma Shearer, Marion Davies, Carole Lombard, all wearing slinky evening gowns, that my mother and father brought home from the Cocoanut Grove every Sunday night when they went out dining and dancing. On Thursdays (Maids' Night Out), they went to Chasen's for dinner. Spencer Tracy, Jimmy Stewart, Clark Gable all had their special tables. My father had helped Dave Chasen start his business. (I truly believed Thursday to be Maids' Night Out in every home in America.) Reality meant lavish parties at the house, with magnificent food, buffets, where various songwriting teams, or Chevalier, Bob Hope, Dick Powell performed. (At Harry Warren's house, you might see the young singer Frank Sinatra, who had just started out in the business, Tommy Dorsey, Glenn Miller.) These parties of music went on till five in the morning, with Bing Crosby singing and George Gershwin or Oscar Levant at the Steinway (I also truly believed every house had a Steinway) and with us kids, sitting on the stairs, listening. Reality was going to the movies on Hollywood Boulevard every Saturday with my best friend, Cookie Warren (Harry Warren's daughter), and being driven there and picked up by the chauffeur. Reality was the movie business.

I came home from school and devoured the trades—*Daily Variety, The Hollywood Reporter.* "Is it true you're replacing Harold Arlen on *Gold Diggers of 1937*?" I breathlessly asked Uncle Harry Warren.

"That kid reads everything," Harry Warren grumbled proudly to my father. It was true: Busby Berkeley, the film's choreographer, could find nothing fanciful to do with the Arlen–E. Y. Harburg score and *had* asked Jack Warner to put Warren and Al Dubin on the picture. It was a sign of the times that one of the lyrics went:

Oh! baby what I couldn't do-oo-oo
With plenty of money and you-oo-oo . . .

In other words, we danced through the Depression. We made people happy. We gave them songs and dances and ice-skating, and polished palaces, shopgirls and heiresses, beautiful people and beautiful music, all for a dime, the price of a movie ticket. Or, for even less, the cost of the electricity it took to listen to radio. Jack Benny and Fred Allen *were* Sunday night. And Eddie Cantor, who was constantly discovering young talent.

"Ladies and gentlemen, a little girl I discovered, who's going to be a big star. She's sweet, she's beautiful—Deanna Durbin!"

He was discovering *everybody*. Oh, couldn't he, please, please, discover me? *She's sweet, she's beautiful—Margaret Whiting!*

But how could he discover me? He already knew me. Mother and Aunt Mag had worked in vaudeville with him. He used my father's song "If I Could Spend One Hour with You" as his theme. The two families dined together all the time. So he couldn't *discover* me. (Later, I did become part of his weekly radio hour.)

We were a helluva lucky, talented community, all of whose members, rivals though they may have been, knew and respected one another. The fathers, like pioneers, had come out west to strike it rich in the studios, whether writing music or words, producing, directing movies, or running the studios. They had sent back east for their families, and they had built their houses, and sent their children to the best schools and sheltered them. Cookie Warren and I both attended Marymount, a convent school that was extremely strict. Hat, gloves, long stockings. Curtsies. Manners. We were not aware, until later, of the prejudice against movie people—new money—by the slightly more established communities of Hancock Park and Pasadena. Cookie can recall, as a grown-up, an irate mother shrilling into her ear over the telephone:

"I want you to know we worship *God* in Pasadena!"

And Cookie replied with asperity, "What a coincidence. We have God in Beverly Hills, too!"

Growing up, as Cookie says, we were *rich*. A thousand dollars a week went a long way in those days. We were very rich, and it was a lovely, lovely time.

Is it any wonder, then, in 1937, when my father asked me what I would like, I replied without hesitation, "A swimming pool, a silver-fox cape, and a trip to Hawaii."

He chuckled and said, "We'll see. You're much too young for a silver-fox cape, but we'll see about the others." (Carole Lombard had worn a silver fox in a movie and I was desperate for one just like it.) Early that January, I came home from school to find a bulldozer groaning in the backyard. And so, a pool. We christened it on a beautiful, cloudless April afternoon (they all were cloudless) with champagne and the first dip, with the weather so cold we had to grit our teeth, but in we plunged, shivering. And celebrating. We had an idyllic summer with that pool; everyone came over and enjoyed it. We were big for parties.

And we planned a trip to Hawaii. My father brought home the travel folders and brochures from the Matson Line. He and I poured over the beautiful colored pictures of yet more cloudless blue skies, spotless beaches, graceful palms. Of course, my mother was around. And Barbara was there. But she was just a baby, and Mother was just a mother. But Daddy was Daddy. Daddy would take me into his confidence and play me his songs. Daddy would play for *me* to sing, and give me advice and encourage me. Daddy would put his arm around me when he was talking with Leo—whether it was the wonderful director Leo McCarey or Leo Robin. He was proud of me, I could feel it. I loved to sing for his friends, I loved to sing for *him*. It was a swell trip on the Good Ship Lollipop.

Safe. We were so safe.

The family did not take the trip to Hawaii. That fall, my father grew ill. It came from the tension, the nerves. He had high blood pressure. I got scraps of conversation, the way children do. Leftovers from the grown-ups' concerns. "It doesn't look good, Ellie." The word *doctor* crept into conversations. "It's more serious than I thought, Mrs. Whiting. He may be going blind." And then Daddy went to the hospital, and when he came back, he was carried up to his room, and then came downstairs in pajamas and bathrobe instead of lovely golf sweaters and slacks. Yes, and no more golf games. No more hanging out with his cronies. Oh, they still visited him, but with that sad pained face cronies have when something is not quite right. My father loved to read, but now he couldn't. His eyes were failing him. He *was* going blind. Blossom, his mother, my grandmother, read to him. Then the pace increased. Nurses came, adding to the household. A nurse to take her meals quietly with the servants. We ate quietly, too, Mother, Blossom, Barbara, and I. Daddy did not join us. Trays were taken upstairs. We were allowed visits. Daddy was always cheerful when he saw me. I would sit on the edge of the bed in the afternoon, with the sun streaming through the window, and watch the patterns of light on the rug and chat with him. I don't remember what we talked about. I just remember how it felt. I was so unaware. I just knew Daddy meant comfort. Safe, I was safe with him.

Then suddenly, there were closed doors. Pacing in the hallway. A doctor visiting in the night. Conferences and more whispered conversations. Daddy was in a coma. What did that mean? That was a fantasy word, from the movies. That had nothing to do with *reality*. His friends, Gus and Grace Kahn, Johnny Mercer, Leo Robin, song-writer Walter Donaldson, sat downstairs soberly. Then at four o'clock in the afternoon, a car went by our house and backfired. It was like a shot from a cannon. Quite miraculously, that brought him out of his coma. My father was crazy about firecrackers of all sizes. Not just for the Fourth of July. He carried them in his golf bag. He would set them off at parties. When Gus Kahn was learning to drive, my father followed in a car behind him and kept throwing out lighted firecrackers. The poor man had to give up his lessons until my father left town.

So the noise from a passing car brought my father out of a coma. *That* was reality. That would have been in one of Leo McCarey's movies. Wishing will make it so. I think we had a merry Christmas. I remember Daddy coming down as we opened presents by the tree. I think we celebrated New Year's. There's a part of me that refuses to remember the details. I can remember the swimming pool, the champagne, the look on my father's face, my impossible girlish demands, and his chuckle. I can remember sitting on his bed. The rest . . . ? I just remember that one day Eleanore sent me over to stay with Leo Robin and his wife, Estelle. Was Barbara with me? I don't remember. Uncle Leo was family.

On the nineteenth of February, early in the morning, he came in and said, "Margaret, I've got something to tell you." And I said, "I know. My father's dead." And he took me home.

Eleanore greeted me at the door, she threw her arms around me. That one time, she threw her arms around me.

"There's just the three of us now," she said. I did not get to see my father. Eleanore felt it inappropriate for us to go to the funeral. Within a few months she had sold the house, and we had moved to another not far away, on Loring. My Aunt Maggie had moved out to be with us. And life continued.

I just did not know then what was happening. I had no idea what my mother was doing, that she was shielding me from the horror of watching a man I loved so much disintegrate, that she was protecting me, that she was determined to be cheerful to keep a household functioning. I knew that my father and she were devoted to each other. But except for the one time she put her arms around me, I was unaware of her *loss*. She was not one to confide.

I did not understand Eleanore. In one small corner of my heart, resentment grew. And rebellion.

I do remember walking through that first house, whispering "Daddy," to myself, to what he had been. Walking out by the pool, calling him, summoning him in the peremptory way a child does. "Daddy . . . Daddy . . ." He did not appear. It was the first time in my life he had disappointed me.

Is there anything sadder than a daddy's girl without her daddy?

When Eleanore was going through his things, she found seven large cans. She thought they contained cigars. She gave them to Gus Kahn. He opened them and found that each can was full of different-size firecrackers.

5

The Kid

There were people to take up the slack. Aunt Mag's vitality, combined with my mother's, made Daddy's death less painful. Jack Haley dropped by often and, of course, Leo Robin and Gus and Grace Kahn. The first time I heard someone laugh in the house after Daddy's death, I was shocked. How dare they? What disrespect! It took some time for me to realize the different shades of grief. And the power of life.

But I was lucky to be surrounded by people who liked to live. Everyone had projects and dreams to be realized. Me too.

First, Aunt Mag decided to renew her career. She needed an accompanist. So she called a friend from vaudeville, Cliff Edwards— better known as "Ukulele Ike." (And even better known as the voice of Jiminy Cricket in *Pinocchio*.) Edwards had always encouraged talent and recommended Skitch Henderson, a young pianist. Aunt Mag made him her accompanist. The first day they started to rehearse, I came home from school. Aunt Mag introduced us.

"Margaret's going to be a singer," she said proudly.

"Oh?" Skitch asked politely. "What do you sing?"

" 'I've Got a Pocketful of Dreams,' " I said, launching into it before he could stop me. Skitch listened for a moment, smiled, and then started to play, and from that day on, he played for both of us.

Aunt Mag was booked into Grace Hayes' Lodge, a night spot in the San Fernando Valley, as a "coon shouter." She came out on opening night, gave the audience one quick grind, hollered, "You ain't seen nothing yet!," tore into "Hard Hearted Hannah," and quickly became a favorite. She was an oddity, a remnant from another era, as was Grace Hayes herself. Grace was at one time married to Charlie Foy, who was one of the Seven Foys. They were all from the vaudeville tradition. You might call them all The Vaudeville Connection. Every weekend, we would go out to the club and I would watch Aunt Mag work. Then, during the week, Skitch would help mold me into a singer. And so, under his approval, I began to flower.

But the main influence was Johnny Mercer. He really took my father's place—as much as one could. Johnny had always been around the house when he was collaborating with my father. To him, I was always The Kid. Now he took The Kid under his protective wing. He listened to me sing. Screwed up his forehead. Gave me his advice. "Listen to singers you like. Who do you like?" I mentioned Garland. Frances Langford. Ethel Waters.

"Good. Study them, their style, the way they phrase. Don't worry about copying them. You'll get your own style. Just listen. And learn."

"What else?" I asked.

He grinned. "Two words, kid. Grow up."

So I did.

One night at Grace Hayes', while we are watching Aunt Mag, she invited me to get up and sing. It was not as though I had come totally unprepared. I may even have said to Skitch, " 'My Ideal'— in A-flat."

I do remember I was a big hit. I had the voice I have now. It's always been the same. Except at fifteen, it was amazing that I sounded like a woman, not some kid.

After that, I sang every week, and Grace slipped me a hundred dollars under the table. Far from disapproving, Eleanore was thrilled. The mother in her was proud, and the businesswoman made sure that I got paid. It wasn't a matter of child exploitation. This was the era of wonderfully talented child stars—Garland and Rooney, Deanna Durbin, Jackie Cooper, Gloria Jean, Jane Withers, and, of course, Shirley Temple. Children were *supposed* to perform for adults.

Grow up. Oh, I would, as fast as I could.

Skitch helped me. He taught me all the songs of the day. We in turn introduced him to everybody in Hollywood. He loved my mother's chocolate cake. In fact, between the two of us, we ate a whole one many times. Since Skitch was like a member of our family, he got to know all the Whiting friends intimately, people like Bob Hope and Harry Warren, Kern, and Jimmy Van Heusen, who used to take Skitch and me down to the Palladium to hear Frank Sinatra sing with the Tommy Dorsey band.

One night after the band had performed, Skitch, Jimmy, Frank, and I went to Franklin D'Amore's Italian hole-in-the-wall restaurant on Cahuenga Boulevard. Over linguini with clam sauce, Frank told us about his plans.

"I'm leaving Dorsey," he said. "I've gone as far as I can go with the band. It was great, but it's time for me to go out on my own. Victor records has offered me a contract. So I'm going to get Axel Stordahl to make the arrangements." And leave he did.

I'll never forget the thrill of hearing those first records issued by Bluebird, Victor's low-priced label. "The Night We Called It a Day" and "Violets for Your Furs." Skitch and I figured that if it could happen to Frank, it could happen to us.

There was a popular local radio program on NBC at the time called *Our Half Hour*. Skitch became the bandleader. Johnny Mercer was a frequent guest on the show. He used to improvise "The News Letter," a musical bit about the current events of the day, and his rhyming abilities just knocked everybody out. One day Skitch called me and said that Johnny wanted to sing "Too Marvelous for Words," and would I join him and do a duet? I raced down to the studio. That was where so many kids had started out—in radio. Rosemary Clooney in Cincinnati, Dinah Shore on WNBC, Helen O'Connell in Lima, Ohio, Frank Sinatra on WNEW, David Rose on Mutual. Well, it worked for me too. NBC was impressed and signed me to a two-year contract. I did a show every night with either David Rose, Bud Dant, or Gordon Jenkins as bandleader. I sang about three songs a show.

Nothing about this struck me as being extraordinary. Wasn't this what every young girl did? Growing up, I didn't know anybody who wasn't famous. But there was one occasion when I felt quite privileged.

Jerome Kern and Mercer were working on a Fred Astaire–Rita Hayworth movie, *You Were Never Lovelier*. Kern called me up one day.

"Margaret," he said, "it's Uncle Jerry. Johnny says you're such a great judge of songs, and your father always said that too. Well, I would like to invite you to tea. I want you to hear the new score and tell me what you think."

I wasn't quite sure what that meant, but I was terribly flattered. I felt very grown up. We made a date. I stood outside on the curb and this huge Rolls-Royce pulled up. Inside was Uncle Jerry. He kissed me and said, "Hop in." We purred our way to his house, where his wife, Eva, a lovely English lady, had prepared high tea for us. I sat there balancing the unaccustomed cup of tea, but both Uncle Jerry and Aunt Eva made me feel comfortable. We chatted about the family, and how I was doing in school, and then Uncle Jerry turned to Eva.

"We're going in to the piano now. I want to play some new songs for Margaret. We don't want to be disturbed."

"Oh, how nice," Eva cooed. And Uncle Jerry and I repaired to the music room. He went to the piano and said solemnly, "Johnny respects your judgment so much. And I respect him so much. I give him a melody and he comes back with a wonderful lyric. He has such fresh imagery. It's a pleasure to write with him."

I nodded. This was high praise coming from a man known to be a severe taskmaster. I sat in my chair.

He played "You Were Never Lovelier," then turned to me. "What do you think?" Through my mind flashed a movie montage of different figures: George Gershwin, his voice echoing down through history, saying, "Kern is the most revered man in music"; my father saying, "There's no one like Kern"; someone else intoning, "Kern brought European theater to the American musical: *Showboat*." All this while the man was waiting for my opinion. I was speechless. He said, "Maggie, what's wrong?"

"Oh, Mr. Kern."

He said, "Stop that! I'm not Mr. Kern. It's your Uncle Jerry. Tell Uncle Jerry what's wrong."

I blurted out, "I'll tell you what's wrong. I just realized who you were. How do you tell Jerome Kern what you think of his songs, when you want to come back for tea?"

He said, "Very simply. Just listen. And tell me." Then he played "I'm Old Fashioned." I was very touched. It was so like Johnny, that lyric. And Kern made the words soar. I told Kern, "My father would have loved that song. And you brought out the best in Johnny. Oh, it's beautiful. Play it again."

He could tell my feelings were genuine.

"I'm so glad you liked it. It makes me so happy." He played the song again, and then he said, "Young Johnny is a genius. You know, I've worked with geniuses before." He had this funny look on his face, always cocked his head, with his neat suit and wing-tip shoes. "I'm very grateful I found him. I have no problems with him. He loved your father very much."

Then he rose. And I rose. The Rolls appeared. Aunt Eva kissed me good-bye.

"Give my love to your mother," Uncle Jerry said. I sank back into the luxury of the automobile.

That day, I realized that the people surrounding me were not just famous. Sometimes they were *great*. And a few could be called legends.

Therefore, it didn't seem at all out of the ordinary for me to be strolling around the Hillcrest Golf Course in 1941 with Harold Arlen, bandleader Bobby Sherwood, and Johnny Mercer, on the day Johnny announced he was going to start Capitol records. He was always saying, "Let's take The Kid along," and I would follow him— gladly—anywhere. Even to a golf course on a Saturday. They teed off, I tagged along. Beautiful morning, glittering sun, fresh green course, birds twittering.

Just as he was about to tee off Johnny said, in an offhand manner, "I've had this idea of starting a record company. I get so tired of listening to the way everybody treats music. I keep feeling they're selling out. And I don't like the way artists are treated either. Bing Crosby isn't the only one who can make records. I don't know. I think it would be fun. Harold, you and I could write some songs. Bobby, I'd use your band, and I'd get Paul Weston to write orchestrations." Johnny had met Paul that year when Weston was scoring the Fred Astaire songs for *Holiday Inn* at Paramount and Johnny and Harold Arlen were writing songs for *Star Spangled Rhythm*. Weston was rather disillusioned with the movie business and was eager to work for a record company, where he could use so many of the brilliant sidemen who had come out to the West Coast. "I've always wanted to use Jo Stafford," Johnny continued. "Maybe I could get Billie Holiday. And we'll let The Kid here sing," he said, grinning affectionately at me.

That sounded reasonable. Had I not heard that kind of dialogue in practically every Garland-Rooney movie where they're going to put on a show, and they do, because everyone pitches in, including Richard Rodgers and Larry Hart? It seemed like a perfectly normal way to found a record company.

Of course, Johnny had been thinking about the enterprise for a long time. He had come up from Savannah as a stowaway on a boat. He arrived in New York, looking for work as an actor, and he had passed a sign outside a theater that said, LYRICS WANTED. He went in and found both his profession and his wife, Ginger, who was a dancer in the chorus. He came to Hollywood, worked with Hoagy Carmichael on "Lazybones," returned to New York, worked with Paul Whiteman, and later, on the radio with Benny Goodman, where he was expected to write a song a week. Then in 1934, he had come back to Los Angeles, collaborated with my father, and with Harry Warren and Harold Arlen. Mercer was a man bursting with talent and always looking for a place to channel his energies. This idea of a record company seemed ideal.

One of his best friends was Glenn Wallich, the owner of Music

City, a record store across from NBC. Wallich had been the man my father and everyone else called to repair their radios, but obviously he had moved up a few notches in five years, for now he owned the biggest record and music store in the area.

One day Johnny went to visit Glenn, who took him into the back room to hear some of the new releases. Johnny shook his head, then blurted out, "How about coming in on a record company with me? Let's try something new." And Glen said, "Fine. You run the company and find the artists." And Johnny said, "And you run the business."

From there, Johnny went to Buddy DeSylva, who, besides being a very good songwriter, had become head of production at Paramount, and had hired Johnny to do the score with Victor Schertzinger for *The Fleet's In*, a musical with William Holden, Dorothy Lamour, Eddie Bracken, and a blond bombshell named Betty Hutton. Hutton had just stolen *Panama Hattie* right out from under Ethel Merman's nose. Buddy and Johnny went to lunch at Lucey's, not a fancy place, but everyone went there because it was close to the Paramount lot.

Johnny described his idea.

"Sounds great. I'm in," DeSylva said. "How much do you need?"

"Fifteen thousand," Johnny answered.

"You better take more, you might have some problems. Here's a check for twenty-five thousand dollars. Put Hutton on the label. She's going to be a big star. She can even do your 'Arthur Murray Taught Me Dancing in a Hurry.' "

Johnny was in business. Sounds easy? Sounds like a Hollywood dream? Remember Mercer's history. He had been performer, lyric writer, songwriter; he had worked on radio shows and with the best bands, the best singers, the best composers: Whiteman, Goodman, Dorsey, Jo Stafford—the list is endless. So both Wallich and De-Sylva, businessmen, knew in whom they were investing.

And what about The Kid?

The Kid here was no longer tagging along, carrying Johnny Mercer's golf bag, so to speak. Jimmy Saphire, who was Bob Hope's agent, had heard me on *Our Half Hour* and offered to represent me. My mother and I thought that was a swell idea. So when Johnny repeated that he wanted me to make records, he was told, "You'll have to speak to her agent." This was Johnny, who had split many a chocolate cake with me and Eleanore at the kitchen table. This was Johnny, who was as close to being family as anyone could be. He did not like being treated like that. And it kind of spoiled the big-brother image. It was the only time we ever had a disagreement. But it was a big one.

Jimmy Saphire, not to be daunted, gathered up a group of demo records I had made, sent them to New York to *Your Hit Parade*. In 1941, *Your Hit Parade* was *it*. The entire nation (including me) waited breathlessly every Saturday night to find out which were the top ten songs in the country. And now they offered me a four-week test contract to go to New York, to sing on the program. I was seventeen at the time, and it seemed as though I had the most glamorous life in the world.

It was all arranged. Aunt Mag would accompany me since my mother had to stay with my sister, Barbara, who was still a young child. There was a lovely party before we left for the train station. Big things were going to happen. Everything wonderful. We boarded the train. I settled back in the comfort of a compartment, and I dreamed all the way east. The snowcapped mountains of Colorado passed by outside my window. I was dreaming of penthouses in New York, big bands and ball gowns, swains falling at my feet. Margaret was on her way. The railroad ties ate up the country. The harvest of Nebraska and Iowa, waving in autumn triumph, passed unnoticed. Not quite. Iowa seemed endless. I could not wait to get to the rhythms of the East. First Chicago, lunch at the Pump Room, change trains. The *Twentieth Century* and that overnight trip to New York. The porter woke us up at six in the morning. Breakfast, as West Point and the Hudson passed before us. Ahead lay those Gershwin-underscored skyscrapers, a jazzy, sophisticated world that was going to fall at my feet. Just like Jeanette, in chemise and mink, I was ready to burst into song!

Then the train plunged into a tunnel. Was it my imagination, or did the rhythm pick up? Oh yes, there was more of a pulse there, a beat.

"Neeew *York!*" the conductor called, and I was ready. New York was there. Crowds, taxis, buses, yelling, pushing. Glamorous gray, needles poking the sky, redcaps, people hurrying by, speaking incomprehensible languages.

Everyone is struck by the power of New York the first time he arrives. But I can't imagine anything more disparate than the easy sunny country-club life of Los Angeles and the frenetic, international, wisecracking double-time pace of New York. It was my first real love affair—and I've never gotten over it, my feeling about New York.

First rehearsal. I was used to radio studios. But here was this orchestra. A New York orchestra. Mark Warnow's. How many times, cozy in the frilly bedroom of my house on Loring, had I heard that name coming out of my radio! And now here Warnow was. And Barry Wood the singer and MC! The world!

I was handed a song. We began. I sang out, taking my time, phrasing the hell out of it.

"Time was
When we had fun on the schoolyard swings . . ."

A beautiful ballad. I filled it with yearning and emotion and plenty of pauses.

Mark Warnow was very impressed. So was the band. This was as good as the Deanna Durbin movie *100 Men and a Girl*. Of course, I didn't have Leopold Stokowski and that symphony orchestra of out-of-work musicians. I had something better. A real live band. This was better than a movie. This was reality.

Performance time. I was ready. I couldn't wait for the announcement. All over America, the radios were being switched on. Saturday night was aglow with radio dials. The theme, the announcement: ". . . and Margaret Whiting."

Oh, I sang. Just a bit nervous when I came out, I bowed to an applauding audience and discovered I was still chewing gum. What to do? I parked the gum on the microphone and sang out! I gave a *performance*. The dress rehearsal had been nothing. I sang, I bent the notes, I held on, I paused.

Unknown to me, forty-five stories above me, the head of Lucky Strike Tobacco, the sponsor of *Your Hit Parade*, the imperious George Washington Hill, was dancing with his secretary. This eccentric genius who had made an art out of advertising danced every week to *Your Hit Parade*. He wanted all America dancing—as well as smoking.

Forty-five stories above the little songstress, George Washington Hill stumbled.

"Goddamn it!" he roared.

"Sorry," said the secretary.

"It's not *your* fault," Hill roared again. "It's *hers*. Who can dance to that?"

Maybe the secretary tried to defend me.

"It's a ballad," she may have said.

"You can dance to a ballad," the great man may have roared.

"She's young. . . ."

"She's not too young to understand one-two-three-*four*."

Meanwhile, the young songstress was taking her bow, acknowledging the encouraging wink from Mark Warnow. Life was too, too marvelous! Bring on the champagne! Bring on the sables!

The first taste of reality came at the next rehearsal. Warnow's smile was wan.

"Listen," he said, "last week was wonderful, but . . . could you sing a little more on the beat?"

"On the beat?" I repeated his suggestion as though he'd spoken a foreign language.

Warnow echoed what must have been Mr. Hill's dictum. "You know—one-two-three-*four*."

"Sure," the seventeen-year-old said.

But the seventeen-year-old didn't have the discipline of singing with bands. She had sung with a combo, usually just a piano. She liked to hold these tones. Besides, singing on the beat was square. Also, the seventeen-year-old suddenly got paralyzed with fear.

"Time was
When we wrote love letters in the sand . . ."

she sang that second week, falling behind the beat and dragging the tempo.

Forty-five stories above came the roar, *"Can her!"*

New York suddenly became cold and grim and heartless. Gray

buildings, gray faces. Gray skies. Mid-November. Two more weeks to fulfill the contract.

I do give myself credit. I let nobody know how humiliated I was. I sang my best, maybe I even got the beat. Who knows? George Washington Hill had stopped dancing.

My Aunt Mag and I got back on the train and headed west across a suddenly frozen landscape. Early winter. A relentless season.

We got off in Pasadena rather than at the Union Station in Los Angeles. That way, we could avoid any reporters. We needn't have bothered.

We arrived on Sunday, December 7, 1941. All reporters were otherwise occupied.

Capitol Records was all set to go, but there were a couple of hitches in their plans. Including World War II.

The American Federation of Musicians, worried as recordings began to replace live music on radio, demanded that the record companies establish a fund for unemployed musicians. The companies resisted. So the union threatened a strike, which meant that not one musician could make a record. Not a terribly thrilling prospect for an emerging record company. Johnny and Glenn Wallich decided to schedule as many sessions as possible before the strike deadline, which was July 31, 1942. At one point, Paul Weston, who was feverishly working on nine different orchestrations, looked up in a daze, and murmured, "I am nine different bands."

The strike did go off as scheduled. From July 31, 1942, until November 1943, not one musician stepped into a recording studio. The results were fairly bizarre. Of course, most of the recording companies had stockpiled releases, but still, there were newcomers arriving on the scene. Vocal groups sang like strings and rhythm sections. There were a lot of tunes with what sounded like flights of heavenly choirs aaahing in the background. Capitol and Decca signed an agreement with the AF of M in November 1943, but the two giants, Columbia and Victor, held out for almost another year. It's strange to think of it now, because we associate the Second World War with big bands and jive and swing, but the strike muffled the recording industry for more than a year.

Capitol's second obstacle was a shortage of shellac. Like Lucky Strike Greens, shellac had "gone to war." Records were made from shellac in those days. Luckily, Johnny had a partner with imagination. Wallich came up with an idea and put an ad in the paper: "Come one, come all. Trade all unwanted records for new. We welcome your shellac."

As a result, Wallich got twenty thousand pounds of shellac. During the war, record companies had to resort to desperate methods to meet the demand. One was to grind up records from other companies. That worked well, except for Columbia's records, which contained a layer of paper inserted between the layers of shellac, rendering them unusable. Meanwhile, Johnny, who was very strict in his artistic standards and was controlling every release, went so far as to sign a band to the label because the bandleader's father was a big man in shellac. For Wallich and Mercer, the worst news of the war was a report that came in about a ship that had been sunk in the South Pacific. "How awful!" I said when I heard the news. "Yeah," Johnny said mournfully, "and it was carrying shellac."

Those two guys had guts. With a war on, a shortage of shellac, a strike by the musicians' union, Wallich and Mercer started production. With DeSylva's twenty-five thousand dollars, the limited amount of shellac, and a few test pressings, Capitol records was in business.

Four records were planned as the first releases in June 1942.

Nowadays, since the record business has become an industry, there are perhaps four hundred records a week released by all the major and independent labels. In 1942, it was another story. Here are the four records Johnny selected:

Capitol release #101 featured the band of Paul Whiteman. The songs Johnny chose for Paul were "I Found a New Baby" and "The General Jumped at Dawn." I think Johnny must have had a special feeling for Paul Whiteman, and that's why he chose him for the first release. The record did fairly well, but it wasn't until release #116 that Whiteman had a million-seller. The song was "Travelin' Light," and the singer was Lady Day. She was, of course, Billie Holiday, but since she was officially signed to another company, this was a *nom de chant*, the name all the musicians called her anyway.

Holiday, not the most commercial, but certainly the most influential vocalist of her time in terms of other artists, found a soul mate in Whiteman, who had, among other things, introduced Gershwin's *Rhapsody in Blue*. In "Travelin' Light," there was a curious intimacy in which each played to the other's quality, almost as though the record had caught an inspired after-hours session.

Capitol's second release, #102, was "Cow-Cow Boogie," featuring Freddie Slack's band and the singing of Ella Mae Morse. Boogie-woogie was still rather "inside," not yet the sensation it was to become a year later. The idea of a cowboy song with an urban boogie beat was nutty, mischievous, tongue in cheek—practically an inside joke. Yet there was enormous popular appeal there. It was infectious, really: the sound of Ella Mae Morse, the joy of the band, the rhythm of boogie-woogie. Who else but Johnny would have thought of such a combination?

The third release was by Dennis Day. It was called "Johnny Doughboy Found a Rose in Ireland." Dennis had his fans, of course, and his record got a lot of play on Saint Patrick's Day—and it probably could become a great trivia question: What was the title of Dennis Day's first Capitol record?

The fourth release consisted of two songs written by Johnny Mercer and sung by him, "Strip Poker" and "The Air Minded Executive," backed by the Paul Weston band.

I went to the "Strip Poker" recording session with Phil Silvers, one of Johnny's best friends. Jimmy Van Heusen was playing piano. The session was ultrainformal—everyone was walking around drinking coffee, smoking butts, and joking. Johnny and Paul Weston conferred for a while; then they nodded and went for a take. Paul had orchestrated the tune in mock burlesque with a lot of *beat*. So much, that when it came to the chorus:

> *"Take it off, take it off*
> *Came a voice from the rear . . ."*

Phil just jumped right up and joined Johnny. The pure joy of it all comes right through on the record. But that's all it was—a lot of fun, and nothing much to it. Nothing important or epic-making. At the end of the session, everybody emptied ashtrays, flipped off the lights, and went home. And that was that.

On a blazing hot day in that summer in 1942, Glenn Wallich, who had never been to New York before, arrived—like Willy Loman—laden down with his sample cases containing these first 78s, shellac releases. He wanted to get his new product to the radio stations. He asked Dave Dexter, who was working for *Downbeat*, to introduce him to the various disc jockeys. Together they trudged around that inferno of a town. Dave would introduce Glenn, who would unpack his case and present a few records. Then it was on to the next station. After a couple of days, Wallich returned to Los Angeles to await the results.

Nobody—not even Johnny—was prepared for what was to come. "Cow-Cow Boogie" was the first one to sell a phenomenal 250,000 copies the first week, and a million within the first month. Then "Strip Poker" repeated the phenomenon. By the time "Travelin' Light" hit, it was no longer a phenomenon. That was a very impressive batting average—first time up, Johnny hit two home runs. (I'm not really up on baseball, but you understand what I mean.)

He had proved his own artistic judgment and calculated the popular taste, but he did more than that. He change the sound of American pop music, and the way it was made.

In the beginning, there were the three major companies—Victor, Columbia, and Decca—all established in New York. New York was where you recorded. New York was where the big bands had their headquarters, rehearsed, planned their tours. Hollywood was a place where you wrote for the movies. If you were a jazz musician, you played little gigs in funny places: Art Tatum playing in a joint on the Strip; Kay Starr singing in a little café; Mel Torme, kid drummer of seventeen out of Chicago, hanging around Music City hoping for things to happen.

Capitol records changed all that. Capitol was new. Capitol was revolutionary. Capitol was West Coast. The music sounded different, and it was fresh and breezy. The artists were new, and they were given greater freedom.

Of course, the Whiting family got into the act. We not only bought a lot of Capitol's stock, but also acted as talent scouts. We had relatives in Detroit who had heard a small combo playing in a two-bit joint. The combo recorded for an obscure label. We were sent the recordings. We listened and loved them and passed them on to Johnny, who immediately signed The King Cole Trio. It was Johnny who represented the first black jazz singer—Nat "King" Cole—to cross over successfully into the commercial field. And that was just the start of the parade. There was the Stan Kenton band. And the singers! Capitol was the girl vocalist's dream world. June Christy. Jo Stafford. Peggy Lee. Anita O'Day. During the thirties, the girl singer had traditionally sat onstage wearing a corsage, dutifully parked the gum behind her ear, stood up, sang one chorus, waited through the trombone solo to sing the last eight bars, and then sat down. Girl singers had toured with the bands, and endured with the bands. But it was Johnny who turned these women into stars. No longer did it read in very small print: "vocal chorus by Peggy Lee." No, the singer was given equal billing.

"And we'll let The Kid here sing." Johnny got over his annoyance. About nine months after Capitol was started, Johnny said to me, "Margaret, you sound like Billy Butterfield when he plays the trumpet. And I think it would be real nice if you made a record with him. I want you to sing one of your father's songs, 'My Ideal.' And since the Les Brown band is in town, maybe Paul Weston can use them on that date." Billy was to play the first chorus and I was to come in on the second. I think Johnny got that idea from listening to a Bing Crosby record with Bix Beiderbecke. It's the only other record I know that used that particular combination. Whatever the inspiration, it certainly worked.

And that's how I cut my first record. Seventy-five dollars a side, and no royalties. I recorded "My Ideal" and the next day went back to classes in high school.

But something happened before "My Ideal" was released. *Star Spangled Rhythm*, for which Harold Arlen and Johnny had written songs, was one of those all-star revue movies so popular at the beginning of the war. It included everyone on the Paramount lot. One segment was a ten-minute screen ballet danced by Vera Zorina. She was to ballet what José Iturbi and Oscar Levant were to classical music. She was Class. Hollywood got nervous, culturally speaking, every once in a while, and it would latch on to the "arts" but not with a terribly secure grasp. *Star Spangled Rhythm* was one of those movies where everything was thrown in. Someone would say, "Hey, here's a great idea," and before you knew it, there would be two hundred girls performing a military tap atop two hundred drums with an Eleanor Powell or Ann Miller leading the way. In this case, Johnny Johnston sang while Zorina danced to "That Old Black Magic." Both Mercer and Arlen wanted the song to have more of a chance. Johnny was going crazy, but neither he nor Harold could intervene. And it was all done to promote this ballet dancer, who glided along with airy purity.

Now, Johnny had this recording company. . . .

Ella Mae Morse was pregnant and therefore unavailable, so whom did they call in? The Kid.

Both Johnny and Harold coached me. Granted, I was an average sophisticated high-school girl; I had no firsthand knowledge of "that old black magic called love" where "that elevator starts its ride / And down and down I go, 'round and 'round I go." But I was nothing if not game. And there was Harold, who had a fabulous style of singing. "Pulsate it," he would say, and show me how. " 'That old . . . black . . . ma-a-a-gic.' Not too smooth. Pulsate it." And I would take it all from him. It seemed the obvious way to sing it. Harold and Johnny wanted the urgency, the highs and lows, crescendos that spelled elevator rides and excitement. So The Kid got the best kind of coaching, and then I was brought into the studio. It took maybe an hour and a half to set up the mechanics. And there were a few decisions to be made. Put The Kid into an isolation booth. Get her away from the band. Get her a little closer. Now let's go for a take.

We did it in three. Again, I got seventy-five dollars a side, and no royalties. But I *did* get split billing with the band.

Because Capitol was Johnny's company, this record came out immediately, before "My Ideal." I was not prepared for my reaction.

The first time I heard the record was on the radio. Al Jarvis was *the* big disc jockey in Los Angeles at the time. I heard him talking with Artie Shaw, who was a guest on his program, about the new

Arlen-Mercer song, which he proceeded to play. And then I heard my own voice, and I thought with horror, What have they done to the record? I don't sound like that. They've speeded it up. No, they've slowed it down. What is that phrasing? I never phrased that way. That's not my voice. And then I thought with even more horror, Oh yes it *is*. That is your voice and it sounds terrible. My response was immediate. I dashed into the bathroom and threw up in the toilet.

The record was over and Artie Shaw began to speak. He could be ruthless, although accurate, in his criticism. I heard him say words like "an instant standard—a great record . . ." And when I heard that, I lifted my face from the toilet bowl and thought, Well, maybe. Then the phone rang and it was Paul Weston, calling to congratulate me.

"Is that how I sound?" I wailed. "I think it's terrible!"

"Yes, that's how you sound," Paul said, "and you're crazy. It's great."

Peter Potter's *Juke Box Jury* was next. The new releases were played on the air before a panel of experts—people in the music business like Benny Goodman, Glenn Miller, Martha Tilton, Jo Stafford, Jule Styne, Sammy Cahn—who would judge each record. "Is it a hit or a miss?" Potter would ask, and that jury would tell him, in no uncertain terms. "That Old Black Magic" was a rarity. It got 100 percent approval.

The record took off, followed by the release of "My Ideal," and quite suddenly I found I was Margaret Whiting, a name, a voice that was recognized, a star—tiny, perhaps, but a star. And I was also still The Kid. I didn't know what to do about that. And neither did anyone else.

The world had changed. But my contract hadn't. It was still seventy-five dollars a side—and no royalties. I was still in high school, but my afternoons were divided between homework and looking over recording material with Paul Weston and Johnny. I still went to those Saturday afternoon movies with Cookie Warren, but I was also besieged by songwriters when Cookie and I went for Cokes on Vine Street. And at school, while I acted in school productions, I was never allowed to sing. Like Alice in Wonderland, the world got curiouser and curiouser.

My success—Capitol's success—was too much to comprehend all at once. I used to drop in at the Capitol offices two or three times a week—The Kid just hanging around, saying hello. The offices were a laugh. They consisted of two rooms in a building on Sunset and Vine. There was the front room, where Paul worked on orchestrations, and a back room that Glenn Wallich and Johnny shared, where big decisions were made. Nine months after the beginning of Capitol's success, the offices remained the same.

Then, one Monday I walked in after school and saw a lady sitting at Paul's desk. I looked at her. She looked at what she assumed to be one more teen-ager.

"May I help you?" she asked grandly.

"Yes, I'd like to see Johnny Mercer."

"Who may I say is calling?"

"Oh, boy, you're new here, aren't you? My name is Margaret Whiting."

"Oh," she said. "Well, go right in to the inner office."

"The inner office?" The back room! Now there were three people crowded into that one office: Johnny, Glenn, and Paul Weston. Music paper was strewn over the desks. Johnny looked up and grinned.

"Hi, kid," he said cheerily.

"Gee," The Kid observed, "we have a secretary now. We're a bigger hit than I thought."

It was true. The success was so immediate and so enormous that the men were too busy to move the offices to a larger space. Finally, when the office resembled the Marx Brothers cooped up in a ship's closet, they moved a little way up Vine Street, right over Glenn's Music City. One of the tiny tragedies of such success occurred one day at a session. Johnny and Paul always liked to use McGregor's, on Western off Wilshire Boulevard, because of the phenomenal sound. Acoustics is something akin to black magic anyway, but in those days—fairly unsophisticated days, technically speaking—the studio was terribly important. The story goes that after a recording session in the morning, everyone broke for lunch. McGregor, feeling flush with Capitol's success and the money it had given him, painted the studio's walls during the lunch break. When the engineers came back, they put on the earphones. The afternoon session began. Suddenly, everyone stopped. The sound wasn't the same. Mercer, Weston, everyone put on the earphones and listened. What had happened? McGregor confessed he had painted the walls. In so doing, something had happened to the acoustics. They never got them back and had to move to another studio. But they kept bringing along with them the old Capitol master records, comparing the sound. It reminded me of alchemists frantically trying to rediscover their formula for gold. Johnny finally found a studio in Santa Monica that suited him, but he always talked wistfully about those halcyon days at Mc-Gregor's before the walls were painted. I guess it was like the South before the Civil War.

During *this* war, life became a carnival—at least at home. On the home front life was a merry-go-round, with the music livelier, the spirit more adventurous, and me grabbing for the brass ring and a promise of better things to come. Everyone felt important. Everyone was "doing his bit."

We weren't bombed like the British or occupied like the French. We didn't have the enemy at the gates of our capital like the Russians. There was no scorched-earth policy. We had problems: getting enough sugar; meat was rationed, and so were gasoline and silk stockings. But this didn't *really* affect anyone. If anything, the war gave us a spirit of togetherness. It's the only time I can recall when the whole nation pulled together with one purpose in mind. I don't mean to denigrate the sacrifices our fighting men made, or the pain and suffering their relatives went through, but I am telling this story through the eyes of The Kid. And The Kid, at the time, was a teen-ager with a budding career, caught up in the excitement of the entertainment industry.

And the entertainment industry was tremendously important to the war effort. The Germans had an enormous propaganda organization, but feeble film and record industries. Most of their major talent had fled the Nazis and come to—where else?—Hollywood. With France occupied, that left the British, who, while producing some noble films, were not nearly as popular internationally as the Americans in either film or pop music. Those of us in the entertainment industry were almost unaware of our power and our enormous influence on morale. Quite simply, just as we had shown Americans of the previous decade how to smoke cigarettes and make love, we now showed them how to sacrifice, go off to war, handle loneliness, accept separations and even death. Remember *Mrs. Miniver*, *Since You Went Away*, "I'll Walk Alone," "Don't Sit Under the Apple Tree"? In Hollywood there was, again, that thin line between reality and illusion. We were all family. And that family included Bette Davis and John Wayne washing dishes at the Hollywood Canteen, and Linda Darnell, Lana Turner, Judy Garland, and Rita Hayworth dancing with the GIs. It was partly illusion, yes, but there was reality there too. We did, indeed, become one extended family. And Hollywood entertainers volunteered for everything.

The Hollywood Coordinating Committee was set up to deliver entertainment to the servicemen who were going overseas. Every week, we met the boys. And we said good-bye to them. I went with my Aunt Mag, and with Al Jolson and Red Skelton, June Allyson, Virginia O'Brien, Nancy Walker, Vivian Blaine, the big bands, small combos, hoofers, comics, jugglers. We went to Camp Roberts, we went to Edwards Air Force Base. We went wherever they would have us.

I have a picture—an example of "family." Four of us at Edwards Air Force Base welcoming the wounded and seeing off the new recruits. Shirley Temple, Pat O'Brien, Louella Parsons, and me. What could be more "family" than that? America's favorite child star, next to Father Pat, everybody's father confessor or football coach. And Louella, the gossipy and sometimes reproving aunt who knew if you had sneaked out behind the barn for a forbidden cigarette. For one last time, America was that small town where, thanks to the movies and radio, everyone knew everybody's quirks and foibles—Bing Crosby's bald spot, Bob Hope's kidding, Louella's chatty gossip, Jack Benny's stinginess. No wonder we look back on those times so fondly. We were saying good-bye to our innocence and didn't even know it.

The boys were eager, afraid and excited, and off to God knew what fate, and the singing, the music, the entertainment, the jokes, the brush with celebrities—or whatever that was—seemed awfully important. I don't think there was one of us entertainers who ever took it cynically, treating it as just another job. We cared. And I think the boys knew we did.

Jule Styne played for my Aunt Mag and then for me. He had come out to 20th Century-Fox as vocal coach, and he gravitated to our house because of my mother's pot roast, my father's piano, and an audience to listen to his songs. That was before the war, and the first time Eleanore heard Jule's music, she said, "You're going to be one of the best. Absolutely. Now, come on and eat."

Jule *was* one of the best. The songs he had written in wartime— "I'll Walk Alone," "I've Heard That Song Before," "I Don't Want to Walk Without You"—certainly captured the spirit of the times. The GIs loved him, and so did we. He was always fun to be with. And, of course, he gave me tips on singing. So did Aunt Mag. Hold the note longer. Bend it a bit. Sing it louder and then let it go. Hands up at the end of the song. Sing it *to* them. They've got to know you're singing right to them. That's how I learned my craft.

Once, at Camp Roberts, we had been sent to entertain and stay overnight. My Aunt Mag and I shared one room in a barracks, and Jule was in the room next door. At dawn, the day started with the enormous boom of the six o'clock reveille cannon salute. Jule burst into our room in his underwear.

"Holy Christ!" he shouted. "What happened? Did the war start?"

There was, during the first few months of the war, the fear of a Japanese invasion of the West Coast. Everyone in Los Angeles took it in stride. If we couldn't have the Blitz like the Londoners, at least we could show some camaraderie. And so air-raid wardens would come around and ring the doorbell to tell us that light was coming through the venetian blinds, and we would invite them in for coffee. We got to know a lot of people that way.

The night of the Great Japanese Invasion Scare, I was performing with Phil Silvers and Rags Ragland. Phil and Rags had come up through burlesque and, once in Hollywood, Phil had made a name for himself as everybody's nearsighted sidekick. He was a wonderful stand-up comic, and he had one routine called "The Singing Teacher" that absolutely blew me away every time I heard it. He would imitate the military directives of vocal coaches. "Chin up-up-up, *squeeze* the cheeks, show us the tongue—where is that *tongue*, I say? I want to see it!"—all performed with the ferocity of the true con artist. He had a number of wonderful routines like that. I had been to several rehearsals with him, so when the girl vocalist who opened the show got sick, I was called to replace her. The boys were doing classic burlesque bits such as "Flugel Street." And since I had learned them from Phil, it gave me a chance to play sketch comedy with two masters.

This particular night, we had to return home over Mulholland Drive, which is on the crest of the mountain chain separating the San Fernando Valley from Beverly Hills and the coastline. Usually the view is spectacular, a million lights glittering out toward the Pacific, but during the war, it was absolutely dark because of the blackout. We crept along in Phil's car, over Mulholland and down Beverly Glen until we were stopped by a couple of military personnel.

"What's happened?" Phil said.

"There's a rumor of a Japanese submarine landing," one of the men answered grimly.

"In Beverly *Hills*?" Phil asked. He never lost his sense of humor. The soldier never found his.

He directed us up the road, where we found a large group of other refugees, all camped in a bar called The Glen. We weren't more than seven minutes away from home, but here we were, all strangers stranded by the exigencies of war at last, and we aimed to make the most of it. The crowd recognized us. We bought everybody drinks. They asked Phil to entertain, and he obliged with "The Singing Teacher," and then I sang "That Old Black Magic" and a few of my father's songs, and then everybody got to singing and carrying on. Why, we were all Brave Americans putting up with the Rigors of War, and we stayed there until the sun came up and it was safe for us to go home. I don't know whether a Japanese submarine ever landed on the coast, but it sure added zest to life on the home front.

The Whiting house of exits and entrances had always been full to overflowing, even before the war. On Saturday nights, people just gravitated to us, lured by my mother's cooking and Aunt Mag's zest for life. The two women were fabulous good-time broads, and they loved a crowd. My sister, Barbara, and I certainly came by those traits naturally. I don't know how those Saturday nights developed. It seemed to start when Aunt Mag came out to be with my mother after my father died. Once Skitch Henderson began playing for her, he brought a crowd around. I got my first job on radio and started inviting the writers over. Jimmy Van Heusen would drop in and maybe bring along Artie Shaw, who would get into an intellectual discussion with bandleader Claude Thornhill on the staircase. And then Johnny would show up, sometimes with Harold Arlen. Then Judy Garland would come along, and maybe songwriters Ralph Blane and Hugh Martin would be with her. Later, Nancy Walker, Van Johnson, and June Allyson—who would form the core of the great Metro musicals of the forties—would show up because they had heard something was going on.

And something always was going on, somebody playing the piano, somebody else singing.

The night I remember best was when Harold Arlen and Johnny showed up around nine-thirty. They were working on a song for a Priscilla Lane movie and wanted to see how we'd like it. Harold sat down at the piano and played a few blues chords and Johnny began to imitate a train whistle. All his life, Johnny was fascinated by trains. He began to sing:

"My mama done tol' me
When I was in knee pants,
My mama done tol' me, Son! . . ."

The room grew very still. I looked around. Mel Torme's mouth was hanging open. Judy had her head down and just her eyes were peering up at Arlen. Everyone in the room knew something great was happening. Just to watch Arlen and Mercer perform was a treat. They "wailed" before the term came into fashion. But this night, we were also being introduced to that extraordinary song "Blues in the Night." We had them play it nine times.

When it was over, we couldn't get Mel Torme up off the floor, and for the first time Martha Raye didn't have anything funny to say. Everyone wanted to sing it. Judy and I rushed to the piano to see who could learn it first. I remember the excitement of that night—and most remarkably, there was not an ounce of envy. People were genuinely pleased for everybody else's success.

And then, during the war years, countless servicemen came to our door, on Aunt Mag's invitation, to sample the hospitality. It got so hospitable at times that the police were called.

"What are you running here—a gambling joint?" they would inquire suspiciously. And Aunt Mag would say, "Come on in, gentlemen. We're just entertaining the troops. Do you know Gene Kelly? Come, let me introduce you." And the party would continue.

With the musicians' strike continuing into 1943, by the middle of that year most of the record companies had exhausted their supply of releases. But there were new shows coming up. *Oklahoma!* had opened in New York, and everyone was dying to record the score. So, in desperation, those "heavenly choirs" were used in place of instrumental accompaniment. Frank Sinatra sang "People Will Say We're in Love" with nothing but *voices* in the background. The result was a lot like trying to make the Mormon Tabernacle Choir swing.

During the musicians' strike, everyone took other jobs. Paul Weston worked on the *Johnny Mercer's Music Shop* radio show. And Johnny himself kept turning out songs with Harold Arlen: "One for My Baby" and "My Shining Hour" for the Fred Astaire movie *The Sky's the Limit.*

Finally, in November 1943, when Capitol and Decca records signed an agreement with the musicians' union, we started to think about the future. I hadn't put a lot of thought into *my* future. Somehow I had managed to graduate from high school. But college? "Forget Vassar," Grace Kahn advised my mother. "The girl is going to sing."

Johnny, Paul Weston, and I went through material—a lot of pretty songs. Some wonderful ones. But Johnny was looking for just the right one. And one day, he called up and said, "Kid, come on down. I want you to listen to something."

I went. I hadn't gotten in the door when Johnny motioned for Paul to play the song. The flow of chord progressions was both sophisticated, and simple and direct. Then I began to listen to the words. They were all picture images. A kind of longing. A warmth.

"It's beautiful," I said, baffled. "But what is it?"

"It's your next record," Johnny replied.

"But I don't understand it," The Kid protested. "What does it mean, 'moonlight in Vermont'? I've never even been there."

Johnny overrode my protests. "Don't worry. I'll go through it with you. Now, what does Vermont mean to you?"

I looked at him blankly. All I could think of was photo calendars. He prodded. "Come on."

"Snow. Lots of snow. Waffles and maple syrup—people sledding. Snow, snow, snow. Real villages, church steeples, leaves, people walking in the leaves. I have no idea what a city looks like there, but there's a lot of snow."

"Now describe spring."

"It's coming from the cold into the first day of thaw. I can see little green things." I was beginning to see it. Johnny led me through the four seasons. I think even Paul was impressed. He just sat there and watched.

"What I want from you is four qualities," Johnny instructed me. "Four seasons. You've got 'pennies in the stream'—that's not literal—that's the wonderful glittering look of metal when sun hits water—"

"Ski tows," I interrupted. "What are ski tows?"

It was his turn to look blank. "How do I know? I'm from Savannah." Then he did the only thing a songwriter like Mercer would do. He called up the two writers, Johnny Blackburn and Karl Suessdorf.

"Hello, Karl? Margaret's here. And she's going to record your song and she doesn't know what ski tows are. Can you give me another lyric—another word, maybe? . . . Ski *trails*?" He looked at me. I nodded. "She knows ski trails. Do you mind if we change it, Karl? No? Thanks."

Life was a whirlwind once Johnny got excited. We worked. Paul did the orchestration, and suddenly there were all the seasons. I was standing in front of the mike, with Johnny talking to me.

"Somehow," he was saying, "I want you to give me the four seasons. Crunchy cold. Then warm. The first smell of spring. Just hit the tone dead sometimes, the way you do, and then add the vibrato at the end. And just think of the images. I trust you, kid."

Johnny had worked so hard with me before we came into the

studio, breaking the song into sections, I could feel the sad warmth of fall, the smell of leaves. I began to sing. The band was wonderful. Then, when Billy Butterfield's trumpet came in, all silver and glittering, it changed my voice. We were like two instruments.

"Telegraph cables they sing
Down the highway
Travel each bend in the road . . ."

I could see the width of the entire country, the road going off into infinity.

We listened to the playback, and somebody said, "Oh my God," and Johnny just nodded his head up and down, up and down, as if to say he knew it all along.

"Moonlight in Vermont" sold two million copies that year, and is still going strong.

There was more to it than even Johnny knew. Nineteen forty-three had been a year when everybody in America was yearning for home. The boys far away, the people who had been uprooted, the people back home longing for the way things had been. No wonder *Oklahoma* had been such a surprise hit. Now, as 1943 ended and 1944 began, "Moonlight in Vermont" answered the same basic need everyone had—a need to belong, for something to hold. A memory of love. It was like a letter from home.

So I became a vocal pinup. Jo Stafford, Peggy Lee, and I were the recording equivalents of Grable and Hayworth. Their pictures were stuck on barracks walls. Our records were spun on Victrolas and beat-up phonographs all over the world. We were that sound of home.

I wasn't The Kid anymore.

By the end of 1944, I was growing up into someone called Margaret Whiting.

6

The Kid
Grows Up

I remember being herded into an army truck at three o'clock in the morning, along with the character actor Frank McHugh; some members of a band; Johnny Coy, a dancer from Paramount; Shirley Dinsdale, who worked with a dummy; and Olga San Juan, who was our sex symbol. We were on our way to entertain the troops, and it occurred to me, as we drove through the desert, *I am on my own. I am very grown-up*. I was eighteen at the time and thrilled to be going out alone, without Aunt Mag or any of the other people who had chaperoned me. I was also thrilled because Robert Armstrong was in the truck with us. *Wuthering Heights* and *King Kong* were my two favorite movies. Robert Armstrong was the star of *King Kong*. And he was in this truck with me. It was all very glamorous. You can see how grown-up I was.

Our expedition had boarded a train in Los Angeles the previous evening, with instructions to tell no one where we were going. These were orders from the Hollywood Coordinating Committee. The train left at 4:00 P.M. At 2:00 A.M. the porter woke us up to say that we would be getting off in an hour. At exactly three in the morning, the train deposited us in the middle of the desert and chugged away. There was nothing there. No station. No road. Nothing. We were twenty-five people stranded in a pitch-black desert without a sound, a light, without anything, except the wisecracks of Frank McHugh. And even those didn't keep out the cold.

In about five minutes, we heard the sound of motors and then we saw lights. Three trucks pulled up. Several officers got out and welcomed us, helped us aboard, and then we were off again, driving through the endless pitch-black night. We drove for about an hour, shivering with the cold. But as I said, I was deliciously happy. It was a wonderful feeling. I was on my own at last. I was seated next to Robert Armstrong! This was adventure! But, God, was I cold.

With a squeal of brakes, the trucks stopped and we were checked through one barrier. A few minutes later, we were stopped at another gate, and then passed through. Finally the trucks stopped. We were told to take our bags and rest in the tent.

"What tent?" I asked, peering into the darkness.

"Here's a tent for the female performers," one of the officers said, motioning with his arm. The girls followed his direction. Sure enough, in a moment, there appeared a tent. There were four or five cots inside. We stumbled around in the dark. I lay down on one of the cots, drew my coat around me, and promptly fell asleep, oblivious to all the mystery.

At dawn, reveille sounded. I jumped out of the cot and headed for the light. Dawn in the desert is always unforgettable, but on this particular day the air was as clean as God ever made it. There was a sudden rosy glow in the east, followed by a burst of orange as the sun rose.

I looked out of the tent. "Where are we?" I asked nobody in particular.

"It doesn't matter," nobody in particular answered me.

"What is this?" I persisted. I could see no buildings at all, but endless rows of tents, stretching almost as far as the desert itself.

Three men came up to me. "We're your bodyguard," they said by way of introduction.

"Who needs a bodyguard?" I asked blithely. They remained tactfully silent. The heat was beginning to cover the desert.

"I think I'll change into my shorts," I said.

"I wouldn't do that, ma'am," one of the bodyguards said, not threatening, just definite.

"Oh." I nodded. "Well, then, just a bit of this perfume. . . ." I was perspiring rather freely.

"Don't put on perfume, lady," another guard warned, as he moved toward me. One could tell they thought they were going to have trouble with us.

At noon, with the temperature hovering around 120 degrees, I said, "Could I please take a shower?"

The man nodded. "So long as we stand guard, ma'am." I was led to an institutional-looking building. What was it doing in the middle of the desert? It was the only building around. It did have showers, and I took one gratefully while the troops stood guard. For all the good it did, I needn't have bothered. Fifteen minutes later, I was a sodden mass again.

They finally let us in on the situation. These troops had been stationed here on the desert for six months—farm kids and mechanics who had undergone an indoctrination course to toughen up for the rigors of desert fighting. For instance, they had not seen an ice cube for six months. Or a woman.

Now they were about to go overseas, and the army was throwing a party. Generals Mark Clark and Omar Bradley were going to attend. The chef from the Waldorf-Astoria had been conscripted (literally), and he was preparing a feast in the desert. Great truckloads of ice had been shipped in from Phoenix. And we were the entertainment. Of course, nobody knew—with the exception of Generals Clark and Bradley—that this was all a prelude to the invasion of North Africa.

It was always the custom for the entertainers to mingle with the troops, to talk to them, carry messages back to the families. In this situation, the guards were leery of the reaction, but we were insistent.

So, acting as nonsexual as possible, with no makeup, no perfume—God knows, no shorts—we walked under the baking sun and talked to the soldiers. It was as primitive a situation as I have ever seen. These guys had been together all this time in the desert. Their faces were burned and cracked from the heat. A lot of them, no older than nineteen, wore beards, because it was easier than shaving. Since we were the first women they had seen, one could feel the vibrations. There was a purely sexual throbbing going on. I had the feeling that, without the bodyguards, they might have just lifted us up and carried us away into the desert. (I don't think this was the *King Kong* influence of Robert Armstrong; I think it was a fact.) But we deflected all this pent-up emotion by asking if they had any messages for home. We took down as many as we could, promised to call or write and tell the families that their boys were all right. From time to time, we had to move in out of the heat, which was like a giant weight pressing down on the camp. It was no cooler in the tents. Our only refuge lay in the quarters where we were to change for the performance. There, at least, we were sheltered from the sun.

And then it came time for the show. The sun had set, the heat diminished. The army had erected a makeshift stage from planks. There was a stairway. The band sat in chairs. There were white lights illuminating us. No gels. No show-business pink. Just blazing white lights.

I can still picture the scene. There was the last purple wisp of sunset in the west, but night had fallen over the camp, and just before I went on, I could catch a glimpse of the audience. There were 100,000 men out there. I have a picture that was taken then, and we entertainers onstage look like miniature dolls, facing an enormous sea of soldiers.

Of course, as entertainers, we could do no wrong. All I had to do was sing, "I don't want to walk without you, baby," and the entire audience ignited. I looked down to see that the edge of the stage was ringed with *more* guards to keep order. I didn't see precautions like this again until the rock concerts of the sixties.

Robert Armstrong emceed, I sang, Johnny danced, McHugh wise-cracked. Poor Olga San Juan tried to reduce her slither to less than a slink, but all she had to do was walk on that stage and the boys roared their approval. Cheers, whistles, cries, applause, laughter blew into that desert night. The sounds of the swing band echoed out into that all-American darkness. We performed for as long as we could, till the dust got into our throats and we were as much in need of ice as the boys were.

Then followed the banquet. Hundreds of cakes filled the tables, huge, magnificent sugar confections, washed down with champagne, properly iced. And we were served fruit cups, the different fruit carved into fantastic figures. There were candles and great tables and elegance, amid all the male laughter and the toasts and the cheers. But what a disorienting experience it must have been for them. Later that night, I thought of all the thousands of kids who had grown up in Petaluma, California, or Pampa, Texas, with Mom and Dad, and maybe a sister or brother, who had worked in the mail room, or at the garage, and who had suddenly been whisked away into the army, where they all were herded together, to sleep, shower, live together, and face who knew what future lying beyond that dark night. Here they were in an empty desert, suddenly plied with champagne, ice, cakes, laughter, and food, and entertainment to dispel the loneliness. Nobody who experienced any of this was ever quite the same, neither the troops nor the entertainers.

The next morning, we waved good-bye to these kids, boarded the trucks, then the train that was carrying us to the next service base. We were let off in Yuma, Arizona, right on the California border, a very popular place for Hollywood folk to sneak off to and get married without the usual notoriety of a Nevada wedding. The press (if there was any in Yuma) was not hip to the Hollywood scene. It looked to me as though there were a main street, two hotels, a couple of motels, and that was it.

Our troupe was all billeted on the same floor of one of the hotels. I was exhausted and prostrate from the heat; there was no air-conditioning in those days. I threw myself across the bed. The springs squeaked. I got up again. I had to have a bath. I went into the bathroom and turned on the faucet.

Thousands of black bugs spewed out of the spigot. I screamed. I thought I was having a nightmare. I hate bugs, and what were they doing in a water faucet? Johnny Coy dashed into my room, thinking perhaps rape or molestation, or possibly murder. Shaking, I pointed at the bugs. He turned off the faucet, started collecting the bugs, and grinned at me.

"Welcome to show business!" he said.

"This isn't *my* kind of show business!" I wailed, sitting on the terrible bed that squeaked again.

And indeed it wasn't. I was used to the best. I had grown up with the best. The best music, the best actors, the best food in the best restaurants, living in the best houses in the best neighborhood of the swankiest little city in the world. I had never trod the boards or done the two-a-day in vaudeville. I had never gone hungry because a booking had been canceled. I had never been stranded in a small town because the theater had been shut down for lack of funds.

And I had never been plucked out of my environment and thrown together with a thousand others and been told when to sleep and when to get up, and denied all luxuries, like those soldiers I had just entertained. *I am on my own. I am very grown up.*

In those four days, I was just beginning to grow up. I had a long way to go.

But I was learning. I had the best audience in the world, albeit a captive one: the U.S. armed services. I also had some pretty swell teachers, Bob Hope and Red Skelton, for starters.

Rehearsing his radio show, Hope said to me one day, "I'm going to give you one of the great laugh lines of all time." I said, "Thank you, and what will I do with it?" He said, "Don't move. Don't move a muscle. Just listen to what I say, wait a beat, *don't move a muscle,* and then say the line. You got that?"

"Yes," I said. He launched into a long description of somebody jumping into a vat full of grapes. The description went on forever with the jumping *on* the grapes and the jumping *around* the grapes. Finally he finished. I moved not a muscle, stared him straight in the eye, and said my line.

"You tell 'em, purple foot."

There was a five-minute laugh. During that time, he just looked at me, as if to say, See, if you do what I tell you. . . . I still don't know why the line was funny, but I did learn *never* to move on a laugh line.

Hope was very particular about movement. One night we were working on a barnyard sketch that Norman Lear and Bud Yorkin had written. There were a lot of animals in the scene and one of the mules bit me.

I said, "That mule bit me!," and Hope said, without taking a breath, "Keep that in!"

"But that mule bit me."

"Right. Just the way you moved when you said that, that was exactly right." Nobody was interested in the fact that the damned mule had bitten me, except me.

I learned how many beats to wait before delivering a line. I learned how the audience absorbs the rhythm; to repeat a line three times, so that the third time it pays off. These men were precise technicians. Red Skelton and I were going to do a piece that involved shaking hands when one of the hands is stuck with chewing gum. The more we tried to extricate ourselves from the gum, the more tangled we became. The frustration of it was extremely funny. After four days' work, we finally got the routine down. Then the network said they were cutting the sketch. Skelton said, "Uh-huh," and under his breath said to me, "We'll do it anyway." And we did.

You can't get that experience now, because no one has the burlesque training, the vaudeville training that Phil Silvers and Rags Ragland, Milton Berle, Hope, and Skelton had. I never saw burlesque. I never saw vaudeville, but these people handed it down to me. You learned from these people unless you were an idiot.

So I learned. Even if I wasn't quite sure who Margaret Whiting was.

For a while in 1943, I was suddenly eclipsed by my sister, Barbara. Barbara is six years younger than I, and when she was twelve and thirteen, those six years made an enormous difference. She was a born performer, and at thirteen, a terrible brat. Gus Kahn was heard to murmur, "If Barbara gets just a *little* bit better, we might get her into Tehachapi," which was a women's prison in California.

No matter what Barbara did, my mother adored her. I remember this was the period when a Mrs. Eager disappeared, and then was found—piece by piece. It made all the papers. With each edition, they found her fingers, they found her torso, they found her toes, but no one could ever find her head. One night, when my mother was being particularly emphatic about knowing what was best for us because she had been through everything so she knew it all, Barbara, hands defiantly on hips, looked at her and said, "All right, if you're so smart, where's Mrs. Eager's *head*?" My mother still loved her. Actually, a mouth like that is very helpful in show business.

A New York producer called my mother. He was interested in me for a Broadway show. Eleanore arranged for him to come over to the house that evening and I would audition for him.

Just as I was about to burst into song, Barbara walked down the stairs and, pausing squarely in front of me, said:

"I hate Margaret.
She'd make a good target.
She sings, she thinks.
But I think she stinks.
I hate Margaret."

And then, on cue, she left the room. P.S.: I didn't get the job.

Small wonder, then, when they were looking for a foil for the lead in the movie *Junior Miss*, they happened upon Barbara. Next door lived Barbara's best friend, Judy Davies, whose father was Val Davies, a well-known scriptwriter. Regularly Barbara would bawl over the fence, "Hey Judy!" George and Phyllis Seaton, friends of the Davieses', were visiting one day when this occurred. George Seaton was going to direct *Junior Miss*. He asked the Davieses to call Barbara over. Barbara obligingly leaped over the fence and into the Davieses' living room, talked for five minutes, and landed the part. In the film, Peggy Ann Garner played the lead and Barbara played her friend, Fuffy. (Later, on the radio series, Barbara became *Junior Miss*.)

While they were making the movie, it was necessary for someone to get up with Barbara, make her breakfast, take her to 20th Century-Fox, and supervise her during the day at the studio. That someone became me. I didn't mind at all, because while Barbara was toiling, I had a chance to pal around the studio, and to sit at the songwriter's table in the commissary with the arrangers and musicians. Alfred Newman and his brother were there. And, of course, Harry Warren and Mack Gordon and Joe Myrow, who were writing all the Fox musicals. On the set, I would be absorbed watching Tyrone Power make love to Alice Faye while Betty Grable stood by. And then they would start to sing. It was always the same. The composer would have written a song for the star, who would pick up the music while the composer sat at the piano. She would read it as if she'd known it all her life, the composer would play eight bars, and on bar nine, the strings would come in—from out of nowhere. I always loved that particular bit of Hollywood romance, and it never changed.

Judy Garland and I used to laugh about those moments of "musical magic." Judy had the best sense of humor in the world and absolutely the most infectious laugh. It would start out as a giggle and then become a genuine belly laugh. We used to get together for lunch during those days. It seemed very grown-up to have luncheon at the Beverly Hills Brown Derby. We were being super-sophisticated. One time, on our way to the Brown Derby, we were driving down an alley, and Judy wanted something out of the glove compartment. Like everybody else's, her compartment was full of maps, bobby pins, cigarette packages, matches, and a couple of boxes. "You really ought to get rid of some of that junk," I observed.

"You're right," Judy said, glancing at one of the boxes. "Throw it out." So I opened the window and tossed the box into the alley. We continued driving down the alley a moment, and then Judy slammed her foot on the brake and screeched, "Oh, my God. What have you done? There goes the career."

"What is it? What is it?" I asked anxiously.

"You threw my teeth out the window!" She started to gasp with laughter. "What would Louis B. say? Fourteen hundred dollars' worth of caps! We got to find them!"

We went back, crawled around the alley on our hands and knees until we retrieved her caps, and proceeded to the Brown Derby.

People often ask me, "If Judy was so difficult, why did anybody put up with her?" I was around during the days she was making *Meet Me in St. Louis* with Vincente Minnelli. They were set to record Martin and Blane's "The Trolley Song" and I had been invited to the set. I've always been a stickler for punctuality. That was Eleanore and Aunt Mag's doing. So I arrived. But no Judy. It was still early in the morning. Vocal coach Kay Thompson was there to practice the routine. Everybody went through the rehearsal without Garland. There were forty musicians waiting around with Georgie Stoll, the conductor. Still no Judy. They rehearsed trolley sounds and dance steps. Ten-thirty. Eleven. No Garland. They broke for lunch. At one-thirty, Judy arrived with her two little poodles. She apologized. She said she had overslept. She flashed that quick, shy grin of hers that melted the hardest heart, and said, "Okay, let's get to work."

"Do you want a rehearsal?" Kay Thompson asked her.

"We'll run it down once," Judy agreed. They did. She was letter-perfect.

"Can we do a take?" Georgie Stoll asked.

Judy said, "Why not?" The music started. That irresistible throb that is the intro to "The Trolley Song" began. Judy listened attentively and then raised her head. Her eyes were shining and she sang:

*"With my high starched collar and my high topped shoes and my hair
  piled high upon my head,
I went to lose a jolly hour on a trolley and lost my heart instead . . ."*

It contained all the delicate urgency of a young girl in love and the joy of performing that was Judy's trademark. It was a perfect take.

"Can we do one more?" Georgie suggested.

Judy shrugged. "Sure."

She did another take. It was as good as the first. She collected her two poodles and went home. She had been there all of fifty minutes. And they had been waiting for five hours. But when she worked she *worked*. And *it* worked. The results were effortless magic.

So, the answer is very simple. The studio put up with her shenanigans because her talent was so extraordinary. And because she made money for them. When she became—perhaps "not cost-effective" would be the studio's term—they let her go.

One day, while Barbara was working on *Junior Miss*, I was sitting around with my pals (Mel Torme was also in the movie, so we had a good time) when George Seaton beckoned to me and said, "Come next door to this rehearsal studio. There are some people there who know you."

He opened the door and there were Richard Rodgers and Oscar

Hammerstein. They were working on Seaton's next project, *State Fair*, which he was producing with William Perlberg, and Dick and Oscar had just completed the score. They were feeling particularly expansive and asked me to come in and listen. I was thrilled.

"You know," Rodgers told me, "I really loved your father. And when I was starting out, I was signed by Remick Music. When the first song was published, it was printed, 'Lyrics by Lorenz Hart, music by Richard *Whiting*.' " He chuckled and said, "Now, listen to this and tell us what you think."

They had already recorded the score. It certainly was lovely, one beautiful melody after another, including "It's a Grand Night for Singing," "That's for Me," and "It Might As Well Be Spring."

"Oh, lovely!" I said when the tape ended.

"What do you think of 'That's for Me'?" Rodgers asked.

"Lovely," I repeated. "But I really like the other one. The spring one."

" 'That's for Me' is going to be our big hit," Rodgers said confidently.

"Oh, they all are!" I enthused diplomatically, and left.

Later that day, when I was home, Paul Weston called me with some bad news. I had recently recorded "Blue Skies," which was being revived by Bing Crosby for a Paramount feature of the same name. And on the back of that record, we had cut "My Intuition," a new Mercer-Warren song from *The Harvey Girls*. But after one of those famous Glendale previews, the producer had decided "My Intuition" slowed down the film and it was cut. The ballad was out of the movie, and we were out of a song.

"Call Barbara Ford," I told Paul. She was the assistant cutter on *State Fair*. "Get her to play the track on a song called 'It Might As Well Be Spring.' I think it would be a sensational number."

Paul did just that and phoned back. "I agree," he said.

Paul obtained copies of the music and we conferred. The tune had been written as a rather brisk schottische.

"I hear it as a ballad," I said rather wistfully, not wanting to go against Mr. Rodgers's wishes.

"So do I," Paul agreed.

We recorded it that way, and with much trepidation, played it for Rodgers and Hammerstein.

Dick Rodgers listened impassively, then looked at us.

"I thought of it as a schottische," he said.

"We know," we said.

He nodded. "Your way is better." And he rewrote the song for the picture.

The record came out and it was a smash. Of course, Fox was delighted. Barbara had completed *Junior Miss* and was assigned to a musical, *Centennial Summer*, with a score by Jerome Kern, his last, and lyrics by practically everyone I knew. Johnny Mercer, for one. Leo Robin, for another. Oscar Hammerstein. And "Yip" Harburg. I had a new group at the musicians' table. They had all been friends of my father's. And now they treated me with respect for myself, but I hardly noticed. My success made practically no impression on me. I was still Barbara's older sister, who was baby-sitting. Or I was Daddy's girl, who was palling around with his cronies. I did see some signs of status. A chauffeur from Fox picked us up each day to go to the studio.

One day I was asked to visit the publicity department. Harry Brandt ran the department, but Shirley Potash was the publicist who introduced me to Bill Eythe, who was working on *Centennial Summer*. He was an actor who had been seen in New York in *The Eve of St. Mark* and signed by Fox to come out to film the same role. Then, it was explained to me, he had completed *The House on 92nd Street* and several other pictures. *Centennial Summer* was his first musical.

Eythe and I were paired up. We made a nice couple, and we were sent to premieres along with Linda Darnell and Victor Mature. Evidently, because of my status as a recording artist, the publicity department considered me important enough to be seen with these new stars. But apparently I had a great deal to learn about Hollywood status.

Because of the war, Hollywood had lost a number of its leading men to the service, among them Tyrone Power, Clark Gable, James Stewart, and Robert Taylor. The studios scoured the country for replacements. Van Johnson came to MGM. So did John Hodiak. Bill Eythe was to be Fox's answer to Tyrone Power. There were a number of other actors who were all friendly with one another, among them Laird Cregar, so memorable in *The Lodger*, and Robert Walker, that sweet, sensitive juvenile still married to Jennifer Jones.

One evening, while having dinner at Romanoff's with Cregar, Bill Eythe, and Bob Walker, we were interrupted by Leo McCarey, a dear friend of my father's. He had been drinking. He raged at me. "What are you doing with those people! You shouldn't be sitting with them!" He continued to fume, saying to my mother, "You shouldn't allow Margaret to go out with those guys. They're the second run. They're not the first cast." Later, he apologized to all of them, but the feeling was there. Hollywood definitely had its caste (cast) system.

Bill and I saw one another constantly. *Centennial Summer* involved a lot of night shots with railroad-train sequences and, of course, I had to accompany Barbara. Because Bill was witty and charming and bright, I gravitated toward him. Those nights passed very quickly. The silly little love story of the film involved two sisters who are rivals for a suitor's affections and the inability of anyone to express his love. I don't know whether or not in my vivid imagination I was setting up a similar sequence, but Bill and I looked long into each other's eyes. We had our intimate jokes. We could do nothing, since we were in full view of everyone, but the buzz around the studio was that we were going together. Meanwhile, Barbara toiled away. Never was there a more careless chaperone. On the other hand, anyone who dared tangle with Barbara would have gotten what he deserved.

The executives at Fox, aware of the success of "It Might As Well Be Spring," kept urging me to listen to the score of *Centennial Summer*. They wanted a recording from me. It was hard to reconcile myself with the personage that was Margaret Whiting. After all, I had been Barbara's baby-sitter. However, I did record two of the tunes, "All Through the Day" backed with "In Love in Vain." The lyric to "In Love in Vain" was Leo Robin's. I knew that Kern did not like working with Leo. This was strange, because if anything, Leo was the president of the Goodfellows Club. But he was a polisher and a refiner, taking infinite pains with every word, and he was too slow for Kern, who preferred Johnny Mercer and Oscar Hammerstein, who could take a tune and toss back a lyric. Not that they were careless in their work. They just, somehow, did it more easily. If anyone was difficult in a relationship, it had to be Kern.

By now, I was not just the vocalist who was called in for a record date and got seventy-five dollars a side and no royalties. I had signed a new contract. Now my name was prominently on the record and I received a two-or-three-hundred-dollar advance against real royalties. That was prestige. So I cut the two songs, and then in a couple of weeks I was told that "It Might As Well Be Spring" had become my third gold record. I was a recording star!

It's only human for anyone to want to be in love,
But who wants to be in love in vain? . . .

By now, Bill and I thought we were head-over-heels in love. We were very romantic. We went to premieres and parties and spent a lot of time alone at his house. Bill was bright enough to know that he would never be Tyrone Power. On his first picture, director Lewis Milestone kicked the shit out of him. Perhaps Milestone resented the fact that Bill had done the role in New York on the stage. He goaded Bill continually, and Bill never got over it. Milestone really undermined his security as an actor. He knew (as they all did) that Bill was considered an imitation of Power, and he lacked a self-image. We would stay up all night and talk and drink wine. Many times we would drive out to a huge house called the Rindge Estate, which overlooked the Pacific. We would sit there at six in the morning, drinking wine and gazing at the ocean. And then he made love to me. Bill was an extremely sexual person and he was a sweet and tender lover, but there was something missing. He said he loved me, but I could never put my finger on the dissatisfaction.

You sit and wonder why anyone as wonderful as he
Should cause you such misery and pain . . .

It wasn't as though I was that experienced a lover. Nor was I a mourner and moaner about life. I have always been very practical.

I had lost my virginity a year or so before, and I had had it all planned.

It was in the guest room of my mother's house. The man was Tom D'Andrea, a Warner Brothers actor, who was full of wisecracks (I am a sucker for a sense of humor) and very attractive. He came over to the house all the time, and often stayed overnight. As a matter of fact, so did a number of other people. Come to think of it, over the years, we always had somebody staying over. There was Peggy Ann Garner, whose mother was a rather unsavory character, and then Jule Styne's nephews, Buddy and Bobby Bregman, and Ed Sullivan's daughter, Betty, for a couple of years when she was going to college. The house was never empty. So one of these evenings I smiled at Tom D'Andrea and led him up to the guest room. I had heard from other women that getting deflowered was not the most pleasant experience in the world, so I was eager to get it over with. Tom was the perfect choice. I adored him; he was a terribly nice guy, but not the kind a girl could get too involved with, because he wasn't really serious. He just wanted a good time. And that's what we had. He led me through that tunnel of love in the gentlest way possible. It wasn't anything terrific, but it wasn't anything so horrible either. And I felt relieved. Now that was over.

With Bill Eythe, I was unsure. Perhaps there was something lacking in me. I wished I had someone to talk to, but Eleanore was not that kind of mother. She adored Barbara and gave her more affection then she gave me. That never bothered me. I understood it; I was harder to handle. I was her alter ego. She had always wanted to perform, to sing. She had a wonderful voice, but she lost it when she went onstage. So she had had to settle for having a career vicariously through me.

Eleanore gave advice, plenty of it, but she never just threw her arms around me and said, "I love you." Oh yes, there was that one time she did. At the time of my father's death, she said, "There's just us now," and held me in her arms. But that was the only time. I don't remember her sitting me down and saying, "You know, you're going to have a menstrual period. It's something that happens to every young girl, and there's nothing to be afraid of." I learned about menstruation because it happened to me at the convent school

I attended, and a nun had to explain what was going on, that I had not developed a suddenly fatal disease, the kind of mysterious ailment that Barbara Stanwyck or Merle Oberon was always succumbing to in the final reel of a film. So the nun explained about menstruation, and then Barbara's baby nurse explained about sex. That wasn't too helpful either. The nurse carried with her a complete catalogue of human lust, but her main warning was that you could get pregnant quick as a wink.

So I was not overly prepared for a love affair. I don't know whether my mother was a terribly physical woman. I know she adored my father and was devoted to him, but I had no idea what she thought about sex. Eleanore did try to equip me to meet the world. She gave cautionary lectures, but they were always too heavy. And, perversely, I would do the opposite. In a house devoted to entrances and exits, there were no private moments. Never, ever, did we share those intimate moments that should occur between a mother and a daughter. Eleanore was always busy visiting people and helping them out, or they were visiting the house and she and Aunt Margaret were helping them out. Years later, Barbara's husband, Gail, said to me,. "Margaret, you're very much like your mother."

"Oh my God!" I said.

"Don't 'oh my God.' Be grateful. Look how far she has come. Look at all the marvelous things she has done. Be grateful for all the wonderful things Eleanore gave you." That was my first insight into accepting the pioneer woman that was Eleanore.

But at twenty, I felt bitter toward the woman who just couldn't sit down and talk to me.

I felt I had to leave home. It was time. I knew by now that Bill Eythe and I weren't going anywhere. We played a great game, but there was always something elusive about the relationship. He said he loved me, but when I went away, he started seeing my schoolmate Buff Cobb, and when I came back, it was never the same. They got married, Buff and Bill, but that marriage didn't work. And somewhere in this period, Bill discovered, or admitted, that he actually preferred men.

I think back to Leo McCarey's outburst, that I shouldn't hang around with these men. Cregar was a homosexual, Bob Walker an alcoholic. And Bill was also a homosexual. Maybe McCarey was trying to warn me about a situation that nobody talked about much in those days, but it wouldn't have helped. I loved all three men very dearly. They were good friends to me.

Bill was interested in producing a stage revue in Los Angeles. He had met a writer, Charles Gaynor, and he was exhilarated by the possibilities of getting involved in stage work again. We offered our house for auditions, and, in turn, he offered me the lead. But my manager at the time, Billy Burton, refused it.

"What do you want with this?" he said. "It's just another actor putting on another revue. Go to New York. You've got a big career ahead of you."

Reluctantly, I turned down Bill's offer. Another blonde came into our house to audition. She had huge eyes and an adorable gawky manner, like a cartoon come to life. Bill hired her immediately. Her name was Carol Channing and the revue was *Lend an Ear*. It played for a year or two in Los Angeles before becoming a smash hit in New York, and it made Carol a star.

Another thing I missed out on was V-J Day. I was in the Weaver Jackson Beauty Salon in Beverly Hills getting a permanent. I was absorbed in *Photoplay* and didn't notice the hustle and bustle. After all, beauty parlors always bustle. But then it came to my attention there was more bustle than usual. Not only that, people were fleeing the shop and running out into the street.

"What's happening?" I cried from under the permanent-wave machine. If anyone had answered, I couldn't have heard it. There was no one to disengage me. I sat there clamped to the machine, looking like Elsa Lanchester in *The Bride of Frankenstein*, while the whole place emptied.

Finally, someone remembered me and set me free.

"What happened?"

"The war's over!"

I cried with relief. I was happy that so many lives had been spared, and that the killing had stopped.

But also because I felt it was my graduation.

I had grown up.

7

The World on a String

I was going to New York again, but alone this time. And this time I was getting the "A" treatment. Margaret Whiting was a record and radio star with three gold records and two hot new releases. The war was over and everybody was happy. And I wasn't going to be absolutely alone; there were plenty of people to take care of me. Eleanore had seen to that. My godmother, Sophie Tucker, promised to get me a room in a hotel and keep a watchful eye over me. The William Morris office was instructed to entertain me, get me work, keep me busy. But as powerful as Sophie Tucker and the Morris office were, together they couldn't find a room in New York. It was the first Thanksgiving after the war and the scene of the Army-Navy game. Keye Luke (forever famous as Charlie Chan's number one son) and I had arrived together at the William Morris office. A very nervous minor agent came out.

"We have found a room for you. It's not a very nice room," he began. Keye Luke and I stared at each other. Were we meant to be roommates, just because we were both William Morris clients?

"One room?" I queried.

The agent blushed. "I mean, one room apiece. It's in a hotel that's a little far west."

I did not have the New Yorker's phobia about geography. "Swell! Take us to it!" The agent bundled us into a cab, and we drove across Forty-second Street to the Hotel Holland.

Just the other day I read in the paper that the Board of Health had condemned the Hotel Holland, which is now a welfare hotel. As far as I am concerned, they condemned it forty years too late. When we arrived with our luggage, we found the lobby filled with sleep-overs from the Army-Navy game. Long-term friendships were being celebrated with flasks and toasts. And new—and I assume very temporary—friendships were being formed before our very eyes. Irate clientele were demanding service, keys, accommodations, information, none of which the Hotel Holland seemed equipped to dispense. Finally, Keye Luke and I were handed our keys. We disappeared into separate elevators, and I never saw him again.

As soon as the William Morris agent left me, I picked up the phone to call Nancy Walker. She came over to the hotel with her boyfriend Murvyn Vye (he had played Jigger in *Carousel*). Tough Murvyn, to say nothing of tough Nancy, said, "Oh no, this won't do. We'll have to get you another place." Nancy called agent Gloria Safier, who immediately invited me for Thanksgiving dinner at her country house in Connecticut. It was a glorious meal and I have never forgotten the warmth of her hospitality.

After Thanksgiving, I called a friend of Bill Eythe's, Jimmy McNaughton, who was a scenic designer for ABC. The two of them had attended Carnegie Tech together. And now Jimmy offered to share his apartment with me. It was a wonderful duplex, right next to the Blue Angel nightclub on East Fifty-fifth Street. Then, as now, there was a housing shortage in New York. I liked Jimmy, and he liked me, so I moved in. We decided I would be his cousin. It made things easier to explain.

What a wonderful time it was! Everyone walked with a spring in his step. The whole world seemed to be smiling. There were thousands of night clubs, lots of live music, brilliant theater, streams of talented people coming to New York to launch their careers. And here was I. In those days Broadway was lined with record shops, all equipped with loudspeakers, and my voice was coming out of every one of them.

> *"I'm as restless as a willow in a windstorm,*
> *I'm as jumpy as a puppet on a string.*
> *I'd say that I had spring fever,*
> *But I know it isn't spring . . ."*

Sing it, Margaret! That was the first time it really hit me, who I was, and what I had done. I was that voice. That voice belonged to me. Practically everyone in America could recognize that voice and knew it was mine. People stopped me in the street and said hello. I was their daughter, their sweetheart, their sister, a friend, the girl next door. I was famous. It was wonderful.

Here was New York, that international grab bag of delights, just waiting for me to discover it, and I did with a vengeance. I wanted to absorb everything.

Fifty-second Street. That was, then, the musician's hangout. Every club was like a shrine. The Famous Door. The Three Deuces. The Onyx. And one night, I was taken to hear Mabel Mercer. She was a very dignified woman who sat in a chair, moved not a muscle, opened her mouth, and spun enchantment. She was economical in everything she phrased, and her phrasing was effortless and graceful. I was listening. I was learning. And so, I gather, were others. Peggy Lee was there that same night. Frank Sinatra, Duke Ellington, and every other singer in town came in to hear Mabel. And in those days you could still hear Billie Holiday. And there were the other clubs —such as Spivy's Roof, the Bon Soir, and the Ruban Bleu. The Blue Angel was right next door. Pearl Bailey was reigning there, sly, smooth, absolutely delicious with her sense of humor. And Burl Ives, the folk singer, turned the club into his personal fireside. These clubs were like an endless cornucopia of music—jazz, folk, special comedy material, Broadway show tunes. It was one giant celebration after another, and no one was exhausted from all the talent and music and energy. The energy only fed energy. No one needed to sleep then. One might miss something.

For me, more than anything, there were piano players. The girl singer always needs her piano player. There were more great piano players in New York than I had ever seen before. And if there was a great piano player around, I either went with him or found him. First I heard Cy Walters play at the Drake Hotel. I introduced myself, told him I loved his records, and we became friends. Through him I got to meet them all—Howard Smith; Stan Freeman; Lester Crosley, who played for Mabel Mercer; Bernie Leighton; Teddy Wilson, who was legendary even among all these legends. I even met Earl Wild, who was a classical pianist, but he could also swing. One night we had a party, and there were eleven pianists there. Before the night was over, all eleven had played "It Might As Well Be Spring" for me, and each one had played it entirely differently. That was the night the illustrator Jon Whitcomb came up to me, smiling, and asked, "How does it feel to be the toast of the town?"

Oh it felt just swell. There was nothing to beat it. I got everything one could get as a new star, dinner at "21," dancing at the Stork Club, drinks at El Morocco, first and second teams of William Morris agents to squire me around. I may have exhausted a whole contingent of agents, but I had a wonderful time. It was Happy New Year every night. And then one night it actually was Happy New Year. It was 1946.

The telephone rang. It was Johnny Mercer. He and Harold Arlen had just finished a new musical called *St. Louis Woman* and they were coming to New York for its Broadway production. He was going to send me a song from the show and I was to learn it forward and backward. I promised I would and I did. Two weeks later, he arrived with Paul Weston, set up the recording date, and I went in to record. Both Johnny and Harold were in the control room, the two of them such terrific singers themselves that just their singing of a song was enough to throw me. They made the most unlikely, wonderful team. Johnny was a true son of the South, and Harold a true son of a cantor from Buffalo. But these two disparate heritages meshed. Harold wrote songs with a marvelous blues chord structure that was sensuous and sophisticated and also primitive. Johnny's lyrics blazed with originality and an American earthiness. They had the same understanding of the same kind of music, so it worked. The song Johnny had given me was called "Come Rain or Come Shine." I had learned it note by note, remembering my father's cautionary words: "Sing the song the way the writers wrote it. They worked hard to get it just right." The very last note of this song was one long note on the tonic. I learned it that way, but when we did a take, something happened in my mind. I started thinking about Harold, the cantor's son. On that last note, I just let it wail:

"I'm gonna love you, come rain or shine."

Well, Johnny burst through the door, mad as hell: "What in God's name are you doing?" He was followed by Harold, who shouted, "No, leave it, leave it! That's the way I should have written it."

That was the first time I dared do such a thing.

The record was released in a couple of weeks and became a big hit. Unfortunately, the show did not. It had a brilliant score, with songs like "Any Place I Hang My Hat Is Home," "Legalize My Name," the ballad "I Had Myself a True Love." The cast included Pearl Bailey and the wonderfully talented Nicholas Brothers. But the book was weak and the show only ran a few weeks. It plagued Johnny that he never had a smash hit on Broadway, although *Li'l Abner* certainly had a respectable run.

By now I was Margaret Whiting, Girl Singer, twenty-one years old, with five smash-hit records to her credit, not to mention the fact that she had been given the opportunity to introduce six great songs (not including my father's "My Ideal"): "That Old Black Magic," "Moonlight in Vermont," "It Might As Well Be Spring," "All Through the Day," "In Love in Vain," and "Come Rain or Come Shine."

This girl singer was hot, and having a ball, going everywhere, seeing everyone, working all the best radio shows, signed to the *Philip Morris Follies. Whoopee!*

I was meeting everyone. I heard a brilliant man playing harpsichord on some Alec Wilder records. I tracked him down. Walter Gross was his name. He worked at Musicraft Records, and he was an incredible piano player. Since he was an incredible piano player, I started going out with him. He was getting a divorce. I found him funny, vitriolic, with a dry, caustic sense of humor. I didn't realize at first that he had a serious drinking problem.

A couple of nights before the Fourth of July, I went to dinner with Walter and some friends at an inn across the river in New Jersey. The dinner was wonderful. Walter drank a lot, but nothing out of the ordinary—everybody seemed to be drinking a lot in those days—and we started the drive back to New York. Somewhere close to the George Washington Bridge, Skitch Henderson's name came up.

"Oh," I cried. "He's an old friend of mine. He taught me my first song."

"Don't mention his name to me!" Walter growled.

"But he was a friend of the family's. He used to play for my Aunt Margaret."

"What did I tell you!" Walter shouted. "I said, don't mention his name. I told you not to mention his name, and you did. Don't you mention Skitch Henderson. He's a lousy piano player!"

By this time, we were on the bridge. Walter was so drunk and so furious that he started to steer for the edge. He was going to drive us right off the thing. I cried, "Walter, stop that!" Someone else in the car grabbed his arm. Together we straightened the car around and avoided an accident. I thought, Piano players are all a bit nuts. But that was all.

On the Fourth of July, Walter came over to the apartment to apologize.

"I feel terrible about the way I acted," he said.

"I didn't know you felt that way about Skitch Henderson," I said. It was like a burlesque sketch. I had mentioned the secret word, Skitch Henderson. Walter headed for the liquor cabinet.

"I don't want to hear another word about the sonovabitch," he said, pouring himself a healthy shot and drinking it.

"Believe me, you won't hear one more word out of my mouth," I promised. "It's not as though we had a love affair or anything."

"Who?" he asked dimly.

"Skitch and I," I explained reasonably.

"Oh."

Walter poured himself another drink. I had been playing a Rachmaninoff piano concerto, not the one with "Full Moon and Empty Arms," but another one. There was a particular passage he found terribly affecting.

Walter said, "Play that again." I obeyed, trotting over to the record player to put the needle down on the groove again. Walter listened. When the passage was over, he said, "Play it again." Fifty-five times we did this. On the fifty-sixth time, I automatically went over and replaced the needle in the groove.

"Who told you to put it back on?" he shouted at me. "God damn it, I'll tell you when I want to hear it." If there had been fifty-five hearings of Rachmaninoff, there had been almost as many drinks. I was looking at this brilliant musician turned violent. He went over to the mantelpiece. On it, Jimmy McNaughton had placed a sculpture. Walter picked it up. If he had hit me with it, I would have been dead. He started to throw it at me. I grabbed his hand and screamed, "Stop it!" He dropped it. Thank God it didn't break, Eleanore's daughter thought at the time. I said, "You're trying to kill me. What's wrong? Fifty-five times you asked me to play the goddamn thing!"

He started to cry.

I said, "You've got to get hold of yourself. You've got to stop this. You're trying to kill me. I didn't say I *loved* Skitch Henderson. I just said he was a friend. He started me off on my career."

This was the kind of crazy conversation that could as easily have led to murder as to meekness. With Walter, it turned to meekness. Abject apology. He said, "I'm sorry, I'll never do it again."

I thought, You're damned right you won't. He left and I went to bed. At three in the morning, I heard the downstairs buzzer. I answered. There was Walter. He said, "I've got something for you." He came upstairs and sat down at the piano and played the sweetest most haunting melody imaginable.

"That's how I feel about you," he said when he had finished. He looked so sad sitting there, so apologetic, so frazzled, and the music was so beautiful, I didn't know what to say. To say "It's beautiful" wasn't enough. Words weren't enough. The music had really come from his heart, from his tortured feelings, and they were something

I could hardly guess at. I really don't know what demons possess people. I can only sympathize. I'm sure there were tears in my eyes—how could there not be?—because the melody was so gorgeous, and because our emotions were so intense. I don't remember what I said. He left.

The next day, Jack Lawrence called again. Jack Lawrence had arrived in town several months back, and had telephoned. "Your mother Eleanore asked me to call," he said by way of introduction. I was always busy, genuinely busy. So for a couple of months, we promised to see each other and never did. But at this exact moment, he called again, and I said, remembering the haunting waltz Walter had played the night before, "You're the man! I know you write good lyrics." (He had written "Sleepy Lagoon" and "All or Nothing at All.") "I've got a song for you. It needs a lyric desperately." He promised to listen to it. I sent Walter over to him. That afternoon, Walter came back and sat down at the piano with the original copy of words and music to "Tenderly." He played it through. I got very excited and called E. H. Morris publishers. I don't know why I was so manic about it all. I think I was genuinely thrilled to see a work like this take life. We raced over to the publishers. Sidney Kornhauser, Paul Barry, and Buddy Morris were there. Walter played the tune and I sang it. They flipped; the contracts were signed that same day.

And I never recorded the song. I don't know why I let it get away from me, but I did. Clark Dennis made the first recording of it, and then Rosemary Clooney had a big hit with it in 1955. I only sang the song in public once, when I was doing a show with Clooney, and told this story about it.

By the time 1947 rolled around, I was terribly in love—with New York City. I never wanted to leave. But the radio shows—the *Philip Morris Follies*, the *Celebrity Club*, and the *Barry Wood Show*—had all come to an end, and I had an offer to appear on the *Eddie Cantor Show*, which originated in Hollywood. I really didn't want to leave New York, but the Morris office said, "This is it. The next stop— Hollywood! It may be pictures, it may be television, but the next move is the *Eddie Cantor Show*!" It didn't occur to me that perhaps they had no idea of what to do with me. It was obvious that I wasn't going to be a movie star. That wasn't the route in those days. None of the girl singers made it in the movies, with the exception of Doris Day. And everyone at the studios knew me. Maybe I had a future in television, which was still in its infancy. Records, yes, definitely. And Capitol was a West Coast company both in origin and feeling.

So, regretfully, I left New York and headed back. I thought of Johnny's lyric "Any place I hang my hat is home." I wondered about L.A. Was it still home?

I found L.A. greatly changed. There were signs that the little box called television might threaten the movie industry. There were also murmurs of signing loyalty oaths and swearing allegiance. I was really blissfully unaware of most of this. During the war, a lot of us had signed anything put in front of us. We had helped out on all causes. But now the House Un-American Activities Committee (HUAC) was investigating "the Communist threat" in Hollywood. The sign of the times became apparent when I told Agnes Moorehead I was going to a party at Gene Kelly's.

"Well, have a good time," she said gaily, "but for God's sake, don't *sign* anything."

I went to a dinner party at Abe and Frances Lastfogel's. He was the head of the William Morris Agency, and they were both good friends of Aunt Mag's and Eleanore's. During the evening I found myself in conversation with the agent George Gruskin. I expressed my doubts about coming back to California.

"It's a good move, Margaret," he said. "A very wise move."

"Why do you think so?" I asked.

"Because I thought of it. I'm your new agent."

Heaven help me, I had found another man with a sense of humor. George was a sweet-looking man and wore glasses. He reminded me of my father. He was very mild, and very nervous. He worked incredibly hard as the head of the William Morris radio-TV department. Among others, he handled Dinah Shore and Danny Thomas. I started going out with him. Then I found he was tremendously jealous. He didn't believe in himself. He thought that every man who looked at me was in love with me. He would say: "I saw it. Danny Thomas is in love with you!"

"For heaven's sake, we were just talking."

"Yes, but I could tell. You were laughing and he was smiling."

"That's true, George. That's what one does when a comic tells you a joke."

"Don't tell me! *I* know what goes on at Hollywood parties."

Well, I suppose he was right there. But, believe me, nothing went on between Danny Thomas and me.

I did become a regular on the *Eddie Cantor Show*. He had changed his format somewhat. Certainly I was not a new talent to be discovered. I was a regular. And, regularly, Eddie would give me this kind of introduction:

"And now herre's—Margaret . . . Margaret *Whiting!*" (*Applause, applause.*)

"Hello, Eddie."

"Hello, Margaret. I must say you're looking wonderful tonight."

"Well, thank you, Eddie."

"And what are you going to say to *me* tonight?" (*Pause, pause.*)

"Hello, Eddie." (*Laugh, laugh.*)

And then I would sing a song, and perhaps do a sketch. It was a formula that worked, and I was grateful for the opportunity to be heard by so many people. But when I was offered the chance to play in the *Lux Radio Theater*'s version of *Alexander's Ragtime Band*, I jumped for joy. The movie had starred Tyrone Power, Alice Faye, Don Ameche, and Ethel Merman. For the radio hour, Dinah Shore was going to repeat Alice Faye's role, and I was to play Merman's part, which had the best songs and was the girl who loved the guy but couldn't get him. I thought that was just great. The extra added attraction was that Jolson was going to make one of his rare appearances. Of course, when he came in everyone practically genuflected to him, including George Gruskin. George had intimated that since his client Dinah was the *bigger* name, she should be given preferential treatment. That did not sit well with me. But I smiled and we started rehearsal. George was sitting in the control booth, and we lowly actors were sitting around waiting for our calls. The director said to Jolson:

"How would you like to proceed with the musical numbers, Mr. Jolson?"

Jolson said, putting his arm around me, "Well, I think we should start with Margaret here. After all, I've known her folks all these years, and I feel I have to take *care* of her."

Of course, it was a childish thing to do, but when nobody was looking, I just stuck out my tongue at George Gruskin, as if to say, "So there!"

Alexander's Ragtime Band turned out to be one of the great shows done on radio. Unfortunately, I almost missed it, being locked in the ladies' room at the time. Fortunately, writer Hy Averback heard my frantic poundings on the door and released me just in time. My entrance was unexpectedly dramatic.

George Gruskin was suffering a nervous breakdown, and I didn't recognize the signs. His own insecurities and the pressure of the business caused it. I realized that the situation between us was growing impossible, but I refused to leave him until he got back on his feet.

If work was the cause of his breakdown, it became my salvation. Exciting things were happening in the music world, including the introduction of the long-playing record and new and different kinds of music. There was also a new Artists and Repertoire (A&R) man at Capitol, Jimmy Conklin. Johnny was far too busy with his writing jobs and overseeing the giant that Capitol had become to handle all the musical projects.

As luck would have it, there was another strike of the American Federation of Musicians. This was crippling to the record industry, since no musicians were allowed to perform with us on records. It did not affect radio programs. I kept on with the radio work. One day Jimmy Conklin said, "When do you get through with your radio show?"

"Around three-thirty."

"Can you meet me at Radio Recorders in Santa Monica at four-thirty? I want you to do me a favor. We're trying out some new recording techniques."

"Sure," I said. And there I was, at the appointed time. Jimmy gave me a pair of earphones, and I heard this musical track that had been laid down. He showed me the sheet music.

"Mmm, pretty," I said as I hummed along. "And a nice arrangement."

"Try singing it a couple of times. We want to adjust some of the balances."

"Okay," I said. God knows, as I look back on my life, I was agreeable to anything. He went back in the control room and I sang two or three takes. I said to myself, Funny, it's in my key. Jimmy came out and said, "Thanks, that's been a great help."

"Anytime," I said and sauntered out.

A week later, a song plugger met me on the street.

"Boy, have you got a hit!" he exclaimed.

"What are you talking about?" I turned around. I thought he must have been talking to someone behind me.

"No, you. That 'Tree in the Meadow' song. It's sensational."

I knew nothing about it. I immediately called Jimmy Conklin.

"Let me explain, Margaret," he said. "Nothing illegal went on. We flew Frank DeVol to London. He recorded the tracks with English musicians. Then we put your voice over it. But there's nothing wrong with that."

Nothing wrong! It was the next million-seller. I'm glad he didn't tell me what he was doing, though. I'm not sure I would have approved.

Frank Loesser had written a song he always played at parties. It was meant to be a duet, with the girl saying she had to leave, and the guy saying it's too cold to go out. For every reason she finds to leave, he finds a reason for her to stay. I always loved that song, and I kept saying to Frank, "Don't forget, that's a great song for Mercer and me to record."

One day while we were rehearsing a radio show called *Club 15*, someone brought in a demo record of Dinah Shore and Buddy Clark singing that song. Evidently, the publishers had issued a license to Dinah and Buddy. I perked up my ears and cooed, "Oooh, let me hear that again. I love it." Actually, I thought the tempo was a little fast. I went right home and called Jimmy Conklin. I had already told Jimmy and Johnny about the song. Paul Weston had gotten a copy and laid down two tracks, one slow and one fast. So now, when I informed Jimmy of the other record, he said, "Well, we better move." Two days later, Loesser and Mercer met at my house, one coming in the front door, the other through the back. They weren't enemies at all, but they were, as songwriters, friendly rivals. Johnny said that day, "Consider me just a singer!"

Frank said, "Terrific!" And away we went. He played the song a few times. We went over it. Frank made suggestions. Then he called Capitol and said we were ready. We went down to Hollywood and Vine in one car. There was a bar in one of the executive offices where people were often invited in for a drink. This had been set up with the recording equipment where we were going to sing to the tape. There were two stools. We sat down, Johnny and I, the microphone between us. Frank stood behind the bar and conducted us. I told Johnny I liked the slow version. He agreed, and that's the way we recorded it. After the third take, Loesser said, "I'll buy that." *Voilà!* "Baby, It's Cold Outside." Our version did better than the Shore-Clark one, and I think it was due to the slow tempo. I was right about that one.

It was a common practice then to try and come out with a competitive record. I'd heard the song first, at Frank's house, and put in my bid. It wasn't stealing; it was healthy American enterprise. Sometimes it backfired.

During the war, Johnny Mercer gave me a cryptic message. "Be down at the studio at seven o'clock. Tell no one where you are going. And be there promptly!" There were a *lot* of these messages during the war. When I got there, I found Johnny, Benny Goodman, Paul Weston and his band, the Pied Pipers, and Peggy Lee all standing around as though preparing to embark on a secret mission. The secret mission was this: Irving Berlin had written a song called "The Freedom Train." Bing Crosby and the Andrews Sisters had already recorded it for Decca. The plan was that if we could record it fast, we could get our version out first. Again, away we went. There was a patter, a riff, where we all had to reel off the names of the performers in rhythm: "There-was-Johnny-Mercer-Peggy-Lee-Benny-Goodman-Margaret-Whiting-the-Pied-Pipers-and-Paul-Weston's-band . . ."

Peggy and I could not get it together. We kept screwing up on the names, and it came out Peggy-Whiting-Margaret-Piper . . . Oh, it was awful, and the more mistakes we made, the more we kept laughing. They finally had to call a dinner break. Everyone looked at Peggy and me as though we were saboteurs. We were certainly not helping the war effort. After dinner, we came back and performed it brilliantly. I was ready to pack up and go home with the rest, when I was told, "Just a minute, you're not through. There's the flip side of the record. You have to sing 'God Bless America.' "

Kate Smith Whiting did her duty. Well, our record came out quickly. And the Crosby–Andrews Sisters record came out quickly. And two bigger bombs were never heard throughout the entire war—which was extraordinary, for this was during the peak of wartime patriotism.

What next, Margaret? I wasn't really worried. I never worried. I just sailed along, and good things happened to me. But what happened next was totally unexpected.

Bob Stabler, the head of press for Capitol, invited me to a party on his ranch in the San Fernando Valley. During the party, I walked outside and gazed at the sky and the mountains and just began to sing for some nutty reason, "Take me back to the Red River Valley . . ."

Stabler said, "Sing some more of that." I laughed. I loved that song. He said, "Did you ever think of singing country?"

"You mean . . . hillbilly?" It was still called that in those days. "You must be dreaming!"

But the next day he called Lee Gillette, the A&R man, and suggested he team me either with Tennessee Ernie Ford or Jimmy Wakely, both of whom were signed with Capitol and very big in the country field. Ernie also sang hymns and folk music. He and I made a tape together, but our voices weren't right.

Jimmy's was. Immediately we had a recording date. I walked into the studio. It was a whole new ball game. I recognized only one musician out of the whole group. And that was pianist Buddy Cole. On this date, he played the organ. They stood me on a box, because Jimmy was so tall, and we sang into the microphone. They were still only using one microphone in those days. I sang lead and harmony. Jimmy sang harmony and lead. Jimmy showed me how to do it. And I laughed and laughed. I thought it was the funniest thing I had ever done. I laughed all the way to the bank.

The song was called "Slippin' Around," and it had been written by Floyd Tillman, who had married numerous women, and that's what the song was about.

To my amazement, it was a hit. It started the whole crossover movement of country/pop. I was invited to Nashville to perform with the Grand Ole Opry. For a month I was briefed, as though I were going to a foreign country and should know all the rules of protocol. I was told I was going to meet Little Jimmy Dickens, Roy Acuff, Red Foley, Minnie Pearl, Hank Williams, and Ernie Tubb. I kept saying, "Yes, yes," and tryng to remember their names. To me, it was like trying to remember the names of Lithuanian royalty. I had no idea who anybody was.

Finally, I took off for Nashville. The trip lasted forever. You couldn't *get* to Nashville then. We eventually landed, were driven to the Opry. I walked into the Ryman Auditorium, where the Opry had been presented for thirty-three years. There were bats still flying around the rafters. Minnie Pearl stuck out a hand and greeted me. That was the beginning of a real friendship. Eddy Arnold was great. What a warm welcome they all gave me. I was afraid they might disapprove, but they loved the fact that Jimmy and I were singing together, that a pop singer was doing their material. A musician came up to me and said, "You sing your way. We sing ours. You use pop arrangements. But, honey, country music can take *anything*." Gee, I hope that was a compliment.

And the audience. Those people would wait for days to get tickets. Then they would file in and the show would start. All these different groups would go on. After fifteen minutes on the show, I felt like Alice in Wonderland again. Things got curiouser and curiouser. But also better and better. The fans loved the coupling of Whiting and Wakely. Even the bats in the auditorium did. They circled around overhead. I watched them warily out of a corner of my eye.

The next day, I performed on another kind of program, *Sunday Down South*, with the Nashville Symphony. Then it was "Moonlight in Vermont" time and "The End of a Love Affair." My music. The reaction was just as good. Very friendly people down there in Tennessee, and blessed with *consummate* taste. Snooky Lanson was the emcee. The tape was flown to New York. They liked his work so much that they hired him for *Your Hit Parade.*

I was in Nashville for a week. I was taken everywhere, even to Printers Alley, where all the good ol' boys hung out. One day, in the middle of rehearsal at WLS, a very tall cowboy, thin and with high cheekbones, opened the door, stalked in, held out his hand, and said in this incredibly deep voice, "Miss Margaret, my name is Hank Williams and I have come to sing you some songs."

Whereupon he took out his guitar, put his foot up on the piano stool, and started to sing. I wasn't a songwriter's daughter for nothing. The moment I heard

> *"Today I passed you on the street*
> *And my heart fell at my feet.*
> *I can't help it if I'm still in love with you . . ."*

my ears went up. Aha! This was a songwriter.

When he had finished, he sang "I'm So Lonesome I Could Cry" and then said, "Miss Margaret, I surely hope you will record some of these."

And thus he left Miss Margaret speechless. But I certainly recorded those songs. Miss Margaret was no fool. Not when it came to music.

Men were another story.

8

My
Ideal:
Strike One

Long ago my heart and mind;
Got together and designed
The wonderful boy for me;
Oh what a fantasy.

Tho' the idol of my heart
Can't be ordered à la carte
I wonder if he will be
Always a fantasy.

Will I ever find the boy in my mind
The one who is My ideal.

That song has always been with me, part of my life. I heard it as a child. It was one of those songs, when I was growing up, that was as familiar as the furniture in my parents' bedroom. And yet, in some way it must have made an enormous impact in shaping my life.

But there were other things.

★   ★   ★

One day, when I was seven or eight, I decided to visit my father in his studio, the one away from the house, the house being too noisy for work. It contained a bathroom, one big room with a little balcony done in very bright sun colors, couches and very comfortable chairs—a place for him to be with his friends. And to work. There was an upright Steinway against one wall. I loved to visit him, to look at all his golf trophies gleaming behind the glass cabinets. I loved to listen to him play. Oh, let's face it. I loved *him*.

On this day, I happily climbed the stairs and I was almost at the top when I heard Walter Bullock, a lyric writer who worked with my father, say, "Tell me, Richard, what are you going to do about Margaret? She looks like a wolf child."

I just stood there. I couldn't move.

"It must be pretty scary to have a daughter like that," he continued.

And then my father said, "She'll grow out of it. She'll be all right. I know she's not too pretty now. But Eleanore will take care of it."

I wanted to die. Walter Bullock was a lot like Clifton Webb in *Laura*. Gay, elegant, he knew how to dress, and how to dress women. As I was growing up, he helped me with material for my act, and made me read books, plays, go to the theater. He taught me how to enter a room. He groomed me. If I have any poise, it's due to Walter, even though I'll never get over his remark. On the other hand, it was that remark that gave me the drive to become a personality.

But what did it say about my father? Did he love me? Did he love me as much as I loved him? Why didn't he say I was the most beautiful child in the world? Why didn't he defend me and knock Walter Bullock down and hit him with a golf trophy?

I guess that day was my introduction to the pain and the wonder of love.

When I got married, what did I know about love? What did any of us know who grew up in Hollywood? We were terribly sophisticated and woefully naïve. (Alexis Smith recalls sitting up in the balcony at the Pantages, just out of high school, smoking a cigarette, which wasn't allowed, and watching Joan Fontaine in *Suspicion*. The next week she was *in* a movie, *The Constant Nymph*, playing Joan Fontaine's older sophisticated sister.)

We lived in a land as strange and as rare as the court at Versailles. There, Louis XIV ruled and created industry. To make lace fashionable, he began wearing it on his cuffs. Everyone followed suit. Ergo, all France needed lace. The lace industry was born. Louis XIV knew what he was doing.

So did Louis B. Mayer. He created products equally exquisite. Judy Garland. Lana Turner. Ava Gardner. Metro-Goldwyn-Mayer was his throne room and Hollywood and Beverly Hills were his court.

Judy and Lana and Ava formed a chain reaction, the marry-go-round in the court of Louis B. One night at NBC I was doing a radio program and Judy was next door, a guest on the *Bob Hope Show*. She was insane about Artie Shaw. They were always together. They were around our house a lot, and they were talking about marriage. The night before this particular show, Artie had run off with Lana Turner and married her. The night of the broadcast, Judy came into my dressing room, threw herself in my arms, and then hit her head against the wall, crying, "I'm going to die. I'm going to kill myself." There was very little I could do for her in the way of comfort. But I started to realize how painful love could be, and how ill-equipped we were to deal with it. Judy banged her head against the wall for quite a long time, then went out and performed. This was February 9, 1940, and Judy, like me, was a teen-ager. She was *acting* like a teen-ager, but *performing* like an adult. That was how we had been trained.

Judy was discovered by MGM producer Lew Brown when she was singing at Lake Tahoe. Already her father, who was rumored to be gay, had run off, and her mother had pushed her and her sisters into performing. Brown brought her to Hollywood. She signed with MGM and was immediately told to lose weight. This father figure, Louis B. Mayer, the lace maker, dictated that she should make this movie, then go out on tour with Mickey Rooney to promote the movie, then pushed her into another movie with Mickey Rooney, and so forth. Judy had very little time to grow up. But, realistically, after having gone so far, having become MGM's biggest money-maker, with the world at her feet, with people (according to Louis B. Mayer's dictates) catering to her, with the publicity department at MGM writing about her, when she had become renowned throughout the world, it was almost impossible for her to walk out on her career. While she knew a lot about life, at the same time she knew nothing. There was a whole set of experiences she had not gone through.

The same was true of Lana Turner. Instead of being able to live as a seventeen-year-old girl with such teen-age problems as where to go to college and whether she was going to be offered some boy's fraternity pin, here was a girl who suddenly had director Mervyn LeRoy saying, "I want to test you for the movies." Then there were a lot of orders. Color the hair, build up the boobs, teach her to *talk*. She was surrounded by all these men on the set who were shaping her, changing her, glamorizing her. The publicity department was unleashed. In those days, that was its own factory. And, boy, did they work. There were the legmen, who would call up Jimmy Fidler, Jimmy Starr, Hedda Hopper, or Louella Parsons and give out the information. Lana and Tyrone are going together! That was front-page news, equal to the war news from Europe. Newspapers all over the country carred the item. Lana made a couple of movies and suddenly every magazine, every newspaper in the world was writing about her. How would anyone treat her? How would she treat herself? She was at the Metro lot, sitting in the same dining room with Mickey Rooney, Garland, Clark Gable, Lionel Barrymore, and Garbo. Everyone was falling all over her at seventeen, and Louis B. Mayer was trying to get her into bed with him, promising her better parts.

And then she met Greg Bautzer. This was a man who loved women, who was older and sophisticated. A handsome attorney who wooed her with flowers, became engaged to her. Then, at least according to Lana's account, there was a confrontation with the older woman, Joan Crawford. One of those scenes right out of a Joan Crawford movie where she says, "He doesn't love you, why don't you give him up? He's mine, mine. I'll scratch your eyes out!"

This is pretty heady stuff at any age. But for a beautiful young girl of seventeen, already wrapped up in the manufactured romance of the movies, it must have been irresistible.

Lana went home weeping. Her teen-age heart was broken. Greg Bautzer called up that night to break a date, pleading an upset stomach. Lana hung up. The phone rang again. She picked it up. Who was calling? Artie Shaw! They had known each other, had made a movie together, and then palled around. Now he called up and asked, "Do you want to go out?" And Lana said, "Fine." She took off the engagement ring Greg Bautzer had given her and she went out with Artie Shaw. They talked and talked. "Listen, I know the shit that you're going through," he said. He was a very bright man, a very *attractive* man. "Honey, I'm on the road all the time, but I don't want this kind of crap. I want a home." And so he was wooing her for whatever reason—whether he really wanted her, whether he wanted to go to bed with her, or whether he wanted to get rid of Judy Garland. Judy wanted to be more than a friend and he didn't want to be anything but. For whatever reason, Artie Shaw was spinning his web. And then he said, "Why don't we get married?" And Lana said, "Fine." They went to Vegas and got married. She sent a wire home to her mother, but she neglected to say *whom* she married. Her mother called Greg Bautzer, who was completely in the dark about all this.

Each of them was playing a role. The problem was they all had their own scripts and the scripts didn't fit together. And worst of all was the publicity department, which fed all these notions. It was like going to war, like a raw recruit who comes in from under a rock in Lima, Ohio, and is given a weapon and taught to kill. There was even a slang term during the time, a "killer-diller." You have a whole new world of *power*. You are invincible. That's what happens when the publicity wheels are rolling. You are invincible—until that damned weapon backfires.

So, if Lana Turner's mother was mystified about these events, imagine how they affected Judy. The circus marry-go-round continued: Greg went with Joan. Lana married Artie. And after her moment of madness in the NBC dressing room, Judy picked herself up and went after the composer and conductor David Rose. She married him in 1941. I know that Judy was very much in love with Tyrone Power, and he was going with somebody else. Lana Turner says that Tyrone Power was the one big love of her life. What made it really terrible for Judy was that Lana Turner unintentionally screwed her up in every way. The situation was mirrored in Judy and Lana's first movie together, *Love Finds Andy Hardy*, with Judy as the Girl Next Door and Lana the Beauty who bewitches Mickey Rooney.

On an additional ride on the marry-go-round, I remember an evening spent with Ava Gardner. I met her through our attorney, Jerry Rosenthal. He and his wife, Ruth, had invited a few friends to their house, including Ava Gardner. She was wearing a pair of jeans, a shirt, and no makeup. She leaned over the table to get a cigarette, and I was absolutely struck by her beauty. I said, "You really have the greatest face I have ever seen. I've been around gorgeous women all my life, but I have never seen a face like yours."

And she said simply, "Thank you," which I thought was very right and pretty funny. We started talking. She said, "I've got to tell you, this is me. I'm from North Carolina. That lady on the screen, that isn't me. I have a face that photographs. I can't act. I married Mickey Rooney because I'd seen him in pictures and I thought he was wonderful and he fell all over me, so I married him."

She took a drag on the cigarette.

"I married Artie Shaw"—it occurs to me that Artie Shaw was so busy running from woman to woman, he must have had a bicycle!—"I married Artie Shaw because I wanted him to like this"—she gestured to her head—"not *this*"—she put her hand to her face. "I'm not a smart girl, but I'm trying. I tried to read. I tried to learn. But that wasn't what he wanted. He only wanted this." And again, with a deprecatory gesture, she pointed to that extraordinary face.

So there we were, four girls in Hollywood—Ava and Lana, the beauties, and Judy, the perennial Girl Next Door, and Margaret, the wolf child, *all* waiting for My Ideal.

Maybe he's a dream and yet he might be—
Just around the corner waiting for me . . .

In any court, whether it's that of Louis B. or Louis XIV, the amount of intrigue is enormous. All the courtiers are vying for social and political power. After World War II, the court changed subtly from movies to television, but the motives of the courtiers remained constant. Get that power!

Which brings me to my first husband, Hubbell Robinson. Hubbell was a power. The new postwar power. When I first met him, he was at Young and Rubicam, the advertising agency, and married to Terry Lewis, a writer. It was the year of my fiasco with *Your Hit Parade* in New York. I met Hubbell at a party given by drama critic Bill Hawkins. Hubbell's first line to me was, "I discovered Dinah Shore."

I replied, "Good for you," and walked away. He must have liked that.

The next time I saw him was at a party in Hollywood maybe six years later. I was on the air with Bob Crosby and the Andrews Sisters in *Club 15* for CBS. My sister was doing *Junior Miss*, also for CBS. Norman Corwin, Cy Howard, and Abe Burrows were all writer-producers for CBS. Ernie Martin (later half of the Broadway producing team of Feuer and Martin), who had started out as a page boy at CBS, was now running the network on the Coast. He called me up because he knew about those Saturday nights at the Whitings'. He was desperate.

"My new boss is coming out to the Coast. Hubbell Robinson."

"I met him," I said.

"I've got to have a party for him. Could you move your party to my house?"

"Why?"

"Don't ask why. Believe me, it'll be good for everybody."

"Okay," I said. "I'll call everybody and have it at your place."

I mentioned intrigue: I was dating Hal March, who at that time was a young comic, teamed with Bob Sweeney. George Gruskin was trying to lure the team of Sweeney and March away from MCA, and thought I might have some influence, so he was delighted about the shift of plans for the party. He thought I might persuade Hal to leave MCA. As you may recall, George and I had been going together but were no longer going together since Hal and I were going together.

Bob Crosby was coming to the party. A night or two before this gala event, he had had too much to drink and had hit his wife, June.

That had made headlines. Bob was coming. June was not. Abe Burrows and Norman Corwin were coming, but they didn't speak to each other. They worked together but hated each other. Announcer Del Sharbutt arrived. He, too, had had too much to drink and had hit a car. This all happened before the guest of honor made his appearance.

Hubbell arrived. He, *too*, had had too much to drink. I was in a bedroom talking to someone when Hubbell crawled in on his hands and knees.

"Hello," he said. "I met you before."

"Yes," I said, looking down at him. "I remember. You discovered Dinah Shore. What are you doing now?"

"Discovering you," he said, with a kind of boozy smile that I found utterly charming. There was a comic quality, a kind of sexuality there. He stayed on his hands and knees just long enough. And then he got up and we started talking. There were a lot of looks in our direction. MCA was looking. Ernie Martin was looking. Sweeney and March, Burrows and Corwin—the number seemed endless. They wanted Hubbell's ear, but Hubbell only had ears (and eyes) for me. Then he got swept away by the crowd. An MCA agent took me to one side, saying, "If you have any influence over Hal March and Bob Sweeney, don't let them leave MCA."

"I don't have."

"You must have."

"I don't know. . . ."

"*I* know."

All the time—although, God knows, no one needed it—strong drink was being consumed as if prohibition were right around the corner.

Hal came over and whispered in my ear, "Let's leave and go to your place."

I had had enough. I said, "Okay."

George Gruskin come over, looking worried. "Where are you going?"

"Hal and I are going over to my place."

"Yes! Yes!" he said fervently. "Go to your place." Then, under his breath, he added, "Use your influence!"

We were almost at the door. The MCA agent approached.

"Why are you leaving?" he asked anxiously.

"Hal's taking me home," I answered.

He nodded. "Good. *Good.*" And, under his breath, he added, "Persuade him!"

I don't want to give the wrong impression. It wasn't that Hal and I didn't make love. We did. But we certainly didn't do it at my house. My mother was there. My Aunt Margaret was there. My sister was there. Hal was tired and he wanted to wake up and have some of Eleanore's eggs in the morning—that's why we went to my place. Eleanore and Aunt Mag were up; they were always up late. Hal went to sleep in Barbara's room. Barbara joined my mother and aunt in the kitchen and we sat around talking. I was trying to describe all the tensions of the evening, when the doorbell rang. It was Cy Howard.

"Someone has stolen my car," he announced. "I had this red Buick parked outside and now it's gone. God, the things that have happened to this country since the war. You can't even leave your keys in the car anymore."

He was interrupted by another ring of the doorbell, and in walked Hubbell. He came straight over to me.

"I got your address, because I wanted to take you out tomorrow, so I drove over." He jingled the car keys. Cy Howard looked at him.

"Wait a minute. Let me see those car keys."

Hubbell looked bewildered as well as potted.

"Those are *my* keys," Cy said.

"I'm driving a red Buick," Hubbell said.

"You're driving *my* red Buick," Cy retorted.

"Oh," Hubbell said. "Well, then you must be driving *my* red Buick."

Cy said, "It sure makes me feel better about the country."

So we all sat around and had yet another drink and talked some more. As Hubbell was leaving, he turned back and said, "What time shall I pick you up?"

"I'm supposed to see Sophie Tucker's opening. She's my godmother," I added parenthetically.

"I would love to see Sophie Tucker," he said gallantly.

"Then seven would be fine."

The next morning, Hal and I had our eggs with Eleanore and he left. Flowers arrived, lots of flowers. From Hubbell.

"Now, *that*'s the kind of man you should marry," Eleanore said wisely.

He picked me up at seven o'clock and further charmed my mother and Aunt Mag. We went out the front door.

"Where's your car?" I asked, looking around at the empty street.

"There," he said, gesturing vaguely to the darkness.

"Where?" I repeated.

He looked. Then he looked stunned. Then he roared with laughter. "You got a *great* sense of humor!" he cried. "You think I don't remember last night? I remember. Okay, now what have you done with my car?"

"I haven't done anything with your car," I said, starting to laugh. I couldn't stop. "Somebody . . . has . . . stolen . . . your . . . ha-ha . . . *car!*" Maybe I was nervous. I don't know what it was, but I couldn't stop laughing. We walked around the block. There was his car parked by the curb. Some of the neighborhood kids had pushed it around the corner.

"You got some sense of humor," he repeated admiringly, convinced that I had engineered the whole business.

That incident really brought us together.

We got in the car and he started driving. He pushed the button on the radio, and my record of "So Far" was being played.

"You engineered that, too," he said.

"Of course. I'm magic. And this is Hollywood," I said, singing along with myself on the radio.

I spent a week going out with Hubbell. He made some decisions. He told me March and Sweeney were very talented and they should stay with MCA. They did.

He left on the train back to New York. Two hours later the doorbell rang. It was a Western Union wire from Hubbell. It read: WHY HAVEN'T YOU WRITTEN? LOVE, HUBBELL. I thought that was funny and charming and gallant. People who knew Hubbell Robinson in business have asked me, "How could you be married to that man?

He was *ice water.*" And he may have been that way in business. He was described as sitting in his office during a meeting, gazing out the window at the New York skyline, and never looking at the person he was addressing. Unnerving, to say the least. But he got what he wanted. That was how he conducted his business. They didn't know the other side. They didn't know Hubbell was really funny and very warm and terribly human. And he had an odd sort of gallantry toward women.

He called me from New York. Often. Then he came back out to the Coast again. We would have lunch together—all very secret, since he was married. The intrigue was romantic too. It was fun. It was exciting. Clandestine meetings. It could have been the script of *Back Street.*

And then one afternoon he took me to lunch at the Beverly Hills Hotel and asked me to marry him. I dropped my fork. He picked it up. In my nervousness, I jabbed him with it.

"I'm sorry," I apologized.

"You mean you won't marry me?" he asked.

"No, I meant about the fork."

"Then you *will* marry me?"

I really didn't know how to answer him. Until this point, I was having fun with the glamour of the affair, playing around with romance and nobody knowing I was going out with him. Suddenly, here was reality.

"I don't know," I said. "You're married."

"I talked it over with Terry. She's agreed to give me a divorce."

I thought, I am responsible. I made him do that. Now I've got to marry him.

He saw my hesitation. "Think about it. Don't say no. Don't say yes. We have time."

He went back to New York.

I did think. I knew that Hal March and I wouldn't get married. I was crazy about him, but he was just beginning his career. And I know enough about show business to know that a marriage wouldn't work out unless the man was established. Otherwise, we would not be equals. But how did I feel about Hubbell? I really wasn't sure. I was in love with love, that much I knew. I loved who he was. He had a responsible position with CBS and he was writing articles for *Esquire*. And he did have a wild sense of humor.

Hubbell came back out to the Coast, and this time he said, "Where can we be alone?" I had a home in Palm Springs and we went there. We were both working at CBS, but we kept our relationship a secret, and would run off to the Springs for three or four days. I found myself really taken with him. The problem was that we would spend a couple of days together and then he would be gone for a month. One of the times we were at the Springs we met a CBS producer, and it became common knowledge that Hubbell and I were involved.

Hubbell asked me to spend the summer with him in New York, and I decided that might be a good idea.

What an incredible summer to be in New York with a broadcasting executive! If Hubbell had tried, he couldn't have impressed me more. There were the presidential conventions to cover. Then CBS called up to ask me to go with Bob Hope to entertain President Truman in Washington. A chauffeur picked me up, took my luggage and my music, whisked me out to the airport and the waiting executive airplane warming up. And there before my dazzled eyes stood Edward R. Murrow, *the* Edward R. Murrow, in his trench coat. I was too impressed to speak. He, however, was not.

"Oh, Christ, a woman," he said on noticing me. Perhaps he thought I was going to spoil some flight-long poker session. However, we clambered aboard, Murrow and Whiting, off the see the president. Once in the air, Murrow relaxed. The shoes came off and it was Ed and Margaret. And Ed started to talk about North Carolina, which is where he came from. And then he *became* North Carolina. And Margaret was fascinated. In Washington, once again it was limousine time. I found myself in the Statler Hotel, unpacking my bags. The phone rang. It was Hope. He said, "Drop whatever you're doing. The president wants to have cocktails with us downstairs."

"I'm not really dressed."

"Margaret, you're not going to miss a moment like this!"

Well, of course I wasn't. However, it seemed I was wearing a dress with one thousand buttons, all of them in unreachable places. I attempted to button the dress. Nothing buttoned. My fingers were like ice. Finally, in desperation, I threw on a coat over the dress and met Ed and Bob in the elevator.

"Are you cold?" Bob asked.

"I can't get the damned buttons to work."

"Here," rumbled Ed, "let me do it." I took off the coat and he fumbled with the buttons in back while Bob started on the buttons in front. The elevator stopped. Two secret service men got on. They frisked us. If the elevator had stopped again, I'm not sure what the picture would have looked like—two men at my buttons and two more prodding and patting, all very intent on the business at hand. Finally the secret service men started to frisk Murrow and Hope.

"I can see why you would frisk me," I said to them, "but why would you have to search two such prominent Americans as Bob Hope and Edward R. Murrow?"

"We don't take chances," one of them said without skipping a beat.

We arrived at the presidential suite. The elevator doors opened and there was Harry S Truman. The president.

"Welcome!" he cried, beaming. "Hello, Bob! Hello, Ed! Hello, Margaret! I'm so glad you could make it. Here, sit down. What would you like to drink?" He winked at me. "I'm the highest-paid bartender in town!"

I burbled something about having a ginger ale. He took our drink orders, conveyed them to *his* bartender, supervised the proceedings, chatting all the while.

"You know, you're not the only Margaret who sings in Washington," he said. His daughter had just embarked on a rather perilous singing career. Paul Hume, the music critic for the *Washington Post*, had been rather critical of her and Truman had gone after Hume, as any proud daddy would have done.

The four of us sat down with the drinks. It was obvious that both Hope and Murrow adored Truman. It was impossible not to be swept up in the sheer gusto of the man. It was a very off-the-cuff conversation. Truman was running for reelection in 1948, and his chances of winning seemed at the moment very remote, but you would never have guessed it from his attitude. He was chipper and chirrupy, and we were having a merry old time, when he suddenly looked at me.

"You must be hot in that coat," he observed.

"Oh, not really, Mr. President," I said uneasily.

"Nonsense, it's hot as blazes. I insist."

I took a deep breath. "Mr. President, I must tell you. Nothing in the world would have kept me from meeting you. But I have to confess. I couldn't get my dress buttoned."

Truman nodded sympathetically. "Let the old haberdasher give it a try," he said. I got up meekly and took off my coat. President Truman very expertly took care of the buttons.

"I can see the headlines now," Hope quipped as he watched. "TRU-MAN BUTTONS WHITING."

"Well, that's better than TRUMAN *UNBUTTONS* WHITING," the president murmured as he finished the job.

That evening the networks and the newspapers were giving the president an annual roasting. It was raucous and funny and terribly affectionate. The press seemed to be genuinely fond of the man. The Girl Singer here did her couple of numbers and had a wonderful time. But no one had a better time than the recipient of the roast, Harry Truman himself. It was my only meeting with a most underrated president.

Later that summer, I met Edward R. Murrow again, in Philadelphia for the Republican convention. Amid all the hoopla, he invited me up to his suite for some blackberry brandy. I sipped. He more than sipped and began singing plaintive North Carolina folk songs in a rich baritone. I was impressed. I was hypnotized. I was practically seduced. When I realized that his eyebrow was arched and that I had just been propositioned, I said, flustered, "Oh, no, thank you," like a deb responding to an invitation to dance. "I'm engaged."

"Oh, to whom?" Ed asked amiably.

Quite suddenly, I couldn't think of Hubbell's name. Ed stared at me.

"Oh, *you* know him," I said hastily. "He's at CBS."

"Yes, but do *you*?" Ed asked. At the time I put the memory lapse down to a surfeit of blackberry brandy. We laughed. And so ended the seduction attempt. But we became very good friends.

Hubbell took me to the Campbell's soup sponsor's house on Cape

My Aunt Margaret Young,
star of vaudeville and records

My father, Richard,
turning out another
big hit

My mother, Eleanore

Jerome Kern plays a new song
for some friends, including Richard Whiting, Arthur Schwartz,
George Gershwin (second, third, and fourth from left),
and Sigmund Romburg (sixth from left).

My father and me

Ann Rutherford, Skitch Henderson,
girl singer, and family friend Warren Mace.
Never stand next to Ann Rutherford if
you don't want to look dumpy.

Johnny Mercer
telling me there isn't a rhyme in
"Moonlight in Vermont"
COURTESY CAPITOL RECORDS

From left: two King Sisters,
Martha Tilton, Margaret Whiting, Jo Stafford, Peggy Lee,
and a third King Sister in the beginning years
of Capitol Records.

Margaret Whiting,
Billy May, the orchestra leader, and Bob Hope getting
ready to record their big hit "Blind Date."
It sold about one hundred copies.
ROTHSCHILD PHOTO

Al Jolson, Margaret Whiting,
and Jack Kirkwood at one of Jolson's radio shows.
I'm wondering, "Where's *my* cup?"
COURTESY OF NBC

Margaret Whiting, Eddie Cantor,
and Mickey Rooney during rehearsal of the Cantor show.
Mickey plays us a new song.
COURTESY OF NBC

June Christy, Margaret Whiting,
Frankie Laine, and Peggy Lee, who look like they're getting
ready to fill in for the Hi-Lo's
GENE HOWARD/STUDIO FIVE

Margaret Whiting, Johnny Mercer,
Janet Blair, Lou Busch at piano, and Danny Thomas
trying out a new Mercer song at a
Saturday night at the Whitings
CHARLES RHODES

Janet Blair, Audrey Totter,
Esther Williams, Agnes Moorehead, and Margaret Whiting,
wondering, "Does anybody still wear a hat?"
CHARLES RHODES

Mr. and Mrs.
Jeff Chandler and
John Garfield,
doing what he
did best—
fascinating
women and
relaxing men

Hoagy Carmichael
running through the words of "Stardust"
for me before we entertain
at an ASCAP benefit
GENE HOWARD/STUDIO FIVE

William Eythe and Margaret Whiting
holding hands at midnight, sighing sigh after sigh

Margaret Whiting
with Hal March at the Hollywood Brown Derby.
He's wishing I'd stop fooling around
with his drink.

Jimmy Van Heusen
and Margaret Whiting listening to Frank Sinatra
sing at the Mocambo

Cesar Romero, Lucille Ball,
Margaret Whiting, and husband Hubbell Robinson
meeting at Ciro's nightclub
CBS

Cod. We had an idyllic time. Life was very exciting. I had never met so many important people. It was like being in my father's living room, only instead of musicians and songwriters, these were politicos and newsmen, the movers and shakers. At the end of the summer, when I had to resume work on *Club 15* in Hollywood, I told Hubbell, yes, I would marry him. Then I left on the airplane.

I thought I was terrifically happy. After all, why shouldn't I have been happy?

Will I recognize a light in his eyes
That no other eyes reveal.
Or will I pass him by and never even know that he is my ideal.

Back in Hollywood, Jimmy Van Heusen started calling me. I went out with him occasionally. Jimmy was very special to me. Once we had been lovers. Now we were pals. So, what was wrong with going out with him? I knew what was wrong. Secretly, I was trying to break up the thing between Hubbell and me. Of course I knew Jimmy wasn't My Ideal. He was an awful lot of fun, but he wasn't the marrying kind. He was not dependable. He would rather go off on a tear with his pal, Sinatra. That's not what a husband should be.

And quite suddenly I found myself totally trapped in that studio morality. Even though I wasn't a studio child, I had been raised in the same way. We had all been educated together. Our intellect stayed for years at about the level of a fourteen-year-old's. Everyone acted on primitive instincts. But the morality of the studio was that marriage was clean and somehow antiseptic. Extra-marital affairs were fun and sexual and sinful and punishable by a broken contract, legal fees, and stern lectures from studio heads. In that world, which was soon to fall apart, the studio managed everything. You didn't really think. You were manipulated. Everything was for the product, whether that was a movie or a song.

And now it was 1948 and the wartime whirl of impulsive marriages had graduated to the postwar whirl of impulsive marriages. Everyone was getting married. It was expected. So there was romance and popular songs, and dancing cheek to cheek and swearing eternal devotion with songs to match that, and boys coming back from the service to girls who had waited a long, long time and, whether they loved each other or not, they got married. Everybody got married. They would learn to live with their dreams. I was no different from anyone else.

For a while I kept the news about Hubbell to myself, but soon my mother knew the relationship was serious. She advised me. "If you are going to get married, you will have to have enough closets." I dutifully informed Hubbell.

He called back. "Tell Eleanore I have found an apartment with eleven rooms and twelve closets. That should satisfy her." He laughed. I laughed—as expected. This is not right, I said to myself, as I hung up the phone. My mother watched me.

"You know," she said, "if you're indecisive, you should tell Hubbell. You should call him and tell him."

"I'm not indecisive," I snapped. "I just can't conduct a romance three thousand miles away."

Of course, Eleanore was right. And of course I wouldn't listen to her. Christmas was coming and Hubbell was arriving on the twenty-seventh. We were to be married on the twenty-ninth.

We had a Christmas party at my house. Jimmy Van Heusen was there. He said, "You gotta come with me. What you're doing is crazy. Come down to the Springs. Come on, get in the car." And I found myself whizzing through the Christmas decorations and merry Santas and stoplights and then the desert night and it was Christmas Eve and I was with Jimmy Van Heusen.

"We're going to spend Christmas Day with Frank and Nancy," he announced.

I nodded numbly. "Nice," I said.

Well, it *was* nice. Sinatra tried to be cheery. Jimmy tried to be cheery. Obviously Jimmy felt something was wrong with the forthcoming marriage. Otherwise, he wouldn't have invited me. Otherwise, I wouldn't have agreed to come.

"Hubbell's not your kind of guy," Frank said. "*We're* your kind of guy. You can't marry a . . . *businessman*."

"You don't understand Hubbell," I said. "He's really terrific."

"Yeah," said Frank, unconvinced, "but he's not our kind. You're our kind. We're your kind. Jimmy's your kind."

Even the Christmas decorations seemed to be nodding in agreement. The lights winked, Yes, he's not your kind.

I went into Nancy Sinatra's dressing room. Nancy was always quiet, thoughtful, and very smart. She was at her dressing table. She looked up at me.

"Hubbell *is* the right choice," she said. "You know you can't rely on Jimmy. He's here today and gone tomorrow. Now, you know how much, God knows, I love Frank . . . but . . ." She shook her head.

"So, why am I crying?" I said, wiping the tears from my cheeks. "*I'm* not Judy Garland."

Nancy smiled and said, "It's hard. You've got a choice of fascinating lives. . . ."

I sighed. "I think I should go back to Los Angeles."

"Dick Steenberg is driving back. You could go with him," Nancy suggested.

I did just that. On the way back, Dick said he knew Hubbell.

"He's a wonderful man," he told me.

"I know," I said, staring out at the dark desert.

Hubbell arrived on the twenty-seventh. The moment I saw him I felt relieved. Everything was going to be all right. We had a lot of laughs that night. 'Twas the season to be jolly.

Two days later, on the twenty-ninth, we were married. My sister Barbara and Hubbell's associate, Harry Ackerman, stood up with us. That night, upstairs in our house, Hubbell started to undress. On his underwear, printed in garish letters, was a parade of my hits: "Moonlight in Vermont," "Tree in the Meadow," "It Might As Well Be Spring . . ."

"That's class!" I said.

"You betcha!" he agreed.

And two days after that, Hubbell got loaded. We were at a party and he drank a lot, so much that Abe Burrows and Cy Howard had to put him to bed. I was standing there and Abe Burrows looked up questioningly. "Why did you do this? Hubbell's a great guy. But he drinks a lot. He's not for you. . . ."

"A fine time to tell me!" I cried.

"Who knew!" Burrows shrugged.

Hubbell went back to New York in a few days. There was something wrong with the whole thing. We couldn't live in the same city. He was based in New York. I was doing this radio program, ironically on CBS, which was very successful. *Club 15* wouldn't let me out of the contract. We conducted our affairs long-distance. Bell Telephone loved us.

Hubbell *was* a wonderful man. He was very respectable. He came from a marvelous background. He was a terrific businessman. He had a great sense of humor. So he had a drinking problem. It wasn't that bad. It was under control.

But I was unhappy. After the marriage, I wasn't running around, but I knew our marriage wasn't going to work. I was so embarrassed. It is still the one big guilt in my life, that I didn't have the guts to say to Hubbell, "I'm not ready to get married. I'm not sure of my love." That's all I would have had to have said. He would have given me all the time I wanted. But I thought I was going to hurt him. And I didn't want to hurt him. So I ended up hurting him all the more.

The marriage deteriorated quickly. Why not, with me on one coast and him on the other? He flew out several times for a few days. Then there were a couple of months when he couldn't come out. The next time he called to say that he was arriving, I promised to meet him at the airport, because I didn't want to meet him at my house. Because I didn't want him staying there. I didn't want him staying with me. I couldn't stand our marriage any longer.

It was late at night when his plane came in. I met him at the gate. We waited for his luggage.

"Is there something wrong?" he said.

"Yes," I admitted. "Hubbell, I made a great mistake. I should have told you this. I'll never forgive myself. I questioned this marriage before. Oh, believe me, there's no other person. It's just that I'm just not ready for marriage."

He was stunned. He had had no inkling that anything was wrong. Oh, the look in his eyes, the hurt, was terrible for me to see. I felt so sorry for him. The luggage arrived. He packed it in the car.

"Do you still have the suite at the Beverly Hills?" I asked him.

"Yes. I'll stay there tonight."

I drove him to the hotel.

"We should talk tomorrow," he said as he got out of the car.

"Yes, we'll talk," I said, miserably.

We did talk the next day. And the day after that. But nothing had changed. The marriage was over. I blew it.

We said good-bye. He went back to New York. I filed divorce proceedings. The divorce became final on August 18, 1950.

Hubbell is dead now, and it's too late for him to read any of this, but I would like everyone to know. I think you were wonderful, a wonderful man.

And I'm sorry.

9

Body
and Soul

Christmas 1949 was approaching. Nancy Guild called me on the phone.

"What are you doing?" she asked.

"Getting divorced," I answered.

"Me too," she said. "Anything else?"

"Nothing."

"Good. Then let's go to Palm Springs."

Nancy was an up-and-coming starlet at 20th, a real beauty, and she was in love with Ernie Martin whose shows, *Can-Can*, *Silk Stockings*, and *How to Succeed in Business Without Really Trying* would soon set New York on its ear. The two of us were really kind of young and innocent—good girls, as they said in those days—but we felt we were ready to check out the action. I called up Jimmy Van Heusen and said, "You don't mind our using your house in the Springs for a week, do you?" What could he say but, no he didn't mind at all. Nancy and I packed a couple of bathing suits and some good dresses and took off. The moment we landed in the Springs, it was—boom, okay, let's have lunch at the Racquet Club. So there we were, lunching by the pool and feeling very grand, when *he* came along.

John Garfield.

John Garfield had been my first screen crush during those Saturday afternoons in the late thirties when Cookie Warren and I (and chauffeur) would trek to the movies. The ritual was always the same. The Brown Derby for lunch. Following that, it was off to C. C. Brown's for dessert consisting of two hot-fudge sundaes with crushed almonds but no whipped cream because we were dieting. Then we would walk the one block to Grauman's Chinese Theater on Hollywood Boulevard, where I would place my feet in Betty Grable's footprints and dream of being a glamorous musical-comedy star. Then it was time for the movie, either at Grauman's or farther along at the Hollywood Warners. It was there, one Saturday afternoon, I saw him for the first time. *Four Daughters* was the name of the movie. Cookie and I sat in the balcony and John Garfield came on that screen— dark, brooding, cigarette dangling from his lips, muttering sentences about fate going around the corner, and suffering and finally ending it all, while my teen-age heart was crying no, no, no. Probably Cookie's heart was saying the same thing, but I couldn't hear because of my sobs. Forgotten were Claude Rains and the Lane Sisters and Jeffrey Lynn. My heart had been stolen by John Garfield. Body and soul.

And here it was ten years later at the Racquet Club, and there he stood, a little rumpled and absolutely sweet, accompanied by another man. He gave us the famous Garfield grin and walked over. Nancy automatically smiled the way beautiful 20th starlets smile, and I automatically thought, Okay, Nancy, here you go with another conquest.

"Hi, I'm Julie Garfield," he said, extending his hand. He was holding out his hand to *me*.

"Oh, sit down," I stammered. *Oh please sit down!* He did and introduced Bob Roberts, the producer of his next movie. The four of us sat and chatted. I don't remember eating any more of my lunch, but I do remember his nibbling at little grapes on my plate, telling me that the doctor wanted him to lose weight, telling me about his heart attack, telling me that he had to be careful now. He wasn't the kind of man to be too careful; he was very restless and liked to move about. Even sitting there, I could feel the energy exuding from him. I thought maybe he wanted to be somewhere else.

"I guess I'll go," I said, getting up.

"Where are you going?" he asked.

I looked at Nancy. "Home. That is, Jimmy Van Heusen's house. We're staying there. . . ."

"Could I come along?" he asked.

Could he! He did. A half-hour later I found myself in the kitchen making him Jell-O because he was hungry and the doctor had said that Jell-O would take away the hunger pangs.

"What a great scene," I laughed. "Here I am with John Garfield and what am I doing? Making Jell-O! Well, so much for glamour."

"I like hearing you laugh," he said. I felt a dangerous tingle. He seemed totally unaware of his impact. *Stir, stir, stir.*

"Nobody laughs out here. Everybody smiles, but nobody laughs," he said. Homesick New York boy, he was sauntering toward the bookcase. Nancy looked at me and shrugged her shoulders. I had to do something with the bowl of Jell-O. Otherwise I would have stirred it all night. I popped it into the refrigerator. *Jell, jell, jell.* Julie took a book off the shelf and opened it.

"Scott Fitzgerald—he's very good," Julie said, as if he weren't too sure about that. "*Tender Is the Night.* Yeah, I like the ending of that." He started to read, very slowly, haltingly, puzzling over the words. At first I thought it had something to do with his being part of the Group Theater, a kind of "Method acting" reading, but that wasn't the case. He had trouble putting the words together. Scott Fitzgerald's words were alien to him the way Scott Fitzgerald was alien to him. Julie had been *told* that Fitzgerald was a good writer. Something about that touched me. I had been used to many facile readings, once-overs of a script and let's rehearse it and that's all. Here was a man reading with a kid's intense absorption, totally concentrating on the words. Finally he stopped and looked up.

"I don't read so hot," he admitted. There was an awkward silence. Nancy excused herself.

"I'll go freshen up," she said, using the classic starlet's exit line.

"Nancy borrowed that line for the day," I said. And Julie laughed.

"You're funny," he observed.

"I'm not really funny. It just comes out that way."

"I like you. You make me laugh, and that's not easy."

"Well, now"—*tingle, tingle, tingle*—"would you like some Jell-O?"

That's how it started. I had left Hubbell and I was looking for a good time. Julie was married but had fallen in love with his most recent leading lady, France's Micheline Presle, who had just run off to marry actor Bill Marshall, damaging Garfield's ego just a bit, so *he* was looking for a good time. And that's what we had. With Nancy and with Bob Roberts—and without them, too—we had a very good time. Julie and I lunched together, dined together, sat by the pool and talked, sunned ourselves and talked, gazed at the stars—and talked. I have not the vaguest recollection of anything we said, but I can picture him exactly. There were the little lines of weariness in the boyish face, lines that disappeared as the days went by. Bob Roberts looked on approvingly. His star was supposed to relax, and indeed, his star was certainly relaxing. For someone with the reputation of a superstud, he was making no move. But that was all right. I would just continue to *tingle, tingle, tingle* by myself.

Looking back, I suppose we were a strange couple. We were such opposites. I was Hollywood-raised, I had been surrounded by all the glamour that goes with the good life of a Hollywood songwriter. The Whitings were not the *crème de la crème* of Hollywood society, merely the plain *crème*. Julie was the New York slum kid, the *dregs de la dregs*, the original gutter hero—serious, brilliant, a natural talent. We were two people who wanted to take a holiday before going on with our lives. We took nothing too seriously and that was wonderful.

For instance, Nancy Guild's father had a drinking problem. Not a huge problem. But he had borrowed a car and taken off for Riverside on a drinking spree. That was what we were told. So Nancy, Julie, and I, went looking for him. Riverside is rather a staid little town, but it does have its share of bars. We walked into the first one, and I approached the bartender. "Excuse us, but have you seen a man—balding, oh about five-eight with glasses and a small drinking problem?" Nancy burst into nervous laughter. The bartender stared at us incredulously, recognizing at least Julie. Then he shook his head wordlessly and we left.

"What's so funny?" I asked outside. By this time, the laughter had become contagious.

"My God," Nancy explained between fits of laughter, "don't you realize you were describing half the population of Riverside, California? 'Five-eight, balding, with a small drinking problem'?" Fourteen bars later, we found her father. She drove him home in the "borrowed" car and we drove back by ourselves.

On our return, there was a message for Julie. Darryl Zanuck had called and Julie was to report back to the studio to reshoot some scenes on *Under My Skin*.

I offered to drive him in.

"It'll only be a couple of days," he said.

"Great. Then we'll drive in tomorrow night."

On the way, we stopped for a drink in a little town called Banning. The bar was decorated with cotton snow and tinsel and lights that went on and off.

"I can't get used to Christmas out here," he said, taking a drag on a cigarette. "Phony trees, phony everything."

"You're talking about Santa Claus Lane and the annual parade," I said.

"Yeah, that's it! Hollywood Boulevard becomes Santa Claus Lane. That's exactly what I mean."

"Well, yours truly is going to appear on one of those floats in the parade."

"Doing what?" he wanted to know.

"I wave a lot. If you're lucky, you can come see me wave."

"Now that's what I like," Julie said, looking directly at me. "You seem to laugh things off. I get irritated."

"Julie, you *have* to laugh," I said. "Besides, remember, I grew up here. None of this seems so bizarre." Then I remembered a Santa Claus made out of a giant plastic orange. "Only sometimes," I added.

The neon blinked and the little colored lights flashed on and off.

Julie began to talk seriously for the first time, telling me about New York, which was so much a part of him, talking about the Group Theater, which he still loved despite its rejection of him. He admired them all—Harold Clurman, Clifford Odets, Elia Kazan. It was odd. He was a much bigger power than any of them and yet he looked up to them with awe.

"They all know so much," he said. "I want to know that much." He was like a young boy.

"But you're famous," I protested, wanting to protect him.

"I know," he said gloomily. "But I can't help *that*." We finished the drinks and continued driving.

When Julie had checked in to the Beverly Hills Hotel, he turned to me.

"Where are you going?"

"My house," I said.

"Could I come along?" he asked. I wondered if he realized that's what he'd said the first time by the pool.

"Of course," I replied. "I'll whip up some more Jell-O."

I went to bed with him that night. He surprised me. His skin was very tanned and very smooth and his body was very strong. What surprised me was that he was so gentle, so caring, so very sweet. Later he clung to me.

"I care for you because you're so alive," he said to me. "And I'm so afraid of dying."

"Maybe it's good you had the heart attack," I told him. "Maybe it was a warning. Look at it that way. Then you'll be more careful."

"You're mothering me," Julie muttered. "Women either want to mother me or fuck me."

"Well," I said philosophically, "now I've done *both*."

He told me about Lana Turner. When they were filming *The Postman Always Rings Twice*, they were the number one sex symbols of the world and, given the steamy subject matter of the film, everyone knew it was only a matter of time before Lana and Garfield would make contact.

"It was in the air. Every day we started a scene, I could see the gaffers making book," Julie reminisced. "I mean, there she was, always dressed in white and her hair bleached practically the same color. And there I was, very dark and everything. Our eyes would meet and we both knew we were going to have to do it. It was like you couldn't let the home team down. Everyone was waiting for it. So one day after work, I said, 'How's about it? Let's go down to the beach tonight.' And Lana said, 'Okay.' And so we went. It was beautiful. I want to tell you even the moon cooperated. The sea was calm and I was getting ready. We kissed in the moonlight. And guess what? No bells. No gongs went off. It was just like on the set. We started to laugh. 'Cause there were no fireworks. These two super sex symbols and no fireworks. Nothing but publicity."

"So you never continued?" I asked.

"Naw, we had to. To see how it turned out. We were right. It was nothing. But we laughed a lot about it and turned out to be really good friends."

A little after dawn, Julie left for the studio and I went back to Palm Springs. Three days later, he phoned to say Zanuck was flying him back. I met him at the airport. This huge plane, which looked about as big as the *Yankee Clipper*, landed and taxied up to the runway and out stepped Julie. He was the only passenger. Zanuck had chartered this whole huge plane just to fly Julie to Palm Springs. That was the part of Hollywood that made me laugh.

The following week, I was scheduled to appear in the Christmas parade. Julie and I were making plans for dinner.

"Who would you like to have?" he asked me.

"Bring Sam Jaffe," I said impulsively. I had adored him as Gunga Din and as the ancient lama in *Lost Horizons*. "I'll get off the float at LaBrea and then we can have a nice quiet dinner at Lucey's." That night, Julie was there with Jaffe, and also John Huston and Edward G. Robinson. "I thought you wouldn't mind a couple of ringers," Julie said. "Besides, they don't talk much."

They did nothing but talk. They were all brilliant men and all fond of Julie. I had never seen four men so devoted to each other. My father had had his friends, but he was essentially a family man and he had saved his serious conversation for Eleanore. Not so, these four. They had a camaraderie I had never seen in Hollywood. They talked of their work and they avoided any discussion of the witch-hunt that was threatening them all.

In 1947, J. Parnell Thomas and the House Un-American Activities Committee had begun its investigation of the movie industry, and this had shaken Hollywood to its not terribly steady foundation. In his "friendly" testimony, Jack Warner had implicated many of the writers who had worked on John Garfield's movies. By 1949, Julie himself was implicated. In 1951, he would be forced to testify, but that night it was like a distant storm. Julie was just having a casual dinner with friends. And I was not very aware politically.

Aunt Margaret, however, did not approve of Julie.

She confronted me. "Why are you going out with a Commie?"

"Oh, come on, Aunt Mag. Julie's not that. Besides, he's been cleared."

"Well, if he didn't do anything, what's he got to be cleared of?" she asked, mirroring the logic of the times.

When Julie came to the door one day, Aunt Mag gave him a curt hello and walked away. Glancing out the window, I saw her car slipping down the roadway.

"Aunt Mag, you didn't put the brake on," I shouted, running out of the house. Julie followed me. We raced across the lawn and he swung around the side of the car, opened the door, got in, and pulled the emergency brake. This was a man four weeks out of the hospital after a heart attack.

"Thank you," Aunt Mag said coldly, when she reached the car. "I have to get that brake fixed." Julie shrugged his shoulders. We walked back across the lawn and he picked up the afternoon paper and unfolded it. His name was spread across the headlines. He was more deeply implicated. HUAC was not satisfied with Garfield's statements.

He rolled up the paper tightly. "What's with them? Why don't they stop? I was cleared years ago. They kept clearing me. They let me entertain the troops. I don't understand any of this."

Nor did I. Julie—who had started the Hollywood Canteen with Bette Davis during World War II, who had donated an enormous amount of time during the war to keep up the morale of the troops—was now being treated like some kind of subversive.

Aunt Mag reached the door at the same time we did. Julie handed her the paper.

"Here," he said. "I bet you believe everything you read."

"Until proven otherwise," Aunt Mag snapped. Julie managed a smile. I sighed. There were some things in Hollywood that even I couldn't laugh at.

I was scheduled to sing for the troops at Oak Knoll Naval Hospital in San Francisco the following week. Julie accompanied me. That night we celebrated at the Blue Fox restaurant. At the time Los Angeles was not noted for its cuisine, but San Francisco was famous for a number of world-class restaurants and the Blue Fox was reputedly the greatest. It was located in an alley across from the city morgue. Julie and I were ushered into the restaurant and shown our table. We watched in awe as champagne popped, fizzed, and was poured. Roast duckling was set before us with a flourish, the champagne deftly replaced by a burgundy of impeccable heritage, the ashtrays whisked away and cleaned as soon as they were sullied by a single ash. With all this we were never aware of a waiter approaching; there was never the inelegant clatter of dishes.

"A perfect dinner!" I termed it when we had finished.

Julie grinned and said, "Yeah, it's all right, if you *like* perfect dinners."

We toasted each other. He raised his glass and said, "Absent friends . . ."

"What does that mean?"

"The British say that. I've always liked it."

We walked up Nob Hill toward the hotel. At the top, Julie turned and looked at the view below us. Across the Bay, the fog was starting to roll in. The night air was a bracing sweet mixture of sea and flowers. Julie raised his arms and cried out to San Francisco, "Hey! I am having fun!"

That was the key to it. Julie and I had nothing but fun. It didn't last. It wasn't supposed to. And when it was over, he went on with his life and I with mine. Three years later he was dead from a heart attack at the age of thirty-eight.

Much later on, at Chasen's restaurant, Johnny Mercer introduced me to Clifford Odets, who, to Johnny's surprise, treated me like an old friend. Odets took me to one side and said confidentially, "Julie told me all about you. You made him very happy. I want you to know that."

"What are you two talking about?" Mercer wanted to know.

"Nothing," I replied. "We're just talking about absent friends."

10

My
Ideal:
Strike Two

—

Often you're not aware of a catastrophe in the making until it hits you smack in the eye. I think it was true of Hollywood after the war. I think it was true of the country. I know it was true of me.

Everything seemed normal to me. The war was over, and I guess I believed all those lyrics I sang. We all had our dreams and our dreams would come true: dream houses, dream weddings, followed by dream marriages, dream children, everything happily ever after, with nothing but blue skies.

I was trying to follow a blueprint that had been set out for me by my mother, by society, by everyone but me. I had gotten married. That had been a mistake. My mistake. But that didn't mean that marriage was wrong, only that Hubbell had been the wrong man for me. Julie Garfield had been a Christmas holiday that had gone on for three or four months. But Julie had not been serious. Julie had been an adventure. Now it was time to go back to the blueprint. A Girl Should Be Married.

I became very busy with beaux, sometimes two or three at a time. I was almost as busy as Artie Shaw, who appeared to marry on the first date, while others were still debating whether to kiss. Artie married *everybody*, even Jerome Kern's daughter, Betty. When I called Betty's mother, Aunt Eva—I suppose to offer congratulations—I was informed that she had taken to her bed on learning the news.

So the war was over and everything was back to normal. But something had happened to the fabric of Hollywood itself. During the war, the movie studios had busily provided "product." They could do no wrong. Everybody went to the movies. Besides, the big studios also owned the theaters. When the courts finally judged this to be a monopoly, and the studios were divested of their theaters, the studio heads discovered they didn't have to supply so much product. So why should they pay the stars on long-term contracts? It would be cheaper and more profitable to hire them by the picture. The studios would have much more control. But that idea blew up when the tax laws were changed. The stars discovered that they could become independent corporations. That gave the valuable stars much more power. The first time that James Stewart's agent got him $750,000 plus 10 percent of the gross, the reign of Louis B. was over and it was the beginning of the end for the studio system. The moguls—the Louis B. Mayers, the Harry Cohns, and the Jack Warners—had lost control.

But then there was that little terror, television, warming up in the bull pen.

If that Reign of Terror was beginning, few were aware of it yet. In 1949, Howard Dietz, the vice-president in charge of advertising at MGM, was saying, "It's our duty to fight off television if it takes the next twenty years." Well, Dietz didn't understand that that particular fight had been already lost.

To me, television was a little box. Actually, it was a great big box with a little screen. When I went to New York right after the war, I was vaguely aware that television existed because my "cousin" Jimmy McNaughton was a set designer for ABC at the old Vanderbilt

Theater over Grand Central Station. I knew that people couldn't wear white on TV. Men had to wear blue shirts, and they had to be careful not to clash with the patterns. I had heard Jimmy discuss such matters over the phone. But my first real encounter with television took place at Harry Warren's house in Los Angeles, and then it wasn't my encounter. It was his. I was visiting Cookie, his daughter, and Harry was very busy, puttering. If there was a new gadget around, Harry was the first guy on the block to get it. He loved to tinker with all kinds of gadgets. Although he was totally unequipped to work with anything mechanical, that never stopped him.

The Warrens had just bought a television set. It was huge and occupied a great deal of space in their bedroom. There were very few programs being shown at the time, maybe one or two a day. Announcements were made in the paper: Television from 1:30–3:00 P.M. And the content of the programs wasn't exactly thrilling either: A woman painted movie stars' faces onto eggs. We watched her as she painted Clark Gable's face onto an egg.

This went on for half an hour or so. And then we would find ourselves staring at a test pattern. Who could take such a thing seriously?

Harry Warren could.

The reception at the Warrens' was not very good. Harry had been told that a rooftop antenna would solve the problem. He had bought the antenna and was now installing it. He and his butler were up on the roof moving the antenna from place to place. And it was Cookie's mother's job to announce whether the reception had improved. Cookie's mother reminded me of Gracie Allen. She was pretty and adorable but kind of ditsy and innocent. Harry was a quite irascible man whose way with gutter language could only have come from growing up on the Brooklyn streets.

So, Harry and the butler and the antenna were up on the roof while Cookie, her mother, and I were in the bedroom. We could hear Harry yell from the roof:

"Is it any better?"

We would gaze at the image of the woman painting movie stars' faces on the eggs. Cookie's mother would yell back in her singsong voice:

"Not *ye-et!*"

Again, from farther away, it seemed, Harry's voice:

"Any better now?"

Again, "Not *ye-et!*"

"Any better *now?*" We peered at the indistinct image on the screen. Both the image and the sound of Harry's voice seemed to be receding.

"Not *ye-et!*" Cookie's mother repeated. Then, for some time, we gazed intently at Clark Gable's features, fuzzily emerging from the egg.

Suddenly we were interrupted by a furious, red-faced Harry Warren, cable and wire entangled around him like seaweed, bursting through the door.

"*Har*-ry!" his wife screamed in surprise. "What *hap*-pened?"

"What *hap*-pened, you goddamned idiot!" Harry screamed back. "I fell off the sonovabitching *roof!*"

The butler emerged unscathed. They finally got their reception. But is it any wonder we didn't take it seriously? Television was a source of frustration. A crazy toy. A fad. It didn't come of age, at least on the Coast, until it dealt with Kathy Fiskus. Kathy was a little girl who fell down a hole in a cave somewhere in California, and they couldn't get her out. Television stayed with the rescue efforts for days and nights, and everybody watched. People bought sets, staying up all night to watch the operations. At first we could hear her voice. And then, as the time passed, it became more indistinct. Finally, they had to give up; the little girl was dead. But that established television. Why? Because it was happening right in front of our eyes. That has always been the attraction of television. Instant reality. Events taking place before your eyes. Volcanoes erupting. Wars breaking out. In those innocent days, and in the early fifties, part of the attraction of live television was to watch the performers goof. There was no refilming or editing then. If Uncle Miltie blew it, the whole world knew it.

Television may have been a menace to the movies, but I was a record star and a radio performer. Nothing seemed so catastrophic to me. There were some changes in the public's taste in records. Country music had become a force. But then I had become a force in country music, thanks to the records with Jimmy Wakely. As for radio, well, that didn't seem to present too many problems. A lot of the shows, like Jack Benny's and Bob Hope's, had always been performed in front of a live audience. Sometimes, now, we performed in the same theaters where we had done radio. The radio studio on Sunset and Gower, for instance, was remodeled for television. It was there that I teamed up with Jack Benny and Isaac Stern for the first (and one of the most brilliant) of the early TV specials. It was an historic occasion. It's a pity no record of it still exists.

About a year later, there was a giant show inaugurating the CBS Television City studios at Beverly and Fairfax. We spent a week rehearsing this huge production, and I can remember everyone standing in line for food. Grips, engineers, Jack Benny, George Burns and Gracie Allen, secretaries, Red Skelton, me, Lucille Ball, the parking-lot attendants, Eve Arden—anyone who was on the network was on the show.

And no one was treated special. Everyone got the same chow. It was like being in the army. But it was wonderful fun, because it was all a lark then, and not quite an industry. Few could envision the kind of giant it would become.

Lucille Ball and Desi Arnaz could. They formed Desilu. And very quietly, all those half-hour shows that had been hits on radio, like *My Friend Irma* and *Our Miss Brooks*, started to make the transition to the new medium. But it was no big deal.

My records were played on the radio, and I was also working on radio with *Club 15*, and later the *Jack Smith Show*—shows that didn't seem to be threatened by TV. But mainly, I was in the recording business, and records were booming.

The swing bands never really recovered from the war. Glenn Miller, along with so many others, had been killed. There had been a great migration of musicians to Los Angeles after the war. The big bands had split up when so many guys joined the service, and these musicians had grown tired of touring. It was an easier life, playing studio jobs and basking in the California sunlight with the family over a morning cup of coffee and not having to worry about missing the chartered bus that was going to Toledo. After the war, it was no longer the day of the big bands. It had become the day of the vocalists. Capitol had established that with all the girl singers—Peggy Lee,

Martha Tilton, Kay Starr, Jo Stafford, June Christy, Betty Hutton. And on other labels, Dinah Shore, Rosemary Clooney, and Doris Day, to say nothing of Nat "King" Cole, Sinatra, Tony Bennett, and Perry Como.

So we all kept singing, figuring all America was dancing to the same beat. Smooth and romantic. The songwriters kept writing the same songs. They were polished and pretty. And again, nobody paid any particular attention when Gordon Jenkins recorded with a folk group called The Weavers. Their first song was a hit, "Goodnight Irene." It was an old Leadbelly folk song. It was a novelty. There had always been novelties. Even in my father's day, there had been novelty songs. So this was tapping the folk vein. Then they followed it up with "Tzena, Tzena, Tzena," an Israeli folk song. Well, hadn't the Andrews Sisters had a big hit with "Bei Mir Bist du Schoen"? I don't think anybody dreamed the beat was changing that much, that something was happening to popular tastes. True, Mitch Miller, that very savvy classical oboist, kept coming up with hits: "There's a Pawn Shop on the Corner in Pittsburgh, Pennsylvania" for Guy Mitchell and Clooney's "Come On-a My House," for example. Paul Weston recorded Hank Williams's "Shrimp Boats," a bayou song, with Jo Stafford. "The Third Man Theme," zither music by Anton Karas, sold four million copies. *Zither* music? Hank Williams's "Jambalaya," another song about the bayou and Creole culture, made an enormous impact, and so did his other songs, "Cold, Cold Heart" and "Your Cheating Heart." Having recorded a lot of his songs, I knew about Hank Williams. Though I was involved in that country crossover, I was still singing the songs my father had written, and songs that were written in that same style, even in 1950. From 1910, there seemed to have been an unbroken chain of songs from writers like Irving Berlin, Jerome Kern, my father, and Harry Warren, men who wrote "novelties" but who also wrote "standards," who adapted to the culture, who even formed the culture. They were songwriters and they wrote by the rules. We were singers and performers and we sang by the rules. For the most part, Hollywood was a place where people still played by the rules. No one realized that this was not a queston of a few novelty songs becoming hits, that there was a full-scale musical revolution approaching.

Life in Hollywood at that time was a really lovely suburban experience. We were surrounded by the smell of eucalyptus and beautiful manicured lawns where the sprinklers went on at seven in the morning every morning. There were barbecues on Saturday nights —not really the lavish parties of my parents' day, because the emphasis was not on glamour. The essence was every-day. We were all intent on getting married and raising families and being normal, so we installed barbecues and barbecue pits and maybe spent more time with the "family" than we had before.

"Back to normal" was a phrase popular right after the war. But I'm not sure anybody was equipped to be normal. There had been a lot of upsetting experiences. Well, we would just have to deal with them.

I describe all this as a way of getting into my second marriage. I had married Hubbell, and I had had several affairs—with Julie and others—so I was not exactly a total innocent, but I was not all that experienced either.

Will I ever find the boy in my mind
The one who is my ideal.

The lyric to my father's song kept running through my head. After all, what was my ideal? I didn't have the foggiest. I knew he had to have a sense of humor. That came before anything else. And I suppose he had to be good-looking. I had had crushes. I had fallen in deep "like." I had not been swept away by love. Well, wasn't it *time*? That's why I was so busy with beaux. The sponsors of my radio show, Oxydol, asked if I would go out with the head of advertising from Procter and Gamble, who was coming west from Cincinnati. He was very important. I said I'd be delighted. And I was. Gail Smith was a charmer. He squired me around town a couple of times, and then asked me to marry him. I was very flattered, but there were a few problems. First, he was already married, but getting a divorce. Second, I wasn't sure I was in love with him, or even that he was in love with me. I wasn't going to repeat the Hubbell Robinson mistake of not giving a relationship enough time.

Gail was bright, like Hubbell, and a good businessman, like Hubbell. He had a sense of humor, like Hubbell. Maybe he was too much like Hubbell. I don't know. But I knew it wasn't right for me to marry him. However, I kept him in the family. Several years later, he married my sister, Barbara, who, I discovered, had had a case on him for years. Before they married, Gail and I sat down and explained to Barbara that what we had was never serious.

"But it certainly was fun," I had to add.

At the same time I was dating Gail, I was also dating Lou Busch.

Lou had been a piano player with Hal Kemp's band, when Janet Blair was the girl singer. They got married and came to Hollywood, where Janet became a movie star, and Lou first worked at Columbia, scoring films, and then got a job as an artist and repertoire man at Capitol. He knew the singing King Sisters, one of whom was married to Jimmy Conklin, who had succeeded Johnny Mercer at Capitol. When Capitol became a big record company, no longer the toy Johnny had played with during the war, and he could no longer issue each record, knowing that it would be exactly what he wanted, he seemed to lose interest. He went on to other things, to writing with Henry Mancini, to his golf game, to fishing. Capitol expanded, and Johnny drifted away, still interested but not so passionately involved. And the product changed. When Jimmy Conklin took Johnny's place, Lou Busch became my producer. We worked on various sessions together. He and Janet came over to the house for the Saturday nights at the Whitings'. We still had those parties, again not such lavish ones, but still a lot of fun. Janet would sing, and Lou would play funny piano, different styles—sometimes ragtime, sometimes swing, jazz, mock barroom piano. He was a very clever guy and his sense of humor came out in his way of playing piano. Then, about the same time my marriage with Hubbell broke up, so did his marriage to Janet Blair.

Lou and I started dating each other. One thing led to another, and I discovered I was pregnant. That brought up The Big Question. Should we get married? Everybody else was raising a family. Lou and I took inventory. I looked at him. He was charming. He had a great sense of humor. He fit a pattern. He was substantial, and a good man. He drank some, but who didn't? He wasn't a mean man. We did have fun together, we did have respect for each other, we both shared a zest for life, and we were in the same business. He was able to teach me the art of putting together an act—what piece of material should go where, how the act should build, how to cut fifteen minutes if the crowd was noisy. He was even good at choosing the gowns I should wear. But love him?

Maybe I've always been a surfacer. Perhaps I don't go deep enough. Maybe I couldn't last at love. But with Lou, I did think we'd be good for each other. People were supposed to get married, and I was going to have a child. I wanted that child. Thank God I had that child. Thank God I married Lou, because he was a wonderful father to her. But, *love* him?

We got married in Mexico, and moved into a very nice apartment in Beverly Hills. And in October 1950, Debbie was born. Debbie was a wonderful baby and I know I loved her. But I wasn't totally devoted to taking care of a baby. Work was what I was trained to do. Performing was it. Eleanore had drummed that into my head. Nothing should really get in the way of the career. And there were plenty of mothers in Hollywood who also worked. They had nurses and nannies, and they continued their careers.

We moved to a house in Glenroy Knolls. Nice house. Nice neighbors. Nice life. Nice husband. Wonderful adorable baby. It all seems like a dream to me.

We did all the expected things, like having birthday parties for Debbie. And, of course, she took her first steps and was toilet-trained and went off to school. But there is nothing to say about that kind of life. There is nothing remarkable about it at all. I loved Debbie and I guess I loved Lou, and I tried to be a wife and a mother and an entertainer and the time went by. Nothing more to declare.

Paul Weston called Lou one day and said, "Lou, you know that funny kind of piano you play at parties? We could use that on a record for Jo."

Jo Stafford was recording "Ragtime Cowboy Joe" with Paul, and he wanted Lou to work on it. Lou came back that day and said, "I just made the *funniest* record with Jo." He forgot all about it, until Capitol called up and said they wanted to give him billing. Since he was an A&R man, he didn't want to use his real name. "How about Joe Carr?" he suggested. "That sounds like a piano player."

They approved of that, but they wanted a little more distinction. "Distinction?" Lou said, "How about Joe *Fingers* Carr?" And they bought it.

That was the start of a whole new career. Lou led a double life. Solid A&R man by day, daring Joe "Fingers" Carr by night. He was called on to do appearances. He recorded an album that was hugely successful. He was very busy, and so was I. Sometimes we worked together. He would come out and play double piano and have a spot of his own. We worked at our business and made a home and raised a child, and that was the way it should be. That was the blueprint.

But it wasn't perfect. No, and maybe it wasn't even good. We didn't stop to look much. I was the dominant one in the relationship. Maybe I have always needed to dominate. Like it or not, from the time I was seventeen, everyone has always known who Margaret Whiting was. If this bothered Lou, he didn't show it. Except at certain times.

Once, we were playing Milwaukee. By coincidence, there were a lot of stars from the Capitol roster in town. Stan Kenton's band in one place and Les Paul and Mary Ford in another. One night they all came in to see Lou and me. It was all very warm and chummy, like folks from the same hometown who met by chance at a convention. At this time, Capitol was negotiating contracts for both Lou and me. I told Capitol I wanted Lou's contract completed before they tackled mine. Lou overheard me.

"Why did you say that?" he asked. He was furious. I didn't know why.

"I didn't want them to use me against you."

"How could they do that?" he asked.

"I just didn't want to be in your way."

"You mean, because you're a big-seller. Is that what you mean?"

"I didn't want them to be influenced."

"God damn it, I'm not Margaret Whiting's piano player. I want to be Lou Busch."

"Exactly!" I agreed. "That's why I want them to sign your contract first. So they can't use you against me, or me against you."

"Why do a thing like that?"

"To protect you."

"Why do I need protection?"

I could see this was going nowhere, so I threw on a coat and got the hell out of the hotel room and went to a movie in downtown Milwaukee until the whole thing blew over. And it did blow over. Life returned to normal. We worked at our careers, had people over for barbecue on Saturday nights, played with Debbie and thought about her future, and didn't really think about our own.

And then, quite suddenly, in the middle fifties, nothing was normal anymore. Everything changed. The Reign of Terror, which had started with television, grew to include the music business.

The Claw. That insistent use of triplets. That was the first sound I heard. It could have been like the opening of Beethoven's Fifth. Fate Knocking at the Door. The Claw was *ta-ta-ta* tapping away. It was rock 'n' roll, saying, "Let me in." "Shake Rattle and Roll" with Bill Haley and the Comets, I guess, was the first huge explosion. And then it was "Rock Around the Clock." And then Elvis Presley and "Heartbreak Hotel." He was on the same *Ed Sullivan Show* as the Tommy Dorsey band and couldn't be photographed below the waist because of his gyrations. And then, before you knew it, Elvis was on television again, and this time you could see him all the way down. And where was Tommy Dorsey and his band?

Nowhere.

It happened *that* fast. In 1945, Dick Haymes and I had headed the bill at the RKO Boston with the Nicholas Brothers and Lord Buckley, the hip comic, giving nine shows a day and busting the house record. We were both associated with "It Might As Well Be Spring," I because of the record, he because he had been in *State Fair*, so we decided that he would sing the song on one show, I on the next. Billy Burton, the manager for both of us, had thought of the idea. It worked out very well, and it gave Bernie Leighton, my piano player, a lot of added income. I paid Bernie five hundred dollars a week to play, and so did Dick. So Bernie was hauling down a thousand dollars a week. That was enough money to send him back to Yale. To this day, he swears that Margaret Whiting put him through college.

That was 1945. And here it was, ten years later, and everything had suddenly changed. And it wasn't that it had changed just for me. Frank Sinatra, who had so confidently mapped out his career over a plate of pasta in that Italian restaurant in the late thirties, and who had achieved more than he could possibly have dreamed, suddenly went into eclipse. In the early fifties, Columbia couldn't give away his records. His throat went bad. He had to beg for the part of Maggio in *From Here to Eternity*. He didn't just beg, he had to audition, to fly in from Africa, where his current wife, Ava Gardner, was making *Mogambo*, and I understand she had to pay his fare. And even then they only paid him a few thousand dollars. But he took the chance, grabbed an opportunity, and saved himself.

Others grabbed what they could get, and through luck and talent, they survived. Dinah Shore got television. Doris Day got the movies. A lot of people, confused, stunned, or frustrated, stopped working. Jo Stafford did. So did Harry Warren.

Times changed. And life changed. I can understand it. The kids were tired of the blandness of Bing, Frank, Doris, Jack Jones, Vic Damone, all of us. We had sung. And we had pleased. But they heard their own rhythms.

When this Reign of Terror hit the record industry, I wasn't exactly a charity case. I worked a lot. I played Vegas, Reno, Tahoe. Those were three places you could always count on, and there was the Cocoanut Grove in L.A., the Sherman Hotel and the Palmer House in Chicago, and Ohio towns like Cincinnati.

It just wasn't the same as it had been.

Nor was our marriage. We were going through the motions. We had money. We had our separate careers. We had our child. We had each other. What was wrong? I began to cough. For no reason. I didn't have a cold. I didn't have nasal drip. I just coughed. I would wake up in the middle of the night and start coughing, great wracking spasms of coughing, and then go back to sleep. I would cough in the morning when I got up. I would cough anytime and anywhere. Except onstage. I could be standing in the wings, ready to go on, and be coughing, and then perform and never have a problem. But it would drive Lou nuts. We were working together. He couldn't sleep and neither could I. My throat became inflamed. I had to cancel two weeks in Denver because my throat was sore from all the coughing. I went to Dr. Martin Covel, who was also Lou's doctor. He could find nothing wrong with me, but suggested I see a throat specialist.

The throat specialist examined me. He could see nothing wrong either, but warned that if I continued to cough like that, I could do permanent damage to my throat. He suggested I see a psychotherapist. I resisted. On my third visit, he introduced me to a patient who had undergone a laryngectomy. The man could talk only by gulping in huge amounts of air and then speaking as he belched. I knew what the doctor was doing. He was trying some kind of shock treatment. I went back to Martin.

"Well, what did the specialist say?" Martin asked.

"He said I should go see a shrink."

Martin got up. "You can go spend your money if you want to. But Margaret, I don't think you need a shrink. You're just trying to be like an average all-American woman and you're not. Maybe you're bored with Lou. Maybe he's bored with you."

"No. We are *married*," I protested. Then he exploded.

"You know, you've got an American flag stuck up your ass. You're different. You don't have to be married. You don't have to stay married. What, are you crazy? You're going to follow everybody else's rules? Because somebody says you've got to stay married you can't have a divorce? Or a second divorce? Who cares, for Chrissakes? You've got to do what you want to do to make you happy. Otherwise you'll cough. It's as simple as that."

And it was. I sat down with Lou. He listened for a few minutes and said, "I don't think we should be married anymore."

I nodded. "We seem to be going in different directions."

"Maybe we better get a divorce."

I said, "Shouldn't we talk it out?"

He said, "If you want."

We talked about it for a day or two, and figured there was nothing left of the marriage. I guess we had just outlived each other. It happens. It happens a lot. I had been trying to live my life like a lyric. Everything swell, everything happy, with the sun in the morning and the moon at night. I had been wrong to do that.

That night, I didn't cough. And I never coughed again.

Let me tell you about Lou. Lou was a buddy. And he was the

most wonderful father. How lucky Debbie was to have him. He was really a *father*. He would say, "No, Debbie, don't you do that," when a lot of fathers might have let her get away with things.

Lou married a lovely woman named Nita and they moved a little ways out of Los Angeles to Ojai. He died in a car accident. I was in Cincinnati at the time. Debbie called. I gave her money for the plane fare to L.A. and she went to the funeral. The King Sisters were there, and Frank DeVol, and all the old friends. Debbie was terribly touched because they all showed up.

I keep pictures and photos, but I don't live on memories. I really do live for the moment. I guess that's why I keep going on.

11

How Do
You Keep the
Music Playing?

As long as I could sing, I was always happy. In a sense, it didn't matter where I sang. I was put on this earth to sing, and that was it. If I wasn't in demand as a recording star, I channeled my energies elsewhere. There were still clubs to work. Records to be made—albums, if not top-of-the-chart singles. I had always wanted to work on the stage, to do "legit" work, as it's rather snobbishly termed. I got my chance when the Dallas State Fair Music Hall decided to revive George Gershwin's *Girl Crazy* with Jack Carson and me. Franz Allers, a most respected musical conductor, was in charge of the musical matters and George Shaefer was the director. It was fun working with George. He was very creative and would take Jack and me up in the balcony or into the aisles and rehearse scenes. It reminded me of football players in a huddle. And then, go in and get 'em again! George was on his way to New York to be associate director of his first play, which John Patrick had just completed. He started to describe it. It had something to do with a teahouse in August. Frankly, it sounded like just another summer-stock dream. But I certainly didn't want to down anyone's hopes. "Where does this all take place?" I asked brightly, hoping he might bring up cherry blossoms, geisha girls, and beautiful pools in Tokyo.

"Okinawa," he answered.

"Oh," I said, and buried myself in the next scene.

So, I was wrong, and *Teahouse of the August Moon* became a big hit, and later George became an important director. What did I know?

Not much, according to Franz Allers. At the first orchestral reading, I was singing along happily when Allers stopped and tapped the podium with his baton. There, in front of all the musicians, he said, "Miss Whiting. I don't know what you learned in Hollywood. But you never learned to follow the beat." (Shades of George Washington Hill!) "Now, you may be a star, but there is one thing I must impress upon you. In the theater, you have to follow the conductor." I was not happy being humiliated in front of the orchestra. Later that day, he apologized.

"You are very talented," he said, "but if everyone is not together in a musical number, it is a shambles and *everybody* depends on the conductor to hold things together."

So I learned, and I also got a chance to sing "I Got Rhythm" eight times a week!

If I was not the recording star I once was, I still had a great many chances to perform. I also felt that I had been given a gift, and that I should share it. In my day I have sung for Catholic Charities, Jewish Charities, the City of Hope, AIDS, Meals on Wheels, arthritis, muscular dystrophy, you name it. If I haven't had it, I've sung for it. (This impulse has led to my being called, from time to time, the Benefit Queen.) I've done 1,500 appearances for the armed forces. I've sung in hospitals and prisons. Most of the time, the rewards have been terrific.

At the Oak Knoll Naval Hospital, I followed the usual procedure. I would go around from ward to ward with a piano that had been wheeled in, I would sing a few songs, and then sit on the hospital beds and talk to the boys. There were a lot of wards and it was very strenuous work, not only physically but emotionally.

In one of the wards, a guy was wheeled up to me. Strange. He couldn't work the chair by himself. He was the first quadriplegic I had seen. He looked at me and said, "I'm okay. I'm all right. But I got a favor to ask. My buddy, he wants to die. He's in a room by himself. We want to get him out here with us. And he doesn't want to live. So we thought maybe you could help us. He's like me, he ain't got no arms or legs."

I said, "What can I do?"

"You can talk to him."

"I'll do anything I can."

So they wheeled in this bed, and the guy in it looked away.

"Hi," I said. "I'm Margaret Whiting." I was onstage now. This was a performance. There was no reaction from him. I started singing anyway. I sang whatever songs I was singing at the moment. He didn't respond.

"What's your name?" I asked.

"Who cares?"

"I care."

"Ted."

"Well, Ted, can I sing something for you?"

"You don't like my kind of music."

"You never can tell," I said. "I sing a lot of things. Except opera."

"It ain't opera."

"Well, swing? Pop? Jazz?"

"I like country," he said.

"Like Little Jimmy Dickens?" I asked, desperately trying to remember those names from Nashville. "Ferlin Husky? Eddy Arnold?"

He seemed to respond.

"Jimmy Wakely?" He really liked Jimmy.

"Well, did you ever hear 'Slippin' Around'?"

"Yeah, that was a good one."

"Well, I recorded it with Jimmy. How about you do Jimmy's part, and I'll do mine."

So we sang. He was a basket case. I discovered they called the men that because they actually put them in baskets, to make it easier to carry them. I stayed with this man an extra-long time.

"Do you know this song?" I would ask, and if he said no, I would say, "Well, let's make it up."

I left him, finally. Two hours later, I was in the rec room when the phone rang. It was the base commander. He said, "I want to thank you for what you did. You got Ted back in the room with the guys."

That was a moment.

I sang in mental hospitals and in prisons. At San Quentin they gave me a poem and a picture. I had been on Queens Row, which is where they put the gays, so they won't get with the rest of the prison population, and they wrote this poem about me standing in front of murderers. Very dramatic. Once, it really was dramatic. I went to one of the locked wards in a mental hospital, somewhere near Los Angeles. Buddy Pepper, the piano player, was with me. As the men came in, they were walking with their heads down. Most convicts walk with their heads up, but the mentally ill walked, heads down, not looking at anyone. There were two or three burly guards in the audience to protect me. I started singing. God knows what it was I sang, but one of the patients got up, started toward me, grabbed my throat. Everybody was in shock. The goddamn guards just stood there. I didn't want to give the man a chance to see what he could do. So with the strength that comes from heaven—and desperation— I pulled his hands away from my throat, right away and down. I kept hold of his hands, and I also kept right on singing, held those hands and kept singing and sang him down to a chair. I think in all the time I have been performing, this was truly the only time I was ever frightened.

Some of the most memorable moments occurred when I was entertaining the troops with Bob Hope. With Hope, you never knew exactly what you were in for. Occasionally we entertained only twenty men on an itty-bitty stage, and other times there were huge audiences. It was always rather mysterious, and with Hope, always fun.

The biggest junket we took was to Thule, in Greenland, and Goose Bay, in Labrador. This fun little jaunt was going to be filmed for a TV special, and it involved Hope, Jerry Colonna, Hedda Hopper, the Les Brown Band, Anita Ekberg, William Holden, and his wife, Brenda Marshall. Marilyn Monroe had been scheduled to make the trip originally, and Nick Castle, in a moment of manic humor, had choreographed "Heat Wave." for Marilyn to sing to our frozen troops in Greenland. At the last moment, she couldn't make it and Ekberg was a more than worthy substitute.

We had been working a week on the show in Los Angeles so that we could just get off the plane and do it. NBC had preceded us with all the equipment. Our troupe left one night from Burbank around eight-thirty. Hope gathered us all together in the plane and said, "Everybody get into pajamas and robes. Get comfortable." I emerged in pajamas and robe. Hedda Hopper came out in a pink robe. We all sat there like kids waiting for her to read us a bedtime story. Instead, Hedda said, "I'm a columnist. I thrive on gossip, but from the moment we take off till the moment we get back, you can sleep with whomever you want to, you can let your hair down, you can do whatever you want. I'll only talk about the good." There was a collective sigh of relief from us. Not that we were planning all that whoopee. But, with a columnist, you tend to keep your guard up and your makeup on at all times. This way, we all felt more at ease.

The next morning we arrived in New York, were put up at the Hampshire House, and then left in Secretary of the Air Force Talbot's plane. That night, Anita Ekberg got up in her pajamas to make her way to the ladies' room. I followed, in pajamas. From the curtains of one berth, a hand reached out and grabbed my rear. It was Hope. He said, "Whiting, it's the only time you ever looked like a bellboy."

The next day we were coming into Thule in almost impossible winds. The major who was flying the plane told Hope he thought it was risky to land. But Hope shook his head and said, "Let's do it." The weather was really unbelievable. Besides the ninety-mile-an-hour gales, the temperature was something like fifty below zero.

It took us almost an hour to make a landing. We would swoop down and then could feel the winds shake the plane like a terrier shakes a rat. We would climb again and try another approach. From where I was sitting, I could see a lot of very terrified famous faces, but nobody said a word of protest. Finally, at the end of an hour, we could feel the wheels touch ground. The engines roared and we came to a stop. An officer opened the door to the plane and welcomed us. Beyond, it looked like a white maze. We all collected our belongings. (We had all been issued arctic gear and looked like refugees from *Nanook of the North*. Hope was the first one out the door.

He was hit by a blast of music. The Air Force Band had struck up "Thanks for the Memory." They had been standing in this cold for two hours for Hope. He realized it. Tears welled up in his eyes and he had to step back into the cabin. He looked at us, shook his head to clear his eyes, and said, "Come on. They been waiting all this time. Let's give them *everything*!" And so we did.

It was amazing how human beings had adjusted to the conditions. First, we were shown through the base. It was an underground city. Very nice rooms, sparse but with beds and showers. Everything was underground. The TV crew had built an entire set there for us. Outside and above ground, there was nothing but the Quonset huts and ice, ice, ice. If you were unprotected, you would die in five minutes out there. In that way conditions were more dangerous than they were in either Korea or Vietnam.

We did two shows for the troops. In the audience there were also a number of Danes, since Greenland belonged to Denmark. They were terribly happy to see a fellow Scandinavian, Ekberg. The shows went off without a hitch, the television cameras grinding away. We could have been back in Burbank in a studio. But, for a moment, while I was waiting to go on, I thought of the incredible logistics of all this. Just the electricity alone. Here we were on this giant iceberg and somebody had brought in *electricity*. That's how the lights could work and the cameras, and the electric guitars. Somebody, actually a lot of bodies, had built this entire base, and they hadn't been sheltered from the winds. How had they done it? And the supplies had been flown in. Sacks of coffee. Sides of beef. Barrels of flour. Where did the water come from? Was it just melted ice? Or was that imported too? And what were we all doing here? Had Hedda Hopper, for instance, ever in her wildest dreams, imagined that she would be in Greenland? Hedda Hopper and her hats in Greenland. It boggled the mind.

While it was true that these troops had an amazing amount of what we call the "comforts of home," it was also true that it was a long and lonely tour of duty. To say that they welcomed us is the mildest of understatements. Since being stationed at Thule, they had not heard a swing band. They had not seen live entertainers. Jokes, songs, dances, costumes—they had almost forgotten what all these things were. That added an enormous excitement to the performances. Anita Ekberg was truly adorable. She was warm, charming, very open, and we had a lot of laughs. Hope did his shtiks with her and she was a wonderful foil. She is truly a talented woman and co-medienne and has never been really appreciated in this country.

The next day, Hedda and I went shopping. In Labrador.

No sooner were we off the plane than we were in the Hudson's Bay store there. From the sound of it, I expected some arctic outpost. Instead we found a terrific department store where we happily shopped for scrimshaw and ivory goods. I will shop *anywhere*. Put me down in a jungle and I will somehow head straight for the local Saks Fifth Avenue.

Three days later, I *was* in Saks Fifth Avenue. We had returned from the Arctic, and we were back at the Hampshire House as Bob Hope's guests, to attend the premier of his new movie, *The Seven Little Foys.* I headed straight from Saks to Sardi's to have tea with Hedda. We were still so bemused by our arctic expedition that we couldn't stop marveling at the napkins, the cutlery, the service, the people. And then, as if on command, Noël Coward appeared at our table. I was, of course, gaga. Noël Coward *sitting down* at our table. He told me how much he loved my father as a songwriter (he himself was not at all bad at that difficult art) and that he admired my singing. And I burbled a few phrases of thanks and admiration. We told him we had been on a tour with Bob Hope. He nodded, got up to leave, and said, "Oh by the way, where exactly were you with Hope?"

"The North Pole," Hedda replied.

"Oh yes. Veddy cold, the Pole," said that peripatetic playwright, leaving with what sounded suspiciously like a line from one of his plays.

So my career went its own way, sometimes with a little help from Fate. Right after the breakup of my marriage to Lou, I regrouped with my mother and my sister. The Saturday night parties were in full swing. Barbara was now The Kid. She would perform. I was the Sophisticate. After all, I had been married. Twice. And Eleanore was the Mother. But she could just as well as have been Auntie Mame. Or Bea Lillie. She had a wicked sense of humor and a surer sense of drama. I wasn't really aware of the effect we made on people until two publicists from Desilu productions came up to me in the middle of a rather swinging party and said, "There's a hell of a TV series." I can't imagine that Eleanore was swinging from the chandeliers or anything like that, but something caught their eye. Of course, *I Love Lucy* was enormously popular. Any program that could duplicate that format was worth a try.

Two of the *Lucy* writers, Bob Carroll, Jr., and Madelyn Pugh, met with us, and before we know it, we were shooting a pilot called—what else?—*Those Whiting Girls*. Mabel Albertson played Eleanore, Barbara played Barbara, and I played me. The pilot was sold, and there we were suddenly shooting episodes. I was the older sister with a lot of boyfriends (I wonder where the writers got that) and Barbara played a funny college kid. I got to sing one song per show, and sometimes Barbara would sing with me. For the next two years, Eleanore and Aunt Mag came to every taping. They were thrilled that they were back in the business again. Perhaps Eleanore thought secretly she could play herself better than Mabel Albertson could, but she seemed so happy with the publicity and fame that went with being a character that she never mentioned it.

Craig Stevens played my main suitor, Mike Connors was in a few episodes, and Charles Bronson portrayed a Hollywood writer. In real life, Bronson was after me, and other women may think I'm crazy, but I found he held no attraction for me. Gorgeous, yes. A lotta muscle, but no sense of humor. I mean, have you ever seen *Death Wish* smile?

No, I was taken up with Hugh O'Brian. He was shooting *Wyatt Earp* on the Desilu lot next to ours, and he dropped by the set to borrow a cup of sugar, you might say. He was right neighborly and he flashed that famous grin, and I immediately went, *Hmmmm*. I had met him a couple of times before, in Dallas, but I had never been able to recognize him. Before he became Wyatt Earp, he played the other side of the hill and range—that is, either an Indian or a Mexican. So his head was always either shaved or he would be sporting a long, drooping moustache. When I saw what he really looked like, I liked what he really looked like—a lot. And God knows, *he* had a sense of humor.

This was not true of some of the cowboy stars of the period. Steve McQueen, for instance. During the period when Jimmy Wakely and I were making records together, we were booked into state fairs. Steve was playing the lead in a western series, *Wanted: Dead or Alive*. He had been booked to play a personal appearance with us. We met backstage. He said, "Hello, how are ya?" without much enthusiasm and dropped, Method-actor-sullen, into a chair in his dressing room. I shrugged and went on my way. Jimmy and I went out and sang our duets, told a few stories, and the crowd loved us. Steve went out in some kind of suit, told a few jokes, and bombed. Evidently they preferred him dead to alive.

When he came off, he looked in rather shyly. I was taking off my makeup.

"What do you think happened?" he asked.

"You don't have an act," I told him, wiping off some cold cream. "You just can't go out and tell jokes."

"What can I do?"

"You got any cowboy gear?"

"I can get some." We found him some buckskin and made sure it was tight in the right places.

"You use a gun. Can you really do anything with it?"

"What the fuck do you think I been practicing all these months for?" he retorted, in his usual charming manner.

"Well, do some tricks, then. Twirl it. Get it out of the holster. Quick on the draw. Now, anything funny happen to you on the set?"

He thought so.

In two hours, Jimmy and I had made an act for him. He went out in his new cowboy drag and said, "Hi, I'm Steve McQueen, but you probably know me better as Josh Randall because I am *Wanted, Dead or Alive!*" (*Applause, applause, applause.*) Then he took out his 1892 Winchester carbine that he affectionately referred to as his "Mare's Laig," told a few anecdotes about times the gun wouldn't go off and they had to keep refilming. The audience loved him.

We were in adjoining suites at the hotel. That evening, Don Crouch, a friend of mine, who was in Albuquerque at the time, was taking me out. During the war, when he had been a flier, I had been Don's pinup. Now he was married to a woman who was a dead ringer for Ingrid Bergman, and he himself was movie-star good-looking. And we were all great friends. Don arrived to take me out after the show. The door to Steve's suite was open. Steve heard my voice and yelled, "Hey, Whiting, come on in here."

We went into his suite. He was in the shower, so drunk he was careening off the sides of the shower stall.

"Hey, baby, come on in with me," he said.

"Not this time," I said a bit skittishly.

"Come on. It'll be fun, I promise you. Hey, there's a bottle out there. Would you hand me the bottle?"

I did, and as I did, he grabbed my arm and tried to pull me into the shower.

"Steve, I'm with somebody," I said. He let go of my arm, and I heard the thump as he hit the other side of the shower stall.

"Oh shit," he said pleasantly. "Well, have a good time."

Don and I left him, drunk and soaking, alone in the shower. It was sad to see somebody so young that disturbed.

Hugh was not disturbed. Hugh was an ex-Marine who had gotten into the movie business. He didn't have that incredible drive that makes for superstars and neither did I. He was a good performer. He had plenty of women. He liked fun and good times and he was very caught up with a charitable organization called the Thalians. That was what drew us together: He wanted Barbara and me to join.

The Thalians was formed of young show-business people—performers, producers, and writers—who hoped to convince the world that Hollywood was not totally made up of dope fiends and drunks. Its members included Hugh O'Brian, Debbie Reynolds, Donald O'Connor and the like, who were smart enough to ask Frank Sinatra, Danny Thomas, and Mervyn LeRoy, among others, to be advisers. Together, they raised money for disturbed children.

Hugh was president, and soon after I started dating him, I joined, too. As a group, we put on benefits, grand and gala affairs, where stars would write and perform parodies of the current musicals. One of the more memorable of these was a parody of *The King and I*, written by Johnny Mercer and Don McGuire, with Sammy Davis, Jr., playing the king and Donald O'Connor the prime minister. They sang the immortal lines

"We kiss in the shower,
At the YMCA . . ."

Later, we developed special shows honoring, say, Jack Benny or Lucille Ball. And for these occasions, Jack Haley, Jr., would take clips from their movies and compile a semidocumentary newsreel of their lives. He later developed this formula into the smash MGM musical called *That's Entertainment.*

When Hugh and I were first going out together, he took me on a plane. We were bound for Las Vegas, Jerry Lewis country. Hugh wanted to persuade Jerry and Sammy Davis, Jr., to perform for the Thalians. We landed and because Hugh was at the height of his fame as Wyatt Earp, Jerry and Sammy challenged him to some shooting matches. Who could be the Fastest Gun in the West? Who could hit the most targets? Well Hugh won because he was in practice, and after all, he was Wyatt Earp. I never spent a more boring afternoon with three men who certainly could be fascinating when they wanted to be. But that day, they just wanted to be little boys.

Hugh was not boring at other times. He was a very sexy guy and I felt very free with him. He didn't want to get married. I didn't want to get married. There was the fascination of an affair. There was the period of getting to know one another, there was the passion and the lovemaking, there was total freedom. He didn't have to answer to me, nor I to him.

I realized I was not playing by the rules. I was not conforming to social standards, but I was very happy. I was not getting married. I was having a hell of a good time. Was this right?

I'm only half facetious in asking this question. It seemed like a lot of people in Hollywood were beginning to question all the rules they had been brought up with. The structure was falling apart. Fast.

Debbie Reynolds was very involved with the Thalians. She was president at one time, as was I. On a certain day in 1959, Jack Haley and I were supposed to meet at Debbie's house. When we arrived, we found a gaggle of reporters outside her door, and a babble of questions. I didn't understand any of this. All I could say was that we had a Thalians meeting. We got inside the door. There stood Debbie.

The news had come out that Eddie Fisher was up at Grossinger's, the Catskills resort, with Elizabeth Taylor. The news had not come from Eddie, but from the reporters. Debbie was wonderful. She said, "Look at me, I can't walk outside because of all the photographers. I'm here with the kids. My life is falling apart. But I think we better get to work."

And so we did. There was a famous picture of her with her hair up in curlers and safety pins in her blouse, meeting the reporters. It was rumored that that photo had been set up. But I can swear that the day I saw her, she was not dressed for any glamour shots. Her life had become a crazy free-for-all, culminating with her climbing over a fence to avoid the photographers in order to meet Fisher, who had promised to explain. He never did meet her that day.

I always admired Debbie Reynolds. When Mike Todd died in 1958, a year before this mess, Debbie sent Eddie right over to comfort Elizabeth. Todd had always regarded Eddie as his favorite "son." Years later, when Elizabeth Taylor was married to Richard Burton, the Thalians wanted Burton as master of ceremonies for a program. So Debbie called up Elizabeth Taylor and said, "Elizabeth, you took my husband. Now I want yours."

And she got him.

But that was in the future. Here we were in 1959. And where were we in 1959? Well, there were no more radio programs like *Club 15*. Variety shows were all on television. Disc jockeys ruled the air waves. Rock 'n' roll ruled the disc jockeys.

Bob Dylan was an unknown scuffling around Chicago.

Barbra Streisand was sitting in the balcony of a Brooklyn movie house watching an Ava Gardner movie.

The Beatles were thumping around Hamburg, Germany.

Jack Kennedy was thinking about running for the presidency.

And I was about to meet my third husband.

Who knew, then, what was going to happen to any of us?

12

My
Ideal:
Strike Three

I hadn't wanted to marry my first husband, Hubbell, but, not wanting to hurt him, I married him. I had wanted to marry my second husband, Lou Busch; that marriage just didn't work out. My marriage to my third husband, Richard Moore, remains an enigma.

I don't know why I married him. I suppose I could blame it on Eleanore, who was always saying, "You go out with the wrong men. Try somebody different."

Richard was certainly different. Here's how we met:

I had become involved with the Thalians because I was involved with Hugh O'Brian. I found it fascinating to watch the growth of so many of these people. For instance, there was a young Swiss named Fred Hayman, who worked for the Hilton Hotels and who was very bright, very affable. He is now the owner of Giorgio's in Beverly Hills, one of the most famous specialty stores in the world. Dave Wolper was a publicity agent. Now he's a very good TV producer. Bob Peterson turned out to be an enormously successful publisher of macho magazines, including *Motor Trend*. Of course, the organization wasn't entirely charitable. Dave Wolper wanted to meet girls. So did Bob. Jack Haley, Jr., wanted to meet Wolper. He did, and went to work for him. I mention these men because they were "networking" before the term was invented. They really did help one another. They helped everybody, in fact. At the time, I was chairman of the Affairs Committee and these men had to answer to me. Did I love giving executive orders! We all had fun, and we raised a good deal of money. Because of this, a lot of people wanted to join the organization.

One was Richard Moore. Press agent Bill Waters, a friend of mine, asked me if I would meet a friend of his who was interested in joining. I said, "Sure, have him come on over." This shiny Cadillac drove up and I said to myself, Mmm, not bad. And then this six-foot-four blond gorgeous hunk walked into the house. He was kind of shy, and totally different from the men I was used to meeting. I said, "Hi, what are you doing?" And he proceeded to tell me.

"My name is Richard Moore, and my partner, Bob Gottshalk, and I created a new company called Panavision. I studied cinematography at USC and that's where I met Bob and we think Panavision is the answer to Cinerama. I work a lot but I also got lots of spare time. I like to swim, fish, ski—"

He was giving me his whole résumé.

I interrupted him. "How wonderful!" (I do none of the above, except swim, but I thought it was great that somebody could do all that.)

We stood there. He continued.

"So, although I'm engrossed in business, I would like to have some fun and help out a charity."

I said, "Fine, why don't you go to the Thalians with me one night and meet Debbie Reynolds and Frank Sinatra?"

And he said, "Great. Would you have dinner with me?"

I thought, Why not? I liked his car, I liked his looks, I liked his manner. Over dinner, I found out he lived in a house in Beverly Glen, loved the outdoors, loved to garden, and knew all about plants and flowers (another subject about which I was woefully ignorant).

At the time I thought he had a sense of humor, although now I don't know where I got that impression. Maybe it was because we laughed a lot.

We started going out together. I got to watch him on the ski slopes, swivel-hipping and schussing. He was wonderful on the slopes! He swam like mad. He was wonderful in the water! In restaurants, he was very gallant, and when we finally made love, yes, he was wonderful in the bed! I introduced him to everybody. He joined the Thalians. Life was absolutely—to put it redundantly—*wonderful!*

One day he said, "Let me introduce you to some of *my* friends." His best friend was Conrad Hall, whose father was half of the team Nordhoff and Hall, who wrote *Mutiny on the Bounty*. Dick arranged for Conrad and his wife to go away with us for a weekend. When we met, Conrad smiled at me and said, "Don't you remember me? I was second cameraman on *The Whiting Girls*." Dick, who didn't like show business, seemed a little annoyed that Connie knew me, but the moment passed. We made a nice foursome and we had fun. We swam a lot. One day, about half a mile out, I found there was a little octopus stuck to my chest. I screamed, "Get that *thing* off me!" I hate underwater livestock. Dick said, "It won't hurt you." He thought he was calm. I thought he was cold. I didn't understand.

I seemed to annoy him. And he was very judgmental about our fellow Thalians, saying, "He's very shallow." "Why does she act that way?" I thought maybe it was because Richard was shy, and that made him uncomfortable. He met my mother, who definitely approved of him. He met my Aunt Mag, who told him a couple of stories in her best vaudeville manner. He met my young daughter, Debbie. We began having dinner together, Debbie, Richard, and Margaret.

"Sit up at table," Richard ordered. "Take your elbows off the table." Debbie would look at him. We would continue eating.

"Finish your food."

"Daddy doesn't make me."

"Manners are important," he would say in an aside to me.

"I agree," I would agree nervously. I would smile. He would not. More often than not, Debbie left the table in tears. These were not pleasant meals. This is just a phase, I would say to myself. It's good that he is disciplined. We all need discipline. Eleanore would approve.

In a restaurant in Santa Monica, Richard asked me to marry him. I accepted. He seemed delighted.

"Where will we live? Your house in Beverly Glen?"

"No," he said abruptly. "You wouldn't like that house."

"But I think it's charming. You've done so much work around the garden. I want a new house."

"Fine. We'll pick out a new house."

He smiled, picked up the check, added the figures three times, once *up*, once *down*, and then once again to check his first addition. He was very thorough. Precise. Teutonic. Looking back, he was the nearest thing to a Nazi I had ever met.

"When should we get married?" I asked.

"When?" he repeated.

"Yes, what date?"

"I hadn't thought about that. I figure . . . May. Or June." It was now November. "That gives us time to work everything out."

Work everything out? Was that so unusual? Perhaps I'm just a different kind of person, more impulsive. And the men I had been with, they were the same way. Maybe that was what Eleanore meant. I needed someone steady, somebody who thought things through. Richard kept his account books very neatly, very accurately. He was absorbed in his business, fascinated by the uses of Panavision. He wanted me to accompany him when he experimented with the capabilities of the camera. He took me on roller coasters, aiming the camera at the bottom of the slide—and *whoosh*, we would go careening down and then up and then whiz around again. Thirty times we repeated this, until he got the right effect. I would grip the sides of the car in absolute terror. I hated roller coasters. "You'll get used to them," he assured me. "Wait till you see how the film turns out." He showed me the film. My reaction to the film was the same as riding the actual roller coasters. I got sick.

"Terrific!" he said. "It works!"

During the next month, Richard and I talked about buying a house. Richard sent a friend of his, a realtor, to see me at my place. I welcomed the man. We discussed real estate for maybe twenty minutes. Then he said he would like to take me out.

"Oh no," I said automatically. "Oh, that's out of the question." I was trying to be nice to the man, since he was a friend of Richard's. But going out with him was the furthest thing from my mind. I took his arm and led him to the door. I wasn't shocked or anything like that. I was used to propositions. It was part of show business. I dismissed it.

The next day Richard took me to lunch. When we had finished eating, he announced, "I really can't marry you." I didn't know what to say. I thought it was a joke, although he wasn't given to jokes.

"What's the matter?" I asked him.

"Ed says you put the make on him."

"Who's Ed?" I asked.

"My friend, the real-estate man."

"I don't believe this," I protested.

"He said you behaved very badly, that you went on the make for him and he wanted me to know, before I married you, what kind of woman you were."

"And you *believed* him?" I asked, incredulous.

"What should I believe?"

"Believe *me*," I said heatedly.

"But why would he say such a thing? You must have done something. He wouldn't just say that, off the top of his head."

"I don't know what his reasons are. I don't know why he would make up a story. He did ask me to go out with him and I refused."

"Why would he ask you to go out with him, when he knows I was going to marry you?" Richard said, pointing a finger at me.

"I have no idea," I said. I felt like a spy under interrogation. No matter what I said, it only corroborated Richard's suspicions.

Gathering whatever dignity remained, I stood up. "If you want to believe that man, fine. Then I guess things wouldn't have worked out anyway. I can't understand why you would take his word against mine, but there's nothing I can do about it."

I left the restaurant and went home. I was heartbroken. I began to cry. I wanted to talk to somebody about it, but I couldn't. I was never able to talk to my mother about such things, about personal things. I stayed home for a couple of days. Then I had to go back to work. I went on the set, filmed whatever I had to, went back home, made dinner for Debbie and me, then locked myself in my room. After two or three days I decided to write him a letter. I was so confused and so hurt. The next morning I went out to the mailbox. There was an enormous envelope from him, addressed to me. I tore it open eagerly. Obviously, he was going to give me some explanation, I thought. Eleven pages. I was impressed. I started to read.

It was no explanation. It was an eleven-page diatribe. He didn't like my mother, or my aunt Margaret; they were too loud, too theatrical. And I didn't have any personality. People didn't really like me, they just used me. It was all phony show-business affectation. There was nothing real, no real feeling. He didn't care for my daughter because she was so close to her father, because she wouldn't sit correctly at the table, and because he couldn't control her. Therefore, the marriage wouldn't work. Signed, Richard.

I was stunned. I found I had no feelings. I couldn't accept any of this, couldn't understand it, had no response to it. Just emptiness. I moved through my day like an automaton. Went to work, performed, came home, performed, took care of my child, slept. On the seventh day, the phone rang.

"How are you?" Richard asked.

"Not very happy."

"I made a mistake. I'd like to talk about it. Tell you what, they're previewing *Raintree County* tomorrow night. They used the Panavision process so I have to go. We could have dinner and talk."

I agreed.

Over dinner, Richard said, "I guess I'm a fool."

"I don't know how you could love me and take that man's word. Richard, what would it profit me to do that in front of your friend?"

"I was crazy jealous. I was suspicious. I'm not used to show business. I have to make adjustments. I know what I said about your family was wrong. They're . . . they're *pioneer* women. It's a different breed to me. Can you forgive me?"

"I love you," I said.

"I love *you*," he said.

We went to the film.

"Let's go to my place," he suggested afterward.

"All right," I agreed. He started to drive.

"This isn't the way," I said.

"No. I bought a new house. Right after our lunch," he said.

"That's pretty fast work for a man who was going to marry me."

"Well, I thought we were finished, and I wanted the house," he explained. To this day, I don't know whether Richard maneuvered the realtor episode to get out of the marriage, so that he could make his *own* decision and buy the house *he* wanted without having to consult me.

"I love you," he said as we drove in the driveway. "You won't like the house."

"It's very beautiful," I said in the dark. I guess I was trying to get him back. "I'm sure it's very beautiful."

I didn't get to see much of the house. Richard began to make mad passionate love to me the moment we were inside the front door. He stripped off my clothes and stripped off his own, and we made love in the dark on a bed I was not familiar with. But I knew his body and I longed for it. He was strong and he was lusty, and he covered my body with his and wrapped his arms around me. He totally contained me. There was no way I could move, nor did I want to. I longed for that too. For once, he seemed out of control, as hungry for me as I was for him.

Usually Richard didn't care about caring, he cared about being taken care of. At the time I thought it was a minor adjustment we would have to make. Time would take care of that. This night, he was insatiably passionate, and I was so grateful and happy that I lay there in bed, thinking how wonderful our life was going to be.

Then he got up out of bed and started dressing.

"Where are you going?" I asked, puzzled.

"I've got a late date," he said. "I thought this wasn't going to work, so I've been dating other people."

I jumped right up out of his bed, where we had just made this mad passionate love, and reached for the phone to call a friend to come get me.

He asked, "What are you doing?"

"I don't have to explain to you. You made love to me and then you say you're going out with someone else. I don't have to say anything."

I left him. I didn't write him, I didn't call him. Eleven days later, he phoned. "You don't know how hurt I was. I made a mistake. I wanted to punish you. I was so upset about Ed."

"You don't know me very well, Richard," I told him. "I can't stand that man. I was only nice to him because he was your friend. . . ."

"We must talk things out."

And so we did. Again, we talked. That was the spooky part of it. We talked out everything. We planned everything. How we were going to live on the money and what we were going to do. We signed the papers. Premarital agreements. I was obviously a bit shaky because two marriages hadn't worked out. Somewhere, in the back of my mind, I must have convinced myself that the failures were all my fault. What was it I was doing wrong? Richard and I decided to go to Palm Springs on our honeymoon. Richard adored Palm Springs.

We got married and went there, and on our wedding night, he asked, "How much income tax did you pay this last quarter?"

"I haven't the slightest idea," I replied. "My accountant writes it out for me, tells me how much I have to pay, and I say, fine, and I sign, and I pay it."

"What kind of businesswoman are you, that you don't know?" he said.

"No kind. I pay that man a lot of money to do my taxes. I don't know my taxes. What the hell do I care?"

That was the start of a big fight.

"Show business! You're all children!" he shouted.

Our wedding night. A fight. He was furious. I should have left him right then. But I didn't.

We bought a house together and moved in. He showed me how to cultivate a garden. He was a miracle worker with flowers. He had marvelous ideas about landscapes. We had grounds, we had space. He was crazy about the garden.

He was also crazy about Mr. Magoo. Mr. Magoo was the parrot Dick brought to our marriage. It seemed he was allergic to everything else. Mr. Magoo got most of the affection. To me Richard was mostly cold, icy, Germanic, disapproving. He wanted me out of show business. He was jealous. "People recognize you because you're in show business. But that doesn't mean they like you."

Then, suddenly, although he hated show business, Richard decided he wanted to be an actor. He studied. He was trying out for the part of Steve Canyon, the Milton Caniff comic-strip character. Dick looked exactly like him. He decided he wanted to give up his business, leave Panavision. He eventually wanted to direct, which is what everyone in Hollywood, including morticians, wants to do. But now acting was suddenly a challenge for him. Dick had the looks, but he didn't have the heart. To be an actor, you have to give something. You have to allow yourself to reveal something. A great actor stands emotionally naked, stripped bare. Stripped bare, Richard had nothing to reveal. Nobody was home in that heart.

I found out he had always gone for waitresses. I hadn't known anything about his background. Hadn't known that for a long time he had had an affair with Movita, Marlon Brando's girlfriend.

Once, during my marriage to Richard, I took a plane from New York to the West Coast. Bob Crystal, a music publisher friend of mine, escorted me into the VIP lounge, only to find it closed for renovations. We were ushered into a small room. Marlon Brando was standing there. We nodded. Bob Crystal and I continued our conversation. The phone rang. Nobody answered it. After the third ring, Brando went over to the phone, picked it up and said hello, listened for a moment, then asked Bob, "Is your name Jack Fuchs?" Bob said no. Brando reported back, "Sorry, there's no Jack Fuchs here." The person at the other end must have asked who was speaking. Brando replied. "This is Marlon Brando."

"Oh yeah, and this is Dwight Eisenhower."

"No, it's Marlon Brando."

"Oh, come on. . . ."

"Sorry, but it really is Marlon Brando."

Then he hung up the phone. I thought that was very funny. He grinned. I grinned. Bob said good-bye. Brando and I got on the plane. I sat down. Richard was going to pick me up at the L.A. airport. After takeoff, I walked up the aisle, and this hand grabbed me.

"You're a great actress," Brando muttered. "You know that? Not just a great singer. A great actress!"

"Thank you," I said. I stopped. Who was going to keep on going after a moment like that? I asked him what he was doing.

"Shooting a pictured called *One-Eyed Jacks*. I'm going back and forth to the Coast trying to cut it. Hey, let's play games, okay? Who wrote this verse?" And he started to sing:

"Little fraternity pin
Studded with tears of sorrow . . ."

I said, "Roy Ringwald."

"That's right!" he exclaimed. "I didn't think you'd know it. Let's play some more." We did. Then he followed me back to my seat, and sat down, and began to eat. And then, just as suddenly, he fell asleep. I began to think, God, I can't stand this. Here was the great Brando, disheveled and snoring. Then, just as suddenly he woke up, smiled at me, and said, "That's a pretty hatbox. Let me carry it off the plane for you."

And that was how I got off the plane to meet Richard with Brando carrying my hatbox.

"Richard," I said, "this is Marlon Brando."

Richard hardly acknowledged the introduction. Marlon Brando went out of my life, alas, forever.

Afterward, Richard snarled at me. "How could you do this to me?"

"Do what?" I said. "I did nothing. The man carried my hatbox." Not only had I no idea that Richard had gone with Movita, I didn't know he hated Brando. I hadn't planned any of this. But if I had known then what I know now, I certainly would have.

Finally, after two years of strife, I said to Richard, "I don't enter into these things lightly. This is my third marriage. This is your first. Obviously, I would like to make a go of this marriage. I care for you very much. I don't know what the problems are, but I think we should go to a marriage counselor."

So then he said to me, "I'll go. But I won't *listen*."

It was time to quit. He had to move out, but he had no place to go. We had bought this beautiful house together. I told him to take his time finding a place. So we continued living together while he looked. In the meantime, he was treating me like shit. And I was taking it.

Finally, he announced that he had found a place and was moving out. That night, the night before he was supposed to leave, he attacked me violently sexually, and when we were through with this sexual thing (it seems to be very common before people break up to have one last fling), he stood up in bed and said, "If only you were taller. If only you were thin. If only you had a ponytail. If only your mother wasn't around. If only Debbie didn't have a father. And these are only some of the things that are wrong. . . ."

That was it. I screamed at him. "You miserable prick! You rotten, selfish bastard! You cruel, inhuman son of a bitch! I *don't* have a ponytail. I *do* have a daughter. She *does* have a father. I *do* have a mother. And there is nothing wrong with any one of us. What is wrong is you are simply a mean, miserable human being—"

"You are *magnificent!*" he cried. "Why couldn't you have been like this all the time?" So now I knew what he wanted. Whips and chains and a black Nazi leather costume to go along with the ponytail.

"Get out!" I shouted.

"Tomorrow," he promised.

That night, I was scheduled to take Richard's mother and Debbie to the ground-breaking ceremonies for the new Thalian building. The three of us went. Debbie was terribly proud of me. So was Richard's mother. When we got home, Dick was there with his bags packed. He couldn't even take advantage of my absence to leave like a decent person. No, he wanted to have one last scene.

"Well . . ." he said, posed at the door.

"Good-bye," I said, and turned away.

The cold son of a bitch! I decided, during the divorce proceedings, to take my revenge. I knew how to fix him. I demanded custody of the parrot. I knew he loved that parrot. That may have been the only thing he did love.

My lawyer said in court, "Miss Whiting—Mrs. Moore—is going to keep Mr. Magoo."

"I beg pardon?" the judge said.

"The parrot. Mrs. Moore has given this parrot a home. And she wants the parrot."

There was nothing Richard could do. I got to keep the parrot *and* give him the bird.

There wasn't that animosity with my other husbands. I saw Hubbell one day at the Bel-Air Hotel. He was driving behind me. I honked and said, "Hello, Hubbell. This is one of your favorite wives." And he laughed. Lou, I saw all the time, until his death. But Richard . . .

When his mother died, I wrote him a note, but he never responded. He became a cinematographer on a television show, produced, as fate would have it, by Hubbll Robinson. Richard did a couple of more pictures. I heard John Huston had him come in and reshoot scenes for *Annie*. He was given cinematographer's credit on that one. My brother-in-law sees him in Detroit, shooting commercials. Somebody else saw him recently and said he looked scruffy. He married again, and got divorced again. And had a child.

Will I recognize a light in his eyes
That no other eyes reveal.
Or will I pass him by and never even know that he is my ideal.

It may be that I am biting the hand that fed me, but I do think that we all got sucked in by those love songs. We believed what they said. I believed it. After all, my father *wrote* that song. There was "My Ideal," just as there was "My Man," "Bill," and "Can't Help Lovin' Dat Man." I grew up with that. Sang it. Lived it.

Never treats me sweet and gentle the way he should;
I got it bad and that ain't good!

Got taken in by it. Almost *done* in by it. But I didn't get done in; I survived. I survived because I was always able to laugh at the ridiculousness of life.

Richard had always complained about my weight. The last time he came to see me, following the divorce, he brought me a present. A giant bag of avocados.

Exit Richard Moore—and not a moment too soon.

★ ★ ★

And it was time for me to exit L.A. I knew it. But I hadn't done anything about it.

I think what finally moved me was The Fire.

The first time I heard about it was from a neighbor, and I said, "What fire?"

I glanced out the window. It was eight-thirty in the morning and I could see some smoke very far away, about fifteen miles away, in Hollywood. I looked at my gorgeous house. All around the grounds were the perennials and the annuals that Richard and I had so carefully planted, and that I, with my lack of a green thumb, had managed to care for. There was the swimming pool we had added. Up the hill was a beautiful stand of pines. Automatically, I turned on the sprinkler system. That should help. Debbie was home from school, sick. The maid, Jean Goode, was there. I kept digging in the garden. From time to time the radio would give reports about the path of the blaze. It didn't seem to have a path. Two houses would burn, and one wouldn't. Laurel Canyon was burning. Coldwater Canyon was burning. So was Stone Canyon. The fire kept advancing toward the beach.

Suddenly, around ten-thirty, it arrived in my backyard. There were fire engines and police. People were shouting at one another, shouting directions, shouting orders. I could hear the throb of engines. Neighbors scurried like animals, bringing out their belongings and dumping them into automobiles.

Debbie suddenly appeared. Frightened. "Why is this happening, Mommy?"

I said, "Go get some things."

I told Jean Goode to take out the dresser drawers and place them with the clothes in the car. I went into the library. The first thing I reached for was two albums of *Madama Butterfly* my father had given me. Now, you figure *that* out. I selected those two albums before my music, before our clothes, before anything. Then it was the music. We put that in my car. Jean also had her car. My mother and my aunt came through the fire lines. Nothing was going to stop them. Richard Moore came by to help protect the house if possible.

That was the nicest thing I ever remember him doing. By this time we were all taking the drawers of clothes and stacking them. Other evacuees dumped their silver and china in the swimming pools, but I didn't care about that. "Leave the silver, leave the new glasses. Get as many suitcases as you can."

As we were moving out, the rats were moving in. The hills above were burning and deer had run down from the mountains. Rats were scurrying under our legs. We just screamed "Aagh!" and stepped over them and kept piling our belongings in the car. Smoke covered the sky. The radio was on and I could hear the bulletins. The fire just swept through the area. Aunt Mag was upstairs with me, opening closets, reaching for shoes, hats, anything, and pulling them out. Suddenly she stopped, pointed her finger at me, and said, seriously, "Margaret, you have too many beige blouses."

As we were leaving, I overheard one of the neighbors attempting to bribe the fire department to look after his house first. I loved the fireman; he just looked at the man and said, wearily, "Mister, you gotta be kidding." The firemen worked without stopping for several days.

Finally we had to go. At that moment, I looked around, I saw the fire engines, I saw the houses in the hills up above me burning. Vic Damone's house. Burt Lancaster's house. As I drove away, I thought, Well, this is it. Everything I have is in these cars. Richard stayed behind with the gardener, to wet down the roof.

The house was saved. The next day, I went back and looked at the damage. There was wreckage all around. I said to myself, Never again are you going to cater to a house and all that. Change your life-style. If you close the door, you don't want to have to worry about a twenty-room house. *You* dictate. Don't let the house dictate. You're the one who counts, not the swimming pool. You're not doing what you should do. You're not growing.

I had the opportunity to do *Gypsy*. I had met the stage manager and he had said, "Why don't you go to New York? There's a whole new world waiting for you." Then, Jean Goode said, "I'll take care of Debbie until you find a place. And she can always stay with her father." I also went to a fortune teller, Mary Young, who lived on

Saturn Street, which I thought was very starry of her. She was a psychic. She said, "I see many changes—a great move, a whole new career ahead of you."

Of course, they always say that. But with all those good omens, I said to myself, How can I fail?

13

Somebody
Loves Me

—

Who was I and where was I going? I'm sure I wasn't the only one to ask those questions in the sixties.

I had been Daddy's Girl.

With Johnny Mercer, I had been The Kid.

I was Debbie's Mother.

I was Margaret Whiting, a record star of the forties and fifties. But what did that mean in the sixties?

I was also Eleanore's Daughter.

But I had to get away from her to find that out.

Records. I had spent seventeen years at Capitol. They were perfectly willing for me to stay with them, but all the men I had worked with, those whom I cared about, had gone. Johnny Mercer had sold the business. I had had both my ballad days and my country days. I had been a pretty fair country singer for a Beverly Hills lady, and when I had been teamed up with Jimmy Wakely on "Slippin' Around," I had been better than that. If you can record and sell, you don't stop. But after seventeen years of selling at Capitol, I suddenly wasn't selling.

So what do you do at that point in your career? Do you move over and wait? Do you give up? Do you stay or do you run away? I stayed. But it was hard, having been on that merry-go-round, to adjust. What do you do? You do your work, no matter where it is. The places are different, the circumstances are different. We played Omaha, San Francisco, and Windsor, Ontario. I got five thousand dollars in the big clubs; Peggy Lee got ten thousand. Peggy was smart. She had developed into a superlative supper-club singer. She had a reputation as a jazz singer. I did not. She *seduced* her audiences with that kittenlike purr. I kept my distance. During this period I played furniture conventions and one-night stands, only without the name band backing me up. Chicago's Mr. Kelly's, the Drake, and the Palmer House were once-a-year engagements.

But you don't *just* wait, dancing a time-step with life. People have new ideas and concepts. Maybe this will work. You listen. You think, Maybe. I had always been recording and I knew how to record. The microphone loved my voice the way the camera loved Carole Lombard's face.

The first idea came from Randy Wood, who had established Dot records. Pat Boone was his find. He was kind of a country crossover. "Find the best of the country songs for Margaret," said Randy Wood. Why not? "If we do it correctly, we might have another 'Slippin' Around.'" Well, maybe. The situation was becoming surrealistic, but I didn't realize it yet. "Listen, Margaret should sing jazz. Margaret should sing the Billie Holiday songs." I should have said, "Jesus Christ, *jazz*?" I can sing jazz now, but I shouldn't have done it then. But it fed my ego. I went along because this very successful commercial record producer, *owner* of a record company, said, "I can do something for you."

"How about," I suggested, "using *six* arrangers?"

"Great idea, Margaret!"

I was allowed to bring in Mel Torme, the Hi-Los, Billy May, Pete King, Pet Rugolo, Frank Comstock, and Marty Paitch. We were a united group of buddies. Thank God I didn't realize the brilliance surrounding me until later, because I couldn't have coped with it. But I went in to record and Mel would be on one side of me, and the Hi-Los on the other, advising me. "Good." "Bad." "Hit that note." "Yes." "Okay." I did "Hit the Road to Dreamland" and they came up with the descending

"Bye, Bye, Ba-by . . .
Bye,
   Bye . . .
      . . . ba-by . . .
         . . . bye . . ."

with the instruments cutting out, piece by piece, until it was just my voice, and then silence. It was an enormously effective way to end the record.

But then the madness started. The A&R man, Milt Rogers, came in with an inspiration.

"This is a jazz album." He sang "I'm Gonna Move to the Outskirts of Town." "Now, that is a song for Margaret Whiting! Here, listen to the Jimmy Rushing record," he said. I took it home. Jimmy Rushing was brilliant. He could slide around there:

"I'm gon-na moo-
      -oo-
         -oove . . ."

I couldn't even get my voice *up* there. I wasn't Jimmy Rushing.

"I can't sing like that!" I complained.

"Just sing it any way you can."

I stayed at home and studied the record and thought, *What am I doing? Who am I?* I don't get depressed; I was getting depressed.

The album was released. On the cover was a photograph of me in an open convertible. Its title, *Going Places.* I was going places, all right. Nowhere, fast. I didn't recognize myself. It was allegedly a jazz album, with songs like "Over the Rainbow" and "Gypsy in My Soul." The company decided to rerelease the album, with a new and more exotic cover. Johnny Engstead, that photographic genius who had worked with Lombard and Dietrich, brought in several makeup people—believe me, it took several—to make me look like a gypsy.

Who is this person? I said to myself, staring at the new cover. And what does she want from my life? That was a question never to be answered.

It was hard for me to create hits anymore. Sometimes I "covered" a song, hoping to cash in or even obliterate the success of the original artist. And then I met Norman Granz. He was the head of Verve records, a company specializing in jazz. He had recorded not only Oscar Peterson but also my very favorite, Art Tatum. I liked Granz. He was very sensitive and very sympathetic and obviously a man of great taste. He came up to me, and the first words out of his mouth were: "I have two favorite singers, Ella Fitzgerald and Margaret Whiting." Why wouldn't I have liked him? He signed me to a contract, then went out on the road managing Ella, and I never saw him again. But I had a contract, so I recorded with Russ Garcia's band. He is a lovely talent, but the pussycat of the world when maybe I needed a tiger. We recorded a Jerome Kern songbook that musicians loved and not too many other people ever heard.

I guess I never found the right genius to have as a manager or an agent. My mother was always saying, "You've got to find the right person. You've got to have another Johnny Mercer to pick the right songs. You need somebody creative." Maybe she was right, but I didn't want to listen to her.

She was driving me crazy giving me advice. She was doing it for my own good, but I had to get away from her, get out on my own. And the moment I did, I started to look at her differently. I was a woman with a daughter. She was a woman with a daughter. What was she really like? And what had she given me?

Eleanore.

Oh, how she wanted to get out of Detroit. She was the youngest of thirteen children. Their father had been deaf, and they had all developed enormous vocal projection, with thirteen of them in the house, probably all talking at once.

Eleanore saw that her sister Margaret had a voice. She saw a meal ticket in Margaret Youngblood. She saw the Shriners' reaction when

Margaret sang. So she booked her. She got her on the bill at the Temple Theater in Detroit and always stood with a glass of water in the wings, telling Margaret to take the second bow. She got material for Margaret—"Oh Johnny How You Can Love," "Hard Hearted Hannah," and "Way Down Yonder in New Orleans." And she met my father while she was looking for material for Margaret. She lived through Margaret, so much so that she was not surprised when Richard was smitten by Margaret, but she was surprised when Richard fell in love with *her*.

They weren't ready for marriage yet, not any of them. Not Richard. Not Eleanore. Not Margaret. Margaret and Eleanore went on the road. Those were the days of vaudeville—the jugglers, the singers, the comics, and the animal acts. One of the acts on tour was called Cheshire's Cats. The cats did all kinds of tricks. The troupe, which was owned by a German couple, traveled with a number of parrots. What fascinated Eleanore was the fact that when the buzzer would ring, to announce half-hour before performance, the two parrots would call out in a heavy German accent, "Haff-hour! Haff-hour! Overture! Overture! Gett rrready, cats!"

Some of the acts were pretty high-class. Sarah Bernhardt performed dramatic sketches, written by playwrights like William Anthony McGuire. Artists like Rosa Ponselle and Maria Jeritza would step down from their coloratura chariots and deign to play the road for, naturally, huge sums of money.

Eleanore loved it when a famous European singer like Jeritza was booked on the bill with Aunt Mag, because my mother had a really fabulous voice. During the rehearsal time before the first performance, Eleanore would stand behind the closed door of their dressing room and vocalize, hitting all kinds of high C's. Soon, invariably, she would hear a shrilling and trilling in the corridors outside, as whatever outraged diva heard the competition. Threats, telephone calls to managers ensued, and accusations to the company manager. "I heard *sopranos*," they would shout indignantly. "Read my contract. I am the only soprano permitted on the bill. Who is this Margaret Young?" And then would come a rapping on the dressing-room door and Margaret Young would emerge, singing in her best bass-style, "Dapper Dan, you're my man . . ."

Irving Berlin heard Eleanore sing. He said, "Why aren't you on the stage. You have a great voice." Eleanore demurred, but Irving Berlin dragged her down to Florenz Ziegfeld.

"I have this terrific discovery," he said excitedly to the great show-man. "Come on, Eleanore, sing."

There was my mother up on the stage, frozen with fear. She dutifully performed a song and Ziegfeld dutifully listened. After-ward, a bewildered Berlin said to my mother, "What happened? You got a great voice. What happened?"

"I lose it onstage. It's no fun anymore."

That was the sad case of it. My mother had a lot of talent, but being onstage was no fun for her, not the way it was for me and for Aunt Mag. And, of course, my father became practically petrified when forced to perform. In his later years, in Hollywood, all the great songwriters were asked to do a concert together: George Gersh-win, Cole Porter, Sigmund Romberg, Harry Warren—the whole bunch. My father shook so that he had to ask Ralph Rainger to play "Japanese Sandman" for him. He just couldn't cut it, and neither could Eleanore. But she knew exactly how it should be done. She conferred with the William Morris agents. After an opening night, they would all meet the next day at the Morris office and Abe Last-fogel would say, "Okay boys, let's start." And one of them would say, "Eleanore, I didn't think Margaret's dress was right. It didn't catch the lights. I think she needs a blue dress, and a simpler dress. And the hat was too big." Everybody wore hats in those days, it was part of the outfit. Then Eleanore would say, "I didn't think the second number worked. Let's put it fifth." Or, "I didn't like the medley at the end. We need something special at the end." And they would go to work.

Eleanore knew the acoustics of every theater on the circuit. All the big-timers did. They zeroed in on a dead spot. It was part of their job, along with knowing how to bow. Long after Aunt Mag had retired, a friend of mine, Larry Carr, was performing at the Orpheum Theater in L.A. He called up to tell us of his triumph. The reception had been thunderous. Aunt Mag was more to the point.

"Do you know how to bow?" she asked him.

"Bow? Of course. I put my hands behind my back and bend over from the waist."

Aunt Mag scolded him. "No, no! Wrong! Hold the phone! I'll be over and show you how."

Well, I'm sure he didn't literally hold the phone. But she was down at that theater in no time, and took him out on the stage.

"Acknowledge the balcony," she instructed him. "Sweep them all in with your eyes. And keep your arms outstretched. So long as you keep your arms up, they'll keep applauding."

Larry did as he was told. The reception after the second show was twice what it had been after the first.

Aunt Mag shrugged. "Of course, nowadays nobody seems to know anything."

In those days, their days, you learned to get to the theater on time for that first day's rehearsal. It was an unwritten law that the first act to get to the theater would get the choice of numbers. Everybody wanted to sing the twenties equivalent of "Feelings," say, so they would rush down, or send their pianist down, to get first dibs. Of course, if you were a headliner like Nora Bayes, Fanny Brice, or Sophie Tucker, there was no question; the headliner got the song. But for the kids coming up, it was a question of first come, first sing.

Eleanore found a conductor-pianist for Aunt Mag. He was wonderful, a genius at the piano. He stuttered a little, but that didn't matter. He didn't have to *say* anything. He really wanted to be a songwriter, and he played some of the things he had written for the girls. They said, "Oh, come on along with us. You'll meet everybody. You'll do just fine." He did, and he didn't. His name was Rube Bloom, and he did write some great songs—probably the best known is "Day in—Day Out"—but inadvertently the girls did him in.

One day, they decided to go to the races and they invited Rube along. He wasn't doing anything that day, so he went. It was like introducing an addict to drugs. There was never a day afterward that Rube wasn't either at the track or reading the *Racing Form*.

Years later, when Eleanore and Aunt Mag attended a funeral, a very natty man came up to them, flashed a diamond ring on his pinky, and introduced himself.

"You don't know me," the man said, "but you've played an important part in my life. I'm Rube Bloom's bookie, and I just want to thank you."

There were marvelous performers on the road in those days, and they were often very generous with the knowledge they had acquired. Julian Eltinge, the female impersonator, taught Eleanore about costumes and makeup. He was straight and married, and had children. He walked like a truck driver and was all business. Eleanore would visit him in his dressing room as he was applying his eyeliner. He would discuss the affairs of the day in a very macho voice. She would eye the sequined gowns—each costing four or five thousand dollars—hung very neatly on the racks, off-the-shoulder items, fetching seductive gowns.

"It's the line that is all-important," Eltinge would say as the rouge went on his cheeks and was skillfully blended. "Most people are not aware of the full line of a gown." Eleanore became aware. That's where she, too, learned about gowns "catching the lights." Then Eltinge would disappear for a minute and return.

"How do you like it?" he would say in his exquisite woman's voice. And Eleanore invariably gasped, which pleased Eltinge very much. The transformation was total. Wig, makeup, gown, gloves. "That man was the most gorgeous woman I ever say," she would declare years later.

Another act was called the Sodas, who were six black guys who sang great and dressed in outlandish costumes. One would say, "I'm Raspberry," and appear in a raspberry satin coat and tails. Next would come Vanilla, and so on. Until the last one, who would croon in a mellow bass voice, "Mmmm, I'm *Chocolate!*" And they would all break into song. "Once you saw them you never forgot them," my mother said with wonder.

Eleanore and Margaret were known as the Double Virgins on the circuit. Perhaps they were given that title by the Marx Brothers, who involved both girls in a lot of horseplay as they journeyed around the country. Every week they were on the road they would be in a different city, staying at a boardinghouse. Eleanore and Margaret always had a kitchen, because Eleanore was a great cook, and would come home after the show and whip up a meal. The Marx Brothers—that is, Groucho, Harpo, Zeppo, Chico, *and* Gummo for a time—usually had the rooms right next door. They loved to play jokes. Their favorite was to get a key to Eleanore and Margaret's room, and when the girls came home to prepare supper, they would find the Marx Brothers, all of them, stark naked in their bathtub.

"What's for dinner?" Chico would say.

"Get out of the tub!" Eleanore would protest.

"Come on in," they would say.

"There's no room. Come on, get out of the tub!"

They would oblige her, and all of them would parade around the room naked.

"Don't walk around like that!" Margaret would say.

"Okay," Zeppo would answer. And they would all sit down to eat, stark-naked. Groucho was more serious than the rest, not at all like he was on the stage. Harpo was the same lovable, sensitive, sweet, charming guy.

That was life on the road. It was fun and it was devil-may-care. But Eleanore was always practical, and she saw to it that Margaret got the right bookings. Sophie Tucker watched my mother do her stuff, and finally made her a proposition. Eleanore became Sophie Tucker's manager, taking her away from the William Morris office, which was like taking the Brooklyn Bridge away from Brooklyn.

But after my mother got married, she turned her sights on Richard. She knew he was talented. He became her ambition.

So, that was Eleanore. She longed to get out of Detroit, and had. When the vaudeville days were through, she urged my father to write for Hollywood. When it seemed like he might not want to leave Detroit, she started selling a line of cosmetics. She got him to go to New York. Then, she said, "Go west." And he went. She handled his business, ran his house, raised his children, and made sure that everything was comfortable for him. She loved parties and having people around. Together, they went dining and dancing at the Mocambo and the Cocoanut Grove. They had a wonderful life together. And when that ended, she nursed him through his illness, saw him through his death, and then picked up the pieces and went on. She did not give up. Ever. She had a great business mind. She had a great wit and an instinct for punch lines.

When someone asked her what happened to Hitler, she retorted, "Not enough."

And, when I performed an entire cavalcade of American song in a flowing Greek gown against classic pillars, accompanied by two (count them) pianists, I thought Eleanore would be thrilled by the elegance of the whole presentation. I went from Stephen Foster through Stephen Sondheim, leaving no composer untouched.

After the performance, Eleanore came back to the dressing room, patted my cheek, and said, "Darling, even Winston Churchill knew when to get off."

Yes, that was Eleanore. She accomplished what she wanted to and let nothing get in her way. She never lost her sense of fun. So she never put her arm around me. No, she wasn't that kind of woman. But she was fierce in her protection of me.

The one time that I sang with a band was right after "That Old Black Magic" was released. Freddie Slack phoned my mother to ask whether I could play the Orpheum in L.A., and two dates in San Francisco and San Diego with his band. The band's regular singer, Ella Mae Morse, was pregnant, and he promised he would take good care of me.

That was not enough for Eleanore.

"Freddie," she said. "I know the road. I have been on the road. And this is wartime. I swear to you if anything happens to my daughter, I will personally come to you, your managers, and your musicians and kill every single one of you." Freddie must have needed me desperately, because he agreed to all these conditions.

I had some wonderful gowns that Walter Bullock, the man who called me a wolf child, had picked out. They had been designed by Adrian and they were certainly of the period: big shoulder pads, beautiful, white-draped. Elegance wasn't my strong point, however. In Los Angeles, I managed to twist my body into some kind of knot, which threw my kneecap out, resulting in my mother and Tom D'Andrea having to rush me to the hospital, where I was told, sadly, that I would never be a dancer. Since I didn't care about that at all,

I hopped off the stretcher and went back to singing the next day.

San Diego was another story, however. That was my first real taste of traveling with musicians. Since it was wartime, there were no rooms to be had in the city. Finally, the management found me a single room, which was very small, but it had a cot and a bathroom, and that was enough. During this period, San Diego was triple anything that you have ever seen or heard about wartime. It was a crowded naval port, full of soldiers and sailors, thousands and thousands of them, knocking girls up against the wall. Lust ran rampant in the streets, in the corridors. In the meantime, I forgot to lock the door to my room. The door opened. A marine came in and asked, "What are you doing in my room?" He was standing there, and I was terrified, remembering only my mother's warnings of wholesale rape.

"It's *not* your room. It's *mine*! Get out! Get out!" I screamed in my eighteen-year-old voice. The marine fled. I locked the door, but I was absolutely petrified with fear. I decided I would not stay in that room alone. I ran down the corridor. I knew where the two trumpet players were rooming and I rapped on the door, shouting hysterically, "Let me in!" They opened the door.

"I'm staying here. I'm not going to stay by myself!" And I jumped into their bed.

This was a situation worthy of Preston Sturges or Billy Wilder, the classic situation of the sweet young thing and two trumpet players. However, my mother had so put the fear of God into the entire band that they never laid a finger on me. Indeed, they stayed up all night, petrified, mumbling, "Don't tell Eleanore, don't tell Eleanore!"

So that is a portrait of my mother. That's what I thought about in the late sixties after I had left Bel-Air, had fled the nest, had rebelled against my mother. Oh, yes, I had rebelled. Slightly.

I had mentioned one day that I wanted a new television set. I didn't mean for her to get it for me. But when I arrived home the next day, there it was, all ready and all installed. Debbie was there and Aunt Mag. And Eleanore.

I blew up. "Why can't you let me do anything by myself?" I screamed. "Why do you feel you have to do everything for me? I'm a grown woman. I can fend for myself." I was blind with rage. Aunt Mag began to cry. She had never seen me like this. Eleanore was stunned. Debbie, later, took me aside, and said, "Mom, you were magnificent. You should get angry more often."

Angry over a television set? I don't think so. I think it was a rage at myself. I don't rage much. I've seen anger, frustration, and bitterness ruin careers. I haven't allowed that to happen to me. Perhaps I have been too soft. I haven't demanded that much. But I don't regret it.

That day, I was angry with myself. I knew I had to get out and do things on my own. I did have to find out who the hell I was.

I was asked to do *Call Me Madam* in Boston at a new dinner theater on the Bradford Roof. I had done some theater, but this seemed very elegant to me. Maybe it was the word *Boston*. Or *Roof*. Anyway, I was a little intimidated and became even more so when I met the owner of the theater.

"You're not in nightclubs now," he lectured me. "We don't want any ad-libbing."

"I'm really not that kind of performer," I said. "I'm not undisciplined. I have been in theaters before. My heart is in the theater. I really know what I'm doing. I'm not a comedienne. I don't go out to break people up. I don't talk to the audience like Jack Carson and Buddy Hackett do." I think I may have gone on for half an hour. I really was crushed. I wanted to be known as a person of the theater. I was here in Boston. I was on my best behavior. I was, for heaven's sake, at the Bradford *Roof*.

On opening night, many Proper Bostonians packed the theater. In one scene where I, "the hostess with the mostest on the ball," throw a garden party, we were all onstage, looking out a window. The Princess Maria was waiting for her lover, Kenneth. It's all very dignified. One gag had a senator running onstage, chasing after various women, goosing them, and running off.

Out of the corner of my eye, I noticed a woman coming up onstage. I thought, I haven't seen her here before. She's not part of the cast. She's quite attractive and could certainly be part of any stage company. But I know she's not. I also know I have been warned not to ad-lib. The woman kept coming closer, weaving slightly.

"Hello," I addressed her nervously. "Welcome to the party. Won't you come in?"

"I want to go to the bathroom," she announced.

"Well, I'll show you where it is. I'll take you to the _loo_." The woman paused and looked around and said, "I think it's kind of pretty up here."

I smiled. "We like it." What the hell was I to do? I _had_ to ad-lib. "I am known for my parties. Princess Maria, this lady wants to go to the loo. Would you show her the way?" The woman looked at Princess Maria a bit doubtfully. "It's okay. You're with royalty," I assured her. She wobbled across the stage. Everyone had frozen. "Just go through that door with the princess and they will take care of you. Won't you, princess?" The woman exited with Princess Maria. I found myself at a loss. At that moment, the Senator came through, goosing the women, and they went, "Awoo!"

I looked at the audience and said, "I could have used that a minute ago." Well, there was a five-minute laugh. When I came offstage, the owner apologized to me. "Forget everything we ever told you. You know what you're doing."

I said, "Who _was_ that woman?"

"Oh, Mrs. Lodge. It's the Mrs. Lodge who drinks a bit."

"You're telling _me_!" I said.

I was learning. In America, we were all finding out about ourselves in the sixties. More than we cared to know, really. I looked at Debbie. She would come to visit me and she would spend the summers with me. She had her father for permanence. She was not living out of a suitcase. She had a home, a school. She had a mother. Did I feel guilty? Yes. She felt her mother had walked out on her. Her resentment was grounded in how I treated her. When she needed me, I wasn't there, even when I was in the same house. _Shades of Eleanore!_ When she wanted to talk about homework, I was out making a record or, now, doing these theater dates.

I knew Debbie was talented. I thought she was going to be a great dancer. When I was doing _Plain and Fancy_ she would watch, and she learned all the routines in one day. Roland Dupree, the choreographer, told me she could do them better than anyone in the cast. She knew all the new songs and rock music. She had a flair for comedy. She was drawn to the business. I encouraged her, but I didn't push her. She had to find her own way.

We did learn from each other, which was important. I listened to her and she listened to me. We kept in touch. She would spend her vacations with me. She would play me Bob Dylan records and Peter, Paul, and Mary. The music was becoming more socially conscious. I was hearing more Brecht and Weill and more Leonard Bernstein being performed. "The times they are a changin'," Dylan wrote. More than I dreamed.

In 1963, I was doing Cole Porter's *Anything Goes* in a dinner theater outside New York for the Thanksgiving period, and I had thought it would be a swell chance for Debbie to come east and visit me. I was in a shopping center (where else would I be on the road?), very happy because Debbie was coming in that night. I was looking at gloves when I noticed a couple of people running and throwing their arms around one another. There was something strange about it. Then I saw more people and I said, "What are they doing? What's going on? Something is happening."

It was a silly rumor: Kennedy had been shot. Which one? I thought. Why start such a ridiculous rumor? And then it wasn't a rumor. It was true. The questions flew all around. "Is he dead?" "I don't know." "What's happening?" People just stopped whatever they were doing. It was a strange sensation. Shopping malls are so impersonal. The escalators kept on whirring, but nobody was on them. The crowd didn't move. They stood in clusters. Camelot has been disturbed, I thought irrationally. Someone said, "They've taken him to a hospital." Why wasn't there a television set around? Suddenly, we heard he was dead.

I realized that Debbie was coming into Idlewild, and I went to meet her. People were walking to and fro in the airport, planes were taking off and landing, but I had never seen people moving so, as if in a dream. It was just coincidence that I happened to be in very public places like shopping centers and airports. I was so aware of the *machinery* that keeps on functioning. Conveyor belts carrying luggage. Escalators. Heating systems. Recorded announcements. All the apparatus was still working, but the human beings were in a daze. I took Debbie back to the motel where the theater was. The performance had been canceled. Debbie and I went down to the bar. Everybody walked around, drinking aimlessly. It was like a funeral, or a wake. Nobody knew what to say or what to do. We sat with ginger ale and watched the television set above the bar.

Television. Television. It brought everything right up close. I couldn't believe what I was watching. The image of Lyndon Johnson appeared on the screen. Next to him was a friend of mine, Jack Valenti. They were flying to Washington. Mrs. Kennedy, always so impeccably dressed, had blood on her skirt. The morning of the twenty-fourth, we were in the bar again, and still watching television. Someone made bacon and eggs, and we were eating and watching as Lee Harvey Oswald was brought out of his cell. A figure stepped in front of the camera and Oswald's face contorted with pain and shock and he bent over. He had been shot. He had been killed. There was a burble of confusion. Nobody on television knew what to tell us. And we didn't know what to say.

But I did say *this* to myself: I'd better grow up. The music is getting louder and louder.

Bogart had been the first antihero. In the sixties the kids discovered him. It started in a theater in northwestern Chicago, where lines waited to see those old movies. The kids discovered the forties too. What a strange time it must have seemed to them.

As strange as these times seemed to me. The furor over the Vietnam War grew, and racial tensions increased. I kept looking around. It had seemed so much easier for us. We had had something to believe in. We had soldiers, we had guns, we had death, we had life, we had letters, we were doing something for the war. Then, in that period, we had a good time. In this period, starting in 1955, what was there, besides the Claw ominously moving into music?

Well, there were the Beatles. I discovered them when I walked into Debbie's room; she had built a shrine to them. I sat down and listened. I liked what I heard. After all, I was a songwriter's daughter. I did have a good ear. But I didn't think of singing those songs. I was entombed in a time capsule. In my own fantasy, I envisioned every singer and musician out of the thirties and forties—Dick Haymes, Helen Forrest, Crosby, Sinatra, big bands, jazz combos—all packed into a space shuttle and whisked off to the moon, not to return for a million years.

Debbie brought me back to earth when I was rehearsing for a personal appearance. Debbie and her friends were outside. There was some giggling and a little whispering. The friends left and I continued working. That night, Debbie approached me—gingerly, I thought.

"Mom," she said, "the kids think you have a swell voice."

"Thank you very much," I replied graciously, the Queen Mother.

"But they can't understand why you don't sing any new songs."

"Like what?" the Queen Mother retorted, piqued.

Well, Debbie played me some songs. What a world was out there! Carole King, Teddy Randazzo's "Going Out of My Head," Buffy Sainte-Marie. Where had they been. Where had I been? I had been out to lunch.

Speaking of "Going Out of My Head," I was performing at a mental hospital not too long into the seventies, when I noticed, as I went from ward to ward, that one woman was following me. I thought she was an employee. She was nicely dressed, very quiet, and seemed very appreciative of my songs. In mental hospitals, it is rather difficult to gauge reactions. Actually, it is in nightclubs too, and on some nights the difference between the two is nil. But in this case, as I went from ward to ward, the music seemed to have a good effect on a number of the patients. At the least, it was one more bit of human contact. In the fourth ward that I visited, I began to sing, "Oh, I think I'm goin' out of my head . . ." The woman who had been following me suddenly joined in the song. She answered me: "Oh, I think I'm goin' out of my head . . ."

By this time, I had performed in enough hospitals to know that something was going on—something good, I hoped. I kept singing, and she kept answering me. I would sing a phrase, she would respond. Finally, the song ended. It was my last song of the day. I thanked everybody. This woman thanked me. As I started to leave, a nurse appeared. She had tears in her eyes. She said, "You don't know what just happened. That woman hasn't spoken a word in five years."

Who knows what the connection was, whether it was the power of the song, or whether it was just in the words "goin' out of my head?" Whatever it was, it came as a breakthrough.

I was about ready for my own breakthrough. I had kept an apartment on the West Coast, and I stayed in a hotel when I was in New York. But there had to be a place to call home. And I wasn't sure where that was yet, because I was just finding out about myself. I knew that I didn't want to be married. I knew that I wanted to perform. I knew I loved the theater. I knew I had talent. I knew I hadn't pushed hard enough, or perhaps worked hard enough. I knew I was doing that now. I was learning in the sixties what most performers had learned when they were growing up. It had all come too easily for me, perhaps. But now I was paying my dues.

I had been booked to play the part of Rose in *Gypsy* in Chicago. I was staring at the script. Rose was the hard-bitten mother of the stripper Gypsy Rose Lee. Rose was a woman who had spent her life in vaudeville, and when vaudeville died, had turned to burlesque. Rose was a woman whose manic ambition to "get her kids *out*," to see them succeed, almost destroyed them. Nothing would stop her, nothing could get in her way for long. She deluded herself that she was doing it for them, until that final moment in "Rose's Turn" when she cries in self-revelation:

> *This time for me!*
> *For me—*
> *For me*
> *For me—*
> *For ME!*

I wasn't like Rose. I had never been poor. I had never had to work, nor push, nor scheme. But now, for the first time in my life, I had set out to leave one kind of life for another. I had to ask myself, Who am I? What am I doing? Of course, that's a technique actors use to involve themselves in a role. But it was particularly necessary for a part like Rose in *Gypsy*. What desperation drove Rose? Did I have something equivalent? What could I find in myself to portray this woman?

Eleanore.

That was the key.

I could use her in my characterization, but also in learning how to deal with people. Without my knowing it, she had taught me many a lesson, and I was certainly about to put them to the test in the next few weeks.

This theater was a new venture in Chicago for its owner, a very wealthy toy manufacturer, whose name, I think, was Marvin. He had a girl friend, Shelly. Marvin, it seems, had decided to promote her career. So he took over Herb Rogers Theater in Chicago. One of the shows he selected was *Gypsy*, so that his girlfriend could play Gypsy Rose Lee. Maybe he thought that, since she was playing the title role, she was also the star of the show. I don't know. I do know that he knew nothing about show business.

There developed an extraordinary situation. Shelly was a brunette. In the show, all the girls in Madame Rose's troupe have to be blondes. So Shelly got a blond wig. Then, when she was transformed into Gypsy Rose Lee, they got her a black wig to put over her own brown hair. Suddenly this show was all about wigs. "Does this man know what he's doing?" I asked Gian Sciandra, the business manager of the theater, who, by now, had become a buddy.

"No, but it's all right. Gus Schirmer will know how to handle it." Gus was the director. "Do you want to go out to dinner?" It was not an odd request, but I looked at Gian. Yes, he was attractive. Yes, I would like to go out to dinner with him.

"One thing you should know," he began. And I thought, uh-oh. What confessions am I going to be privy to now? "My phone is tapped. My uncle was in the rackets."

"Oh, are you a card-carrying Mafia man?"

"No."

"Oh, well, then let's go. Besides, I love spaghetti."

Marvin the Toy Man invited us all out to his place for dinner— Gene Rayburn, who was playing Herbie, my fella, in the show,

Shelly, and Gian. Over dinner Marvin asked me, "How's Shelly going to be?"

"Fine. If you'll leave her alone, she'll be fine."

Plates dropped. Silence reigned. Well, he'd asked.

"You did all this to build her career. Now get away. She's got talent, but she's watching you out of the corner of her eye. Forget all the wigs you've given her; it's your constant taking her aside and giving her notes. That's what's wrong. Let Gus direct her. I promise you, she'll be fine."

He took that. "Yeah, she'll be great." He smiled. But then I let him have the truth.

"However . . ."

"Yes?"

"I promise you, the play is mine. Anybody who plays Rose, it's her play. That's what the play is about. It's in my hands alone."

Maybe Marvin didn't think so. On opening night, he imported three real strippers to supplement the three that we had in the cast. Two of the three were content to perform as characters in the play, but the third kept flashing away like a two-bit hooker. That was only the first surprise of the evening.

Second, came a million dollars' worth of diamonds for Shelly to wear. And with the diamonds came the Pinkerton men. Of course, no one had told me. Traditionally, Mama Rose makes her first entrance through the audience, telling her daughter, "Sing out, Louise!" That night, as I started to make my way through the auditorium entrance, I was stopped by a Pinkerton man with a gun. He said, "Where are you going?"

"Onstage," I said.

"Oh no you don't," he said.

"If I don't, there's no show. Now get the hell out of my way." I had also noticed two more Pinkerton men with guns on the roof. I thought, This is going to be a rather strange evening. At the time, I wished Gian had been just a bit friendlier with his Mafia relatives. I could have used a little protection myself.

The evening progressed. The ringer strippers flashed-flashed away and Gypsy sparkled and dazzled when she came out. The last scene, the denouement, was about to take place. Gypsy has become a star and Madame Rose is about to hang a cow's head on the set to remind Gypsy of her humble beginnings as the front end of a cow in Madame Rose's Adorables. The set started to come in on cue. And then it reversed and went out. Somebody was sabotaging this show. No Pinkerton men were helping out now. I found I was out there alone on the stage. The music had stopped. Nobody knew what to do.

I yelled, "I've got my cow's head here, Gypsy, and we're going on!" Nothing moved. This girl, with her million dollars' worth of jewelry, was too frightened to appear. I was there alone. There was no way that I could play the scene by myself. I turned to the audience.

"Ladies and gentlemen, we have to stop the show. The set did not move on. This is a scene that requires two people. Now, if you will just bear with us . . . ." I called to the stagehands. "Gentlemen, bring on the set where it belongs." And then to Shelly, "Gypsy, honey, Mother says get the hell out here on the stage!" The audience, which loves disaster anyway, applauded for five minutes. Gypsy appeared. And we went on.

By the time it came to "Rose's Turn," I was like a woman demented. All the frustrations of the evening came out. I don't believe there has ever been a version to equal that one for pure energy and fury.

When I walked into my dressing room, Marvin the Toy Man screamed at me, "How dare you do that? What *happened*? You are trying to ruin the show for my Shelly!"

Cats in Sheboygan could have heard me.

"You son of a bitch, how dare you! What would it profit me to sabotage this show? Why would I order the sets changed? I wouldn't. What would it profit me, the star of this show, with people coming to see me—not your girl—why would I tell them *not* to move the set? For what purpose, please? Why? This show has no finish without that scene. Screw you. Who cares about you? Or your girl? For God's sakes, she's not even smart enough to walk out onstage when I read the dialogue where she's supposed to come out. She's a bum. And so are you!"

Very quickly, Gian discovered someone had been sabotaging the show for some reason. He told Marvin the Toy Man, who came to apologize. But it was too late. I did give Shelly a little advice, however, from what I had learned in the past few years.

"Honey. This last scene is for the both of us. We don't need anything but each other. To hell with the sets. If they don't come on, you *do*."

After all of this drama, I flopped down in my chair in the dressing room and looked in the mirror. What had I done? And then I thought, Yes, what *had* I done? I had made the goddamn show come off. I hadn't let anything stand in my way. Eleanore would have been proud. Yes, and that's where I got it from. I had gotten that strength and that determination from her. My God, and how long had it taken me to acknowledge the debt I owed her!

There was a knock on the door. What now? "Come in," I said, in a voice drenched in fatigue. The sweat was still running into my eyes.

The door opened. I was looking at Gypsy Rose Lee. I couldn't believe it. It must have been some trick of the mirror.

It wasn't, because she said, "Hello, I'm Gypsy Rose Lee. I just want to tell you, you are the most like the real Rose of anyone I have ever seen. Mama was warm, you know. Determined, but *warm*. I wondered whether you ever knew her."

"No," I said. "But I have a mother too."

We laughed. We understood each other very well.

Later that night, Gian Scianda said to me, "Come to New York. You're ready for it now."

I knew he was right. I wasn't sure exactly what kind of life my life would be, but I was sure, at last, that it was going to be *my* life.

Two weeks later, we were walking by a building on Central Park South. Gian said, "This is where you should live. It's a wonderful building. There happens to be a vacancy."

We walked in and looked at the apartment. The next day, I signed the lease. That was in June 1968.

Like Eleanore before me, I had made my move.

14

Anyone Can
Whistle

—

I signed the lease and the next two years were like a kaleidoscope of events. First, Martin Luther King, and then Bobby Kennedy, killed. The Chicago convention. Cops with billy clubs. Kids in the streets with their heads bleeding. Old-time pols acting like gangsters. Gangsters acting like politicians. Woodstock, and a kind of sweet mud wrestling and peace and harmony and rock music. Jimi Hendrix screeching out "The Star-Spangled Banner" on the most amplified guitar I had ever heard. Naked bodies, *Easy Rider,* youth culture, Kent State following the invasion of Cambodia, the Manson murders, Altamont where a guy watching a Rolling Stones concert was stabbed and killed by a Hell's Angels bodyguard.

Eleanore blamed it all on the Beatles.

"They've been hired by the Russians to destroy the minds of our youth," she had said the first time she saw them on the *Ed Sullivan Show*.

Eleanore's mind was brilliant, but politics wasn't her long suit.

She had been raised in a world of solid furniture, solid futures, solid people. To her way of thinking, America had presented marvelous opportunities and had given her husband great success. She would brook no criticism of the country. Her sister, my Aunt Harriet (a human filing cabinet if ever there was one), had been Henry Ford's secretary and was honored by being the first woman ever to ride in a Ford automobile. Harriet never forgot that, nor were we allowed to. Eleanore may have hated Detroit, but there was a lot of Detroit still left in her. And she saw a Red under every bed.

"Look at those girls screaming! They have lost their minds!" She had pointed to Beatles fans reacting to "I Want to Hold Your Hand."

"Sinatra had the same effect," I tried to point out.

"He was *American!*" Eleanor retorted.

"Well, Ed Sullivan is American," I reminded her.

"Well, they must have gotten to him too" was Eleanore's answer.

There were times during the next two years when I wondered whether maybe Eleanore wasn't right. Everything was so *crazy*. At first I thought it was just my moving to New York.

I signed the lease in June and moved in in October. During that time I had wanted some repairs made in the apartment. Gian assured me that he would oversee all the reconstruction. I had hired a ship's captain, who had been a carpenter, to design and construct built-in shelves for the records and books that would fill my den and to build a niche for the bed in the bedroom, allowing for extra closet space.

On a wonderfully crisp New York night early in October, I arrived, I turned the key in the lock of my new apartment and switched on the light. Nothing happened. The lights weren't working. They hadn't been connected. But there was enough light from outside for me to see. The place was a shambles, the den filled with sawdust and the remnants of molding that had not been installed. There was no bed in the bedroom, only a mattress on the floor. I was tired from the long flight and the packing and crating, and I admit I was scared. What had I done? Had I made a ghastly mistake? I sat on the mattress and started to cry.

Then I realized that was nonsense. It really wasn't up to Gian to take care of me. It was up to me to take care of myself.

I got up off the mattress, went downstairs, and found somebody to turn on the lights. In the morning I made friends with Jules, a workman in the building who, for a lot of money, would build everything I needed. That's a great thing about New York apartments: There are people who will *do* for you. Porters. Handymen. Superintendents. For a former house owner like me, this was a glimpse of paradise.

Then I went about my business, which was going to be the theater. I was ready for it. Well, maybe the theater wasn't quite ready for me. It was changing. The new trend in musicals was for somebody—or everybody—to shed his clothes. I was not about to shed mine. The Youth Culture had taken over. The actors, singers, directors, even producers, looked about ten years old.

None of this bothered me. I was having a wonderful time. I was really on my own, learning what it was like to be a working woman. The Woman's Movement was on, and everybody's consciousness was rising, like so many loaves of bread.

If my entrance into the world of New York theater wasn't the triumph I had imagined, the record scene was brighter. A very talented composer-arranger named Arnold Goland got me together with record producer Jack Gold. The result was a new single called "The Wheel of Hurt," which they sold to London Records, and that became so successful that it spawned a series of albums on London. I found it very nice to be back on the best-seller charts. But there was one thing I should have learned from the sixties. Andy Warhol said it gave everyone a chance to be famous for fifteen minutes. He was right. In the old days, one could have stayed on the charts for months with a best-selling record. In 1969, you were lucky to be up there for eight weeks. But the length of time didn't really matter to me. What mattered was the fact that I could do it! My confidence returned in a hurry. By the summer of 1969, I was booked into Disneyland, where I would share the bill with Freddie Martin's band. Disneyland! That would be a first. Margaret in Disneyland. Like Alice in Wonderland. Little did I know.

Before going to Los Angeles, I was booked to play two weeks at the Shamrock Hotel in Houston. When I arrived, a tremendous wind and rain storm had left everyone nervous about the weather conditions. There was talk of a hurricane, although it wasn't the season for hurricanes. What did I care? I had landed. I went to the hotel, checked in, drew the curtains, went to sleep, woke up the next morning, and, before rehearsal, decided to check the weather. I drew the curtains back and spied a man standing on the roof of the Shamrock, holding a shotgun. I didn't believe what I was seeing. I took a more careful look. There were men stationed everywhere, all of them armed. I thought I must be in some South American republic at election time. I decided to go down to the lobby. That was not easy, I found.

Spiro Agnew was staying at the Shamrock. There were pickets with signs saying AGNEW GO HOME! and there were police guarding the pickets. Then there were secret service men guarding Agnew. This made for a very crowded lobby, with nobody moving around much, except in circles. I could certainly understand the need for all the security, but this was the first time I had ever been faced with such a tense situation.

We all went about our business. Agnew gave his speech in the Grand Ballroom. I performed my opening show at the Shamrock's nightclub without incident and afterward was talking to a fan, when a very attractive man with dark hair, a sweet smile, and very aware eyes approached me.

"Vice-President Agnew would like to see you," he said.

"How do you know?" I wondered.

"I'm his secret service man."

He could have been anyone, but I didn't doubt his word. I just followed him through the picket-packed, guard-packed lobby and was ushered into the Grand Ballroom. There sat Agnew and Senator John Tower, his Texan host. They both rose.

"Well, it's Miss Moonlight in Vermont," Senator Tower said. We shook hands and Agnew invited me up to his suite after the second show.

"How do I get through all this security?" I asked.

"Don't worry about a thing. Andy here will pick you up after the show."

So it seemed I now had *my* secret service agent. Andy was very attentive. He stood in the wings while I sang and afterward led me around the back way and up to the suite. I walked in. The vice-president greeted me warmly, and this time—unlike the experience with Harry Truman—nobody had frisked me.

I didn't need my own secret service man, but I had one. I think he had a crush on me, which was just fine. It certainly got me through the crowds. The next night, Maxine Messenger, the gossip columnist from the *Houston Post*, and I were scheduled to catch Tom Jones's show. He was also being guarded and given police protection! Houston was the kind of town to be expansive in, and maybe they overdid it. Tom Jones had a police car come to pick us up. We sped through the city, past the fans, and then went into the theater where he was appearing. This did not pass unnoticed in the Houston press. For the next two days the papers were filled with comments chiding the police for gallivanting around with us, and joyriding while civic responsibilities were being neglected. I'm sure they were right, but it only seemed to be a sign of the times, those police cars and security men and politicians and flashing lights. And it was fun not having to obey the speed limit!

After Houston I boarded the plane for California, got off, rehearsed with Freddie Martin for the following night's opening at the Pavilion, which featured name bands playing weekly. I got my identification tag at Disneyland and then drove off to Newport Beach's Newporter's Inn, where I checked in and unpacked. I drove back around eight-thirty in the evening. When I arrived at the gate, I saw perhaps a thousand uniformed policemen and motorcycles, and again those flashing lights.

I was stopped. I rolled down the window and asked what was going on. A very grim officer informed me.

"The Orange County underground newspaper just printed the threat that Mickey Mouse must die," he said.

I thought, This isn't Disneyland, this is Looneytuneville.

"How?" I asked.

"Twenty-five long-haired hippies have infiltrated Disneyland and at the moment are camped out on Treasure Island. Their objective is to kill Mickey and Minnie Mouse."

"Whatever for?"

"To destroy the spirit of Disneyland." This sounded like dialogue straight out of a comic book.

"But I'm supposed to be performing tonight!"

"I'm sorry, lady. Disneyland is closed!"

There was such a hurt quality in his voice. A boyhood dream destroyed. Although actual humans walked around in Mickey Mouse garb, showing tourists the sights, the idea of assassinating Mickey Mouse was ridiculous. On the other hand, the presence of a riot squad was real. Walt Disney, incidentally, had insisted that no guns be permitted inside Disneyland, so there was no way that these riot troops could shoot the intruders. Not a bad law, when you come to think of it. At the same time, these twenty-five kids were holding Treasure Island hostage. And Mickey and Minnie maybe *were* in danger. I went back to the Newporter's Inn. The troops advanced on the kids that night and took them in custody. Order was restored the next day, and we performed as scheduled. But for the two weeks I was working there, I had to display my identification card every time I went in or out. And the dress code was changed. No blue jeans or long hair was allowed. Huck Finn and Tom Sawyer would have been banned from Disneyland.

The one good thing about that engagement was that I never had to wait in line for the rides. A boy who escorted me to the stage every night and helped me find my way through the maze of Disneyland also sneaked me through all the back doors after I had done my show, so I could ride without waiting. Rank has its privileges.

During the engagement, Freddie Martin mentioned that he was interested in putting together a touring package and bringing back the big bands, including swing music, maybe with somebody like Frankie Carle and myself. Was I interested?

I thought it was a good idea. Pop Art had Andy Warhol painting Campbell's soup cans and people going crazy over Kleenex boxes. All of that was around us. Everyday objects like comic strips and Coke bottles were being glorified. Why not the big-band sound? And the girl singer? I wasn't sure whether Warhol and all these artists were satirizing the period. Was it "camp"? Would we be considered "camp" or back in fashion? Soon Bette Midler, that Peck's Bad Girl of music, would come out with her version of the Andrews Sisters' hit "Boogie-Woogie Bugle Boy of Company B" and it wouldn't matter. The rage was on.

So I told Freddie Martin that I was interested. Bring back the big bands!

I was sitting in a coffee shop in Beverly Hills, reading a paper, when I learned about the death of Judy Garland in London. Such a sad end for such a brilliant woman. I had really loved her. I had loved her for her talent, of course, but also because no matter what was happening, or how desperate the situation got, she never lost that outrageous sense of humor. I sat there with tears in my eyes and looked out the window at Sunset Boulevard. Now it was called the Sunset Strip, filled with barefoot boys and girls from Nebraska or wherever, walking aimlessly up and down, cadging money from stopped cars. How everything had changed from the days when Cookie Warren and I went to the movies on Saturday afternoons and Judy and I went for real grown-up lunches. Now Judy Garland was dead, the first to go, the first of the group we had been thirty years ago, very young and very eager, and most of us talented. She, superbly talented.

That carnival at Woodstock gave me hope. Thousands upon thousands of kids descending on that little farm community of Bethel, New York, and having a ball for three days. Joy and peace and "good vibes" and everything else that they talked about seemed to be a reality. I found that very moving.

And then, in August, the Manson murders occurred. One August weekend, when Sharon Tate and the others were found tortured and stabbed, wiped away all those good vibes. They were ritual murders with blood messages smeared on the walls. Insanity. All the grotesqueries of Disneyland and the threats of assassinating Mickey Mouse had become a horrible reality. And what was the song that had inspired the Manson family?

"Look out! Look out! Helter Skelter"

A Beatles song. I couldn't believe it. I thought of Eleanore. It was impossible that she was right. But who could understand what was happening? It was so cruel and inhuman. Los Angeles fell into a panic. All the security dogs and security systems seemed unable to stop the paranoia. Later, with a little "Sympathy for the Devil" still ringing in the ears, a Hell's Angels bodyguard for the Rolling Stones murdered a spectator, and Altamont rolled in on us. Drugs, fantasies, horrors.

What was a girl singer (now a little old to be called a girl singer) doing in the midst of this madness? She was singing and paying the bills and worrying about her daughter, now nineteen.

Debbie had come to New York, deciding that she wanted a career in show business. She got a job in an off-Broadway show, where, in one scene, she was supposed to appear nude. That didn't bother me. *Hair* had made nudity respectable and *Oh! Calcutta!* was making it commonplace. The Living Theater, an avant-garde troupe headed by Julian Beck and his wife, Judith Malina, had toured Europe and the United States performing a theatrical piece called *Paradise Now!*, where actors mingled with spectators and stood up and said things like:

"I am not allowed to travel without a passport."

"I cannot move about at will!"

"The Gates of Paradise are closed to me!"

"I don't know how to stop wars!"

"You can't live if you don't have money!"

"I'm not allowed to smoke marijuana!"

"I am not allowed to take my clothes off!"

"The culture represses love!"

And then everybody stripped. And mingled. Until the cops came and broke up the proceedings. Untrammeled emotion! Let it all hang out!

I could go along with that. Debbie's nude scene wasn't nearly so political as the Living Theater's. Actually, it was rather adorable. The producer was not.

Buddy Bregman, Jule Styne's nephew, was now going after my daughter. Years ago, Buddy had practically lived at the Whiting house. He had always been a horny kind of guy. He had been after me, and then after my sister, Barbara. I finally found a girl he could go out with, because he seemed like a desperate teen-ager. Now he was not a teen-ager, although he still seemed desperate. I shouldn't be harsh about Buddy. Actually, I was fond of him. In a way he was like a relative, but he was after my daughter. And he got her.

Oh, yes, it was her life. I didn't really have the right to interfere. Nobody was supposed to interfere during that period. "Do your own thing." How dated it all sounds now, like samplers, rather smug samplers of a fatuous age.

Debbie had her affair. And then she started going with an artist who did imaginative things with seashells. Do you think anyone, reading this in the year 2010, will understand? I'm not sure *I* understand, here in the relatively sedate eighties. This guy was "into" Scientology and also into drugs. He wanted to introduce Debbie into Scientology. I believe he had already introduced her to drugs.

"Oh, Mother, there is nothing wrong with pot," she assured me. I wasn't at all sure. It was a time when the laws were much stiffer than they are now. I knew that, whatever was happening, I didn't want Debbie to be involved. I told her that, but why would she listen? Would I have listened if Eleanore had said it? Probably not. Thinking, perhaps, I was not being "with it," I asked a friend of mind, who ran the Rainbow Grill, where I frequently appeared, to meet Debbie and her artist. Debbie's boyfriend had in the meantime asked me to sign a paper, allowing him to "audit" Debbie into Scientology. I read some of the literature he had brought me. First, Scientology allowed no use of drugs and no alcohol. What was this guy thinking of? I protested to him. "You're not being honest. You're doing all these things." I told him I wouldn't sign a thing.

Then my friend Tracey came over. Debbie announced that her boyfriend had a little "gold" and we should try it. I really didn't want to have anything to do with it. Tracey also refused.

"A little gold won't hurt you," Debbie's boyfriend said, and they went into the other room. Tracey was a man with a mind like a computer. He was as sharp as anyone I knew. He could remember great lists of facts and add up sums in his head. He was brilliant.

"You know," he warned me, "you shouldn't have anything to do with this. It could be dangerous for you. For your career. Suppose they get busted."

"I'll really have to stop them," I agreed.

The boyfriend smiled at us when we went into Debbie's room. "Why are you so *paranoid*? Do you really think pot is so dangerous?"

I left. Tracey stayed. Evidently they talked him into trying it, for he took the stick, the joint, whatever it was called, and it flipped him. Maybe there was something else in it besides marijuana. His mind was like a computer gone berserk. He started spouting facts, but they made no sense. His mind was racing, and so was his tongue. After a while I couldn't understand him. Then he said he had to leave. He went over to Carter and Amanda Burden's, where they had been planning some benefit. He entered their house and began walking in a rectangle, squaring the corners, almost in military fashion, and never once stopping his insane talk. Carter Burden did not know how to handle him. Not that Tracey was violent, just uncontrollable. Burden telephoned the police and they took him to Bellevue Hospital. My manager, Lloyd Greenfield, and I had to get him out. Tracey went back to work but eventually returned to his hometown. I will never forget the experience.

Debbie was horrified at what had happened.

I was furious.

"Now listen, Debbie. That's the end. You got to get rid of this guy. You got to get rid of these drugs. I don't want them around. I won't have him around. Now either he goes or you go. Get rid of this guy," I said. "Get rid of him, or get out!"

"I can't leave him. I love him."

"How can you love him? Debbie, this is the hardest thing I've ever had to do in my life. But if you don't leave him, right now, I want you out of this house. I can't deal with it, and I don't know how to bring you to your senses."

She left. The guy had decided they should take a trip cross-country by car. They departed. Debbie promised to call.

I got on the phone with her father.

"Lou, I really don't know what to do."

"You did exactly the right thing," Lou said. "We'll just stay in touch every day until she gets out here. You call if you hear. I'll call if I do."

In the beginning of May 1970, President Nixon announced the government's decision to invade Cambodia. Demonstrations exploded on college campuses. Students were shot to death by the National Guard at Kent State, and the streets of the cities boiled with infuriated young people. There were bomb scares and bombings, and I kept waiting by the phone for a call.

Debbie did call, from Stephens College, in Missouri. She had once attended the college and had gone back to see what it was like.

"Mother, they're blowing everything up here."

What was I supposed to say? "That's nice, dear"? I felt totally frustrated, inadequate, and angry. But relieved. Debbie was all right. So far.

"Mom," she said, "I'm scared."

Should I say, "Come home. It's okay. You really don't have to worry about anything. You can do anything you like. There are no consequences for behavior"? I couldn't say it.

"Take care of yourself" is what I did say. "And call your father. Keep calling both of us."

When she next called, she said, "Hi, Mom. Listen, I'm not high. And yet I am high. I'm one mile high." She was calling from Denver. Okay, a bad joke was good enough for me. For a parent in 1970, it was good news to know that your kid wasn't high and hadn't been blown up, was not killed in a war, nor injured in a riot.

Debbie got to California and stayed with her father. The guy lasted maybe a week after she got out there. Lou saw to that. And Lou straightened her out. I am everlastingly grateful to him for that.

John Meyer came into my life at exactly the right point. It was in the winter of 1971, and my agents had asked if I would care to audition for a new musical trying out at the Bucks County Playhouse in May. Of course I was interested. They arranged for me to meet the composer, John Meyer. I went to the twelve-room apartment he shared with his mother and father on Park Avenue. He made some coffee and started talking. He didn't stop talking, even when I started talking. We found we were finishing each other's sentences. We thought alike and we knew a lot of the same people. He had taken care of Judy Garland during one of the last desperate periods of her life. He had gotten her a job for a hundred dollars a night at Mary McCarthy's supper club, and had brought her home to his apartment because she said she needed a bath and hadn't been able to take one in a week. She emerged from the bathroom and he introduced her to his parents. "Mom and Dad, this is Judy Garland." They practically fainted, and she went into the living room, curled up in a bathrobe, and proceeded to charm them. I told him about the Judy I knew.

This was all apropos, because the musical Johnny had written was about his experience with a legend like Garland. It was called *When Do the Words come True?* He played me some of the score. There were beautiful songs. I told him so. He thanked me.

I didn't get the part; Gloria DeHaven did. Instead, I got the composer. John Meyer phoned maybe a week later, wondering whether I'd go out with him. He had a great sense of humor, in addition to which he sure could play the piano. If we were ever at a loss for words—or anything else—he could always play the piano.

Well, John and I were never at a loss for anything. But when he came into my apartment, I was convinced he was gay. He wore this huge hat, and a cape that was mink-lined. "Flamboyant" hardly described him. He swept in, went to the piano, played some obscure Rodgers and Hart (a *sure* sign), and then asked a little hesitantly whether I would go to a gay bar with him. I assured him I had been to one or two in my time.

We walked in, and the bartender said, "Hello, Margaret, long time no see." I said, "Hi, Nick," and shrugged at Johnny. "You see?" I said airily. "I have been everywhere."

Johnny was not gay. He really loved to jump into the feathers. He was divine in bed, except maybe "jump" is the key word here. Like a little kid, he would jump up and down, up and down. Hyper. He never stopped. Never stopped anything. Never stopped talking. I asked him once, "What is the matter with you?"

He laughed. "I'm like a guy who's waiting for a taxi. I'm just so anxious I won't get one." He was. He was always in a rush. Always enthusiastic. We started singing and playing. He would sweep in and say, "Today, my favorite composer is George Gershwin," and then we would sing Gershwin songs. The next day it could be Cole Porter or Arlen. Rodgers, Kern. Sondheim.

One day, practically in midchord, he stopped and turned to me. "I can't figure you out."

"Why? I'm not so complicated."

"No. I see you. I hear you. You've got a great voice. Garland had a great voice. You've got a great voice. You perform. You understand a lyric. But somehow it doesn't all come together."

"What do you mean?"

"You got all the pieces. And you haven't put them together, all together, so that everything works at one time."

He grabbed a song sheet off the piano.

"Here, take this one." It was "Make the Man Love Me." "Now, what do you think about lyrics?"

"Johnny Mercer always said a song was like a one-act play. Exposition, development, then the big crisis and the denouement."

"Well, he's right. But you have to take every bit of it moment by moment. You can't play the end at the beginning. You shouldn't even be aware of what's going to happen at the end. Tell us the story. And it has to be like it's the first time. That's really the great thing about a Piaf or a Garland, you never knew what was coming next. Anything could happen. That's the key to being a storyteller."

We started working. Not that we realized we were working. We were just going through something together.

"Take an event that happened today. Use it. That will keep everything fresh. Did you get hurt? Did you love something—someone—especially? Tell me what happened. No, don't tell me. *Sing* me."

He was asking me to let go. I wasn't sure I could do that. I had been trained by my father to respect the songwriter. I knew how carefully all these songs had been crafted and put together.

"But they don't *sound* like they've been crafted," Johnny Meyer countered. He was right. The songs just flowed. Emotionally, that was what I should do.

Amazing things started to happen. I lost control. I started to cry. I wasn't sure why. I didn't stop singing. I sang through it. Another emotion took over. I couldn't sort my feelings out, but my voice started to get stronger, and then more caressing. In a way, it didn't belong to me. I couldn't think about it. There was a power inside me I had never known. It scared me. I stopped singing.

"I don't think I can do this," I said. I was trembling a little.

"Of course you can." He was bouncing on the piano bench. Bouncing with excitement. He grabbed another piece of music. It was "Anyone Can Whistle," a Stephen Sondheim song.

"What's this one about? It's about how easy it is to do anything. Relax, let go. Just whistle. Everybody else can do it, why can't I?"

I started to sing it. Yes, that was right. Relax, let go! I wasn't singing for Daddy any more. Nor for Eleanore. Nor, for that matter, was I singing for John Meyer. I was singing for me, and the feeling was overwhelming. So much had happened to me. I was no longer the little girl in front of a microphone. I had been hurt, and I had also hurt people. I had been angry and crushed and jubilant. I had known failure and also great success. I had been in love and I had fallen out of love. What a wealth of feelings there was to work with! One feeling led to another. Sometimes humor was mixed with wistfulness. I wouldn't stop singing.

"Anyone can whistle . . .
Easy . . ."

Johnny Mercer came into town a few weeks later, He had established the Songwriters Hall of Fame, and now, in return, the organization was inducting him and two other songwriters. Mercer wanted me to sing three songs. One for Leo Robin, one for Dorothy Fields, and one for him. I couldn't wait. My God, it was a chance to try out what John Meyer and I had been working on.

For Leo, I chose "Beyond the Blue Horizon," which he had written with my father. For Johnny, "Too Marvelous for Words," ditto. For Dorothy Fields, I said I was going to sing "Make the Man Love Me" from *A Tree Grows in Brooklyn.* She was furious. She wanted something *up,* like "On the Sunny Side of the Street." I said, no, this was it.

I sang the three of them. Here I was, performing in front of all these songwriters. In a sense, I was performing in front of my father. Lightning might strike me if it wasn't right. But I just didn't care. I was that excited. The first two songs, I had sung all my life. But "Make the Man Love Me" was another story. It was the first time I had ever performed it. I just let go. The response was overwhelming.

Backstage, Bobby Scott, the musician, said admiringly, "You sang from your *ass!*" Musicians are so descriptive! I beamed at John Meyer. He had been right. I had found something terribly important within myself. Johnny Mercer flashed that adorable, almost elfin grin that he smiled when he was secretly very pleased. Oh, but it didn't matter. I knew, myself, what I had done. I didn't really care what anyone else thought. I knew this was right.

And what had it boiled down to? Things I had learned from Johnny and from the times and from the kids. Nothing was gospel. Lots could be challenged. And the important thing for a performer was to bare himself. I really don't mean like the Living Theater's taking off their clothes. But performers bare themselves in other ways. They strip off the pretensions. Get right down to the basic feelings and show them. Let the audience see you naked, emotionally naked. Trust them. Trust it. It was scary. It was easy. It was hard. It was exciting. That was the sixties' gift to me. And it took Johnny Meyer to bring it out.

With Johnny, I went to an annual Christmas party given by Ron Antoine, head of BMI at the time, at his house in New Jersey. There I met all these new and vibrant—and then unknown—performers. A girl named Melissa Manchester. And there was some guy playing piano and singing. I asked him, Could he sing that a little louder? He did. He sounded pretty good. So then I asked him his name.

"Barry Manilow."

"I love the way you play," I said as I left. Then I began to see him around town, playing piano. He had done an off-Broadway show, *The Drunkard*, and was working at CBS as a piano player. All the time he was writing songs. I said to him one night, "You play contemporary music so well. I should sing it, and I know I don't sing it well. Could you come over to the house?" He did.

"Teach me contemporary music," I said.

He shook his head. "Margaret, I'd rather do 'fish gotta swim, birds gotta fly.' "

I said, "No, no. You sing with another feel. You read the lyrics in a different way. This contemporary stuff isn't coming to me honestly." So he played "Up on the Roof" and some Beatles songs, and made wonderful arrangements of them for me. But after each lesson, he would say, "Let's sing the songs *I* love—'Losing My Mind,' 'It Had to Be You.' "

One day, he called up and asked, "Will you do me a favor? It's my birthday. If Johnny Meyer doesn't mind, would you go out with me tonight?" He had two tickets for Carole King's concert at Carnegie Hall. That evening he picked me up, and as we walked toward Carnegie, he became very apologetic. "I didn't have enough money to buy the best seats," he said.

I reassured him. "That's all right. We're gonna love it."

We had to sit in almost the top row, like two kids looking around. "Do you think James Taylor will be here?" Barry asked anxiously. Carole had backed up Taylor on one of his albums. It was the time when everybody was backing one another up—Mick Jagger on Carly Simon's album, and so on.

And then out James Taylor walked. We were like two teen-agers.

Later, outside, Barry said, "I have to go to work. It's a strange place, but if you want to go there, I think you'd have a lot of fun."

I said, "Let's go."

He explained he was musical director. "I hope you don't misunderstand where I'm taking you," he said. We went to the Ansonia Hotel and walked downstairs into the baths. This was the first time I had ever been in a gay baths. Men were sauntering around with towels wrapped around their waists. I was introduced to the owners. There was one section roped off, and that's where I sat. Barry, so concerned, asked whether I was all right. I was fine. I was the only woman there. He played with his trio through the steam, and men walked around. Then he whispered to me, "The show's about to go on. Tell me honestly what you think of this girl."

Until this moment, people had been in the pool or sitting around, eating. But with the announcement of the up-and-coming attraction, everyone found seats, and the baths turned into a kind of impromptu theater. The announcer said, "Ladies and gentlemen, we think we have a new star on the horizon. Miss Bette Midler!" I had never seen anyone take over an audience as Bette did. She took instant command and had instant magic. She pulverized them. She was making her nightclub debut in a gay baths. But it didn't matter. There was no question in my mind that she was going to become the most sensational act in the business. When the show was over, she winked, looked at me, and asked me to get up and perform.

I sang a very strange chorus of "Moonlight in Vermont" amid the steam and naked bodies. I kept thinking, This would not have been believed ten years ago. Then Bette and I took a bow and walked off. We chatted after the show, and I said, "This may become the hottest room in town." Which indeed it did—in both ways. I loved Bette because she could combine camp and fun, or be tacky, then raucous, then vulnerable. She is so marvelously varied. And that's what I told Barry when he took me home. "Don't lose her, whatever you do."

He became her musical conductor. They went on tour. Barry knew how to arrange for her. They spent a lot of time in the Brill Building, looking over old standards like "Boogie Woogie Bugle Boy" and "Don't Sit Under the Apple Tree." The act was a smash.

Barry wanted to sing, and Bette, being the kind of lady she was, let him. At the beginning of Bette's second act, Barry would get up and do two or three songs. In the next year or so, as I followed them on the road with the Big Band Cavalcade, I would read the reviews of her show, praising her to the skies and calling him a wonderful musical conductor, but advising Bette to see to it that Barry never sang again.

Two years later, he had become the biggest record star in the country.

When Barry started making records, he brought one to the house. He sounded great, but the record didn't sell. He'd signed a deal with a record company and Clive Davis wanted to let him go. Barry said, "No, you owe me an album. I want to do it."

Davis said, "Only if you'll sing the songs I want you to." Davis brought him "Mandy," and the rest is history.

Good things started happening. Freddie Martin called to say he had booked the Big Band Cavalcade to tour the country from the middle of September through the middle of December. Besides his band and me, there would be Bob Crosby and his Bobcats and Frankie Carle. Those names alone filled me with nostalgia.

Johnny Meyer and I were going to Europe. He had written a second musical, the first of the musical spoofs of horror movies, called *The Bride of Glockenspiel*. There were some American producers in London who wanted to hear the show, including Arthur Whitelaw, and Ernie Martin and Cy Feuer. Since I knew all the songs, Johnny figured the two of us should audition the show. We did, and the reaction was great. But you never know what that means in show business, and here I was with The Man Who Was Waiting for a Taxi! He was just too impatient. So we decided to take a three-week tour of the wine country, ending up in Paris.

Johnny knew wine. He wasn't pretentious about it; he just knew it. He could really tell when a bottle, even though from a great vintage and a good château, was not up to par. He didn't mind speaking out either. Once, at Scandia in Beverly Hills, he had ordered four different bottles and sent them back. Each one of them had turned. The management didn't believe him, but they tasted, and sure enough, he was correct.

Just before we left for Europe, Freddy Martin called me, inviting us to San Clemente to perform for President Nixon. More than anything, it was an invitation to a party, a celebration. Nixon had defeated George McGovern in the presidential election. He was riding high, and he loved Freddy Martin's orchestra. It would be a blast.

"You're going to miss *some party* at President Nixon's," Freddy said.

"Another time," I said blithely. I was going to have a blast myself. With Johnny.

From London, we flew to Nice, stayed at a little hotel behind the Carlton in Cannes, poked around the Riviera, went to Saint-Paul-de-Vence to look at the Dominican nuns' chapel Matisse had so joyously filled with his stained-glass windows, murals, and altars. Then we went to lunch at a restaurant called La Colombe d'Or on one of those heavenly days with a Matisse-blue sky and everybody dining out under the shade trees, escaping the Mediterranean sun that was beating down. Bees droned around the half-filled wine-glasses, attracted by the sweetness and the smell of flowers. The atmosphere was romantic and earthy and luxurious all at the same time. So absolutely European. Yes, I want more of this! I said to myself. To John, I made a comment. "I think this is the place Yves

Montand and Signoret love so much." Just as I said it, I looked up and saw them coming in. Okay, I had had a couple of glasses of wine. But there they were—she tawny tiger and he sleek panther—sitting down and eating lunch! Okay, so I had had more than a couple of glasses of wine. But they sure looked wonderful. We all watched the *bocce* games, although I guess in France they're called *boules*. Afterward, John and I drove back to the hotel and made dinner reservations. Was there no end to all this excess?

We started to climb the hill behind the Carlton, wandering through winding streets searching for yet another fabulous restaurant. Then my eye caught a glimpse of my absolutely favorite flower. There, in a restaurant arcade, was the most magnificent bunch of tropicana roses, orange- and peach-toned, absolutely *glowing* at me! "Oh, stop! Look! Johnny, look!" I believe everything about that trip was in exclamation marks. I ran over to the flowers and inhaled the aroma. We stayed there for dinner. I don't know about the other fabulous restaurant, but this meal was wonderful.

There's no way to describe the feeling of an adventure like this. What I want to suggest is the brilliance of the country, the shock and delight of coming across so many pleasures packed together so tightly. The senses reeled.

We were leaving on the train *Le Mistral* the next morning for Lyons. Johnny was in a hurry, but there was something amiss with the bill. He made a fluent and convincing argument with the management, and they were changing it. In the meantime, we were missing the train. I was getting anxious, so I waved my arms and a cab appeared. Thank God. John was still settling the bill. In desperation, I called to him. "John, you're the man who's always waiting for a taxi! Look! The taxi's waiting for you. Move it!" That broke him up. We sped to Lyons.

Bocuse, Troisgros. Three-star nights and a chain of delights. Even the croissants in the morning were three-star. We ate, we *dined*, we tasted, we sniffed, we quaffed, we made love. Between courses and meals and renowned restaurants and *amour*, we giggled a lot.

And then we started the wine tour. We rented a car. John had brought along Frederick Wildman's wine guide, and we were going to follow it exactly. There was even a map at the beginning of each chapter for us to gaze at.

Mâcon, Beaune, Chagny, Chambertin. These were just names to me. They were wines to him. And I don't know what we were to those winegrowers. John told them that we were writers for *Cosmopolitan* magazine, researching the different vineyards. That seemed to work like a charm. We were given entrée everywhere and shown the *caves*, always, always sampling the wine. Long glass *pipettes* would be introduced into a cask, the wine brought out into glasses, and we would again sniff, quaff, and *spit*! I found out why. After a day or two, you could lose your mind if you actually swallowed all that wine. As it was, I had a bit of a buzz, just like those bees in Vence.

At Chambertin, wine expert that I had just become, I was given a taste of wine.

"Welch's grape juice!" I cried in horror, only to discover that the wine had not been given a chance to ferment yet. Well, what did I know?

Every night we stayed in a charming inn, walked the streets of the little villages, made love, awoke the next day to drive through the countryside. Summer was just ending and autumn about to begin. The green and gold of the countryside swept past my eyes. Every so often, the gray ruins of a castle turret would rise above the slopes of the vineyards. And so we made our way to Beaune and the Hospice de Beaune.

There is still, in the center of this Burgundy wine country, a real hospital with nuns in their great colorful surplices and broad-brimmed hats, and with ancient scales to measure the pharmaceuticals. And, of course, there are the vineyards. John explained all this to me. Unlike the other sections of France, where the châteaus and *domaines* grow vast amounts of wine, Burgundy has many small vineyards. This is because the *seigneurs* had parceled out acres to the Catholic church to appease the hierarchy. Also, the wines come out differently because the grapes are grown on different parts of the slopes. Some get more wind and less sun. The Girl Singer nodded and kept quaffing.

Every year in November, a wine auction aids the hospice. Wine buyers arrive from all over the world to taste the new crop and speculate on the value of the year's vintage. There are banquets called *les trois glorieuses*. The prestige of buying and owning wine from the Hospice de Beaune is enormous. So during the *vendange*, or the wine picking, there is great excitement. Nineteen seventy-two was supposed to be a terrific year for Burgundies, although the rest of the French wines suffered. So there was enormous anticipation even before the *vendange*. I was surrounded by beaming Burgundians. For some reason, I kept thinking of the sketch I had done with Bob Hope: "You tell 'em, purple foot!"

I *still* have no idea why that was funny.

We tasted other vintages, stayed at the Hôtel de la Poste, and chatted with Charles Cheviot, who had opened a wonderful restaurant, La Petite Ferme, in New York. I even tried out my not-so-terrific French. Observing a fly that had fallen into my glass of wine, I said, "There's a *mouche dans mon vin*." Heavens! Everything in French sounded like the title of a Feydeau farce!

The next morning, when we came downstairs for breakfast, the headlines in the papers read: ARAB TERRORISTS KILL ATHLETES AT MUNICH OLYMPICS. Once again, there was that absurd feeling of living in an incomprehensible world. Great revelry and shocking tragedy.

I was to remember that feeling often during the months to come.

From Paris to Los Angeles with only a week between. I was a little breathless. Three days of rehearsal with the Freddie Martin Band at the Roosevelt Hotel, before the Big Band Cavalcade took to the road for its three-month tour. Twenty-two men and Miss Whiting on a bus for three months! I had missed touring the first time around in the late thirties. Now, conditions were evidently much better. There was a bathroom on the bus, which certainly helped. I never had to pack my costumes. My gowns were all hung on a rack in the back of the bus, and I merely had to say, "Take out the blue and the red, we'll wear those tonight." And Rex, the bus driver, whom I dubbed "Captain Greyhound," carried out orders. I took a tote bag with my makeup and jewelry. That was simple.

I don't mean to say that that was all my luggage. No, I have never been one given to "Travelin' Light," as the Mercer song says. The morning we set out from the Roosevelt Hotel for Bakersfield, California, our first date, I arrived with eight suitcases. Rex, that wonderfully sweet and patient man, took one look and said, "Jesus H. Christ!" But he loaded the bags on. And away we went to Bakersfield.

Autumn. I was seeing the countryside again, this one so different from the French. There, everything was very neat and orderly, with packets of land, trees, and narrow lanes dividing properties. Here, there were vast stretches. Mountains and desert off in the distance. Great rows of . . . what were they? Orange lumps. I finally figured it out. They were ripening pumpkins—thousands of them. California is impressive for many reasons, but none more so than the quantity of produce. I think I saw enough pumpkins to feed all France.

Thus started the ritual of traveling with the band. Every day it was the same. Check in at the hotel. Columbia Concerts had booked these engagements, and they were terrifically well organized. Every day we were given our key in an envelope, sometimes the best rooms, sometimes a suite, many times a motel room. Howard Johnson's. The Ramada. We'd take the hand luggage out of the bus. The costumes were hung up in the theater. The stage crew would set up. The rest of us always headed either for the drugstore or the nearest fruit market. Fresh fruit was a must for the next day on the bus. Then back to the hotel or motel. Once inside the room, the first thing to do was turn on the television so as not to be alone. I always carried a lot of books and magazines with me, and these I put out on the coffee table, along with a couple of pictures. Then it was home. I also carried with me a stuffed animal, a mole someone had given me. I had stuck a gold star on his behind. I would prop Moley up on the sofa and then get ready for the show. So, unpack, and then quickly repack for the next day's departure at nine in the morning.

My only real problems were my hair and how to get the daily *New York Times*. I needed a hairdresser every other day. Sometimes Columbia Concerts had to wire ahead and locate a hairdresser, who would then be waiting for me in, say, Ottumwa, Iowa.

The shows started at eight o'clock. Every night we were at a different theater and sometimes not even a theater, but an auditorium or a gymnasium. Often, we were booked into small towns. But there would be five thousand people wanting to see us. So we played gymnasiums. I dressed in locker rooms and bathrooms. It didn't matter. It was wonderful and we were a big hit. The audiences loved us. The big-band sound was back with a bang. Kids who couldn't have been older than fourteen or fifteen had memorized all the big-band arrangements and could quote obscure riffs to us. Their parents (sometimes their grandparents) would end up dancing in the aisles. It was a festival of fun, for all of us.

Freddy Martin and The Martin Men opened and played all their big numbers, including "Bumble Boogie" and "Tonight We Love." Then I came out for my first segment, a medley of forties tunes— "I'll Be with You in Apple Blossom Time," "Boogie Woogie Bugle Boy," and some of Jule Styne's great wartime ballads, like "I've Heard That Song Before" and "I'll Walk Alone." Then Frankie Carle was introduced, and he wowed them with his "Sunrise Serenade," "Sweet Lorraine," "Piano Roll Blues," and "Tea for Two."

After intermission, Bob Crosby described to a rather awestruck generation the intricacies of "dipping" while dancing, and then drove them wild with great swinging renditions of "Big Noise from Winnetka" and "When the Saints Go Marching In." I came out again, with a second gown and some contemporary songs like "Never Say Goodbye" and "What Are You Doing the Rest of Your Life?" mixed in with the standards and of *course* "It Might As Well Be Spring," "Moonlight in Vermont," and a medley of my father's songs. Then we ended with a salute to the theme songs of the great bandleaders. By that time, to borrow from the Fats Waller vernacular, "the joint was jumping."

Then back to the hotel. If the town was big enough, I would have reconnoitered and found the best restaurant, and we would all eat. Otherwise, we persuaded the hotel or motel to keep the dining room open so we could get a meal. Then it was to bed and up again the next morning. I had to get up especially early because I never let anyone see me in curlers. The Girl Singer had to keep up her standards! Then it was back on the bus, a "Good Morning, Freddy," "Good Morning, Margaret, and how are you, Moley?" We kept up the amenities. We always said a good morning to one another as we set off on another 250-mile jaunt, and the whole procedure started over again.

Mostly we had a good time. I was working with the *best* band, the *crème de la crème* from both New York and Los Angeles. Start with Babe Russin, one of the jazz immortals on sax. Babe began with Red Nichols and went on to play with both Tommy and Jimmy Dorsey and Benny Goodman. There was Ray Linn, the great Chicago trumpet man who joined Tommy Dorsey at eighteen, and later played with Woody Herman and Artie Shaw. What about Peanuts Hucko, one of the great jazz clarinetists? Peanuts served his apprenticeship with Glenn Miller's Army Air Force Band before becoming a star of *The Lawrence Welk Show*. And there was John Cochran, who played the sweetest trombone. He had been with Freddy over twenty-five years. Because of his beautiful gray hair, I dubbed him the "Lorne Greene of the Band Business."

I think the biggest surprise was Frankie Carle. Freddy had spent hours on the phone convincing Frankie to come out of retirement. He turned out to be the hit of the show, especially with the ladies. Every night they'd line up at the stage door to wait for his autograph. At sixty-nine years young, Frankie was a joy.

One night I saw a very lovely fan and her daughter waiting at the stage door for Frankie. I thought, Hhmmm. The next morning, I saw the lady and the daughter emerging from Frankie's hotel room. I thought, Hmmm. Hmmm. He certainly was a joy.

However . . .

By the end of three months, nerves got a little frazzled. But there was only one guy who got on everyone's nerves. He was a very religious man who constantly read (and quoted) from the Bible. He had a parable for every cornpatch, it seemed. He was also a fuss-budget. He would cry "Close the window" while everyone else was stifling or "Open the window" when everyone else was freezing. Finally, one morning in subtropical Florida, toward the end of both the tour and my tether, Mr. Religion ordered the windows closed again. I said, "You can take that Bible, stick it up your ass, and close your own window!" The band burst into spontaneous applause. It was one of my finer moments.

Such was traveling on the road.

As the autumn went by, one town blurred into another, one week into another. Only one image began to intrude—and it became a constant intruder.

When we started out, the band members described the party I had missed at San Clemente. Musicians love a good blast, and evidently that had been one of the best. They couldn't stop talking about the setting, the food, the drink, and President Nixon.

News bulletins began to appear on television, and, as I said, the first thing we did on entering a motel room was switch on the TV. There were news breaks, featuring the name of a hotel in Washington called the Watergate. Soon, the Watergate was shortened to just Watergate. News releases described revelations of a break-in. Burglars had ransacked the Democratic National Committee's headquarters on June 17th. Who paid it much mind? There was a show to do. The news was interesting, but it was just the game of politics. Boys would be boys. The important questions were: Where was the hairdresser for the night's performance, and would I be dressing in a gym again?

Then, mornings on the bus, beyond the hello-Margaret-howdy-Sam routine, there was the same curious question. "Did you hear the latest?" Men were being indicted. They weren't your common criminals. There was a Gordon Liddy, who was general counsel for the Committee for the Reelection of the President, and E. Howard Hunt, Jr., a "former White House aide," as the newscasters described him. Then suddenly they were known as part of the Watergate Seven and they were standing trial.

Meanwhile, every night, we were going out and performing "Bumble Boogie" and "It Might As Well Be Spring," and people were dancing in the aisles, bringing back the good old days. And every night after the performance, we went to our television sets to listen to more "disclosures." A new word entered our vocabularies.

Here we were, a bunch of musicians, touring the country, every day in a different town meeting grocery clerks at check-out counters, druggists, waiters, motel clerks, stagehands, students, concert committee members, bankers. And no one could understand, no one could believe what was happening. It was impossible that members of government could behave like that. Burglary? Wiretapping? But, in the dark parts of our mind, we thought, Yes, and we couldn't believe the assassinations either. We couldn't believe we were capable of this.

Americans are not really naïve, but we do like to believe the best about people. It's hard to put much stock in stories about "misdemeanors." But as we made our way from Kansas to Illinois, "misdemeanors" turned to "crimes" and "credence" turned to "guilt." There was that incredible mixture again that I had experienced in France. Revelry followed by what began to look like a national tragedy.

Autumn started turning to winter. The band kept playing, the joint kept jumping, the revelations kept coming, the nation kept reeling.

It was like a dream. . . .

HOLDREGE, NEB. (POP. 5, 635)

MARGARET: (*singing*): You're just too marvelous, Too marvelous for words . . .

NBC NEWS: . . . latest reports. Five of the Watergate Seven plead guilty. However, G. Gordon Liddy and James W. McCord . . .

MARGARET: . . . That say enough, tell enough, I mean, they just aren't swell enough . . .

CBS REPORTS: . . . in Washington. Before the reconvened grand jury, Jeb Stuart Magruder, assistant to John J. Mitchell, former attorney general, has changed his testimony . . .

PAMPA, TEX. (POP. 21,726)

MARGARET: You're much too much, And just too very very! To ever be In Webster's Dictionary . . .

ABC NEWS: . . . perjury at the instigation of Mitchell and John W. Dean III, counsel to the president . . .

The culmination of this for me came one night in Champaign, Illinois, in 1973. I call it the Night of the Knives. It was the night the news announced that Nixon had fired Archibald Cox, the special prosecutor who had refused to stop the judicial process investigating the conversations secretly recorded in the president's office.

By this time the Big Band Cavalcade had almost completed two tours. We went out one more time in 1974. By then, the administration had collapsed, Nixon was out, Gerald Ford had taken his place, while Margaret was still singing:

> *"To tell you that you're marvelous,*
> *Too marvelous for words."*

Something had happened, though, a change in character. I can't put my finger on it. But just as there was a feeling of togetherness during World War II, and a feeling of resurgence during the Kennedy days, now there was a kind of national shrugging things off. I kept thinking about that later, when Cliff Robertson brought to light executive David Begelman's forging of checks, and later still, during the collapse of United Artists following the financial fiasco of *Heaven's Gate*. The first question always was: Who would have allowed such a thing to happen? And in the answer was always a reference to Watergate, which became an excuse for bizarre behavior.

During these tours, Johnny Meyer would often fly out to meet me and travel with us for a week or two. It was always fun, but I think by now both John and I knew we'd had it. It wasn't really serious anymore. Johnny was always a man on the go, never at home. He was looking at other women the way he was waiting for a taxi. At the end of 1973, we split up and he moved to Greenwich Village.

We still see each other all the time, and I will always be grateful to him. He taught me the greatest lesson in my professional life—that anyone can whistle.

Easy.

Gian Sciandra introduced me to another man who was to become important in my life—Greg Dawson. The two of them were among the partners opening a restaurant called the Ballroom on West Broadway in the Village. The Ballroom started out as just a restaurant with incredibly good food, but then branched out as a cabaret. Greg's fascination was with performers. We would meet each other at every opening. He saw everything and so did I.

He then inaugurated a series at the Citicorp Building called the Salute to the Great American Songwriters. Greg asked me to see the salute to Johnny Mercer. I did, and then he asked me to perform in one. That was the start of a real friendship.

Johnny Mercer. Nobody was more American than Johnny Mercer. A romanticist, and old softie sometimes. Never terribly political, he didn't get swept up in causes. He loved to talk, the way he loved to cook bouillabaisse and drink J&B and paint watercolors. He loved to talk about fascism and communism, Mussolini and chocolate ice cream and sailboats. He was a dreamer and a poet, not an activist. His genius had been in keeping his finger on the American psychic pulse, perhaps. He seemed to know what America was feeling and could express it in pop songs that people cherished.

We had kept in touch through the years, talking to each other almost every week. Johnny always liked to play his new songs for me. He valued my judgment, which was a terrific compliment. When he and Henry Mancini wrote a song for the film *Breakfast at Tiffany's*, Johnny called me. He wanted me to hear it. Hank played while Johnny sang:

"Moon River, wider than a mile;
I'm crossing you in style some day. . . ."

I listened, entranced, until he came to the lines

"We're after the same rainbow's end, waitin' round the bend, my
Huckleberry friend. . . ."

Johnny finished.
I said, "Gee, I don't know."
"What, kid? What is it? Don't you like it?" (I have never met a really *secure* songwriter.)
"I love it. . . ."
"Margaret, I know you. I know you well. There's something wrong."
"Okay. You asked me. I think it's a very simple song. It tells a beautiful story, but I just don't like 'huckleberry friend.' What is a

'huckleberry friend'? That particular phrase throws the whole thing out of context for me.''

He said, "Oh . . ." I looked at Hank Mancini, and he just slumped over the piano and said, "Oh my God."

And Johnny said, "Do you really think so?"

I said, "Johnny, I do. It changes the whole song. It simply won't work.''

He looked at me and said, "Well, I'll tell you what. I'll think about it. But, boy, I really liked that lyric.''

So I went home, and about three hours later Johnny called me and said, "Kid, I gotta go along with my instincts. I gotta keep 'huckleberry friend' in.''

I said, "Well, *okay*! If you feel *that* way.''

About six months later, I bumped into my mother at the Bel-Air Market, and she said, "Oh Margaret, I've just heard Johnny's new song. I think it's wonderful. It's beautiful. It can't help but be a big hit.''

I said, "Which one is it?"

" 'My Huckleberry Friend,' " she replied.

I was very pleased that Johnny had thought enough of me to ask my advice.

Thank God he didn't take it.

I never said I was perfect.

Nor was Johnny. There had always been a dark side to John. One that he kept to himself. He could see that changes were happening in the world, and he was not convinced he could cope with that. After the break-up of the Beatles, Paul McCartney expressed an interest in working with Johnny.

"I dunno," he said, sitting in his rocking chair. "I don't know if I could do *that*.''

"The publishers think you could," I said helpfully.

"Yeah. What do *they* know?" was his reply. He loved John Hartford's "Gentle on My Mind" and the songs of Jim Webb, but he also felt out of touch with these new times.

He would drink, and when he drank he would say things that hurt. I'd rather think he didn't believe what he said. When he came with Harry Warren to see me at the Playboy Club, he said, "You sing too goddamn loud. You're like Streisand. Why don't you sing the way you used to sing?" The next day, he called to apologize and sent me flowers. He said, "I know you have to get up and perform. I don't know what got into me." Well, I knew. He had helped create me. He just liked those soft pretty tones.

In 1974, Johnny was in London collaborating with André Previn on a musical called *Good Companions*. He was getting off a bus and there was an accident. It was thought he had hit his head getting off the bus. When he came to, he was in a hospital and he didn't know what had happened to him. All he could say was, "I tripped and I hit the bus." But he was having dizzy spells and he was scared. He didn't want to go to a doctor. In England, the medical men said something about pressure on the brain. He didn't want to listen.

When he got back to New York, he called me, but I was busy in California and taking the time to visit my mother. A few days later, Eleanore and I went to a meeting of the American Guild of Authors and Composers at songwriter Johnny Green's house, and there was Johnny Mercer with his wife, Ginger. I looked at him. He had lost a lot of weight. He looked awful. He was stumbling. I thought, Oh my God, but I said, "How are you?"

"Fine. Fine. Let's the four of us go out to dinner."

"Okay."

After the meeting, Ginger and Eleanore were talking as we walked out toward the car. Johnny started to weave. I gave him my arm to steady him. He stopped and leaned on a tree. Then he put his arms around the tree and looked at me.

"Isn't this awful, Mag? I'm scared."

"You got to see a doctor, Johnny."

"I know. I've been putting it off. Bill Harbach said I had to go. Ginger says so. You do. I'll go tomorrow."

He did. The first doctor said, "I'll send you to another doctor. There's a pressure on your brain, but I don't know what it is."

Johnny went to six different doctors. They said it was a brain tumor, but couldn't be cancer, because he had had it so long, for two or three years. But they were going to have to operate.

Mercer said, "If there's something wrong, I don't want to be a vegetable. I want to die."

When they did operate, they found that it was cancer, and that it was terminal. He didn't want to see anybody. Ginger took him home.

He lived for about a year. We weren't allowed to see him, but I kept hearing stories that the nurse who was with him would come in and listen to a song that was coming out of the TV set and ask who wrote it, and Johnny would say, "I did." And most of the time he was right.

Around seven o'clock at night on June 25, 1976, Jim Lowe, my close friend at WNEW, called me and said "Johnny's gone."

A part of my life went with him. The Kid. The Kid. I knew he had been dying, but it hadn't made any difference. I hadn't believed it.

The cruelty of cancer was unbelievable and I grouped that together with the Manson murders, and the terrorists, and random killings.

It was all part of life that I had never known before, and that now I guess I had to learn to live with.

Exit Johnny.

15

4 Girls 4

"That's the craziest idea I ever heard," I told Bill Loeb, who had phoned me from Los Angeles.

"What's so crazy about it?" Bill countered. "You, Rosie Clooney, Rose Marie, and Barbara McNair do a week at the Beverly Doheny Theater in L.A."

"And what do we call ourselves?"

"Four Girls Four."

"And what do we do?"

"Twenty-five minutes each—and then go home."

"Go home?" I protested. "Oh no. We've got to have a closing with the four of us."

"That means you'll do it?" He sounded eager. "I booked the theater for the week after Labor Day." It was already August 15.

"You must be crazy," I said. I found I was repeating myself. "I must be crazy."

"So you'll do it?" he asked.

"What about billing?"

"Don't worry about it. We'll work it out."

"And who goes on first?"

"Don't worry about it."

"And who sings what?"

"Don't worry about it."

He hung up. I began to worry about it. So I was right on the phone to Rose Marie.

"We gotta have a closing number together," I said.

"Of course we do," Rose Marie agreed, "but you know Bill. He's nuts."

I did know Bill. He was Clooney's manager and Rose Marie's, and evidently, Barbara's. I knew he had been very loyal to Rosie when she had gone through her breakdown, a severe one that had put her into a hospital for a long time. He had comforted Rose Marie when she lost her husband. And he had a way of dealing with all problems by saying, "Don't worry about it." Later, that was going to cause us problems, and plenty of them. But at the moment, the whole idea was so preposterous we took it very lightly.

"How about 'together wherever we go . . .' " Rose Marie sang to me over the phone.

"Good," I said. "Or 'Side by Side.' "

"Also good," she said. "You got someone who writes special lyrics?"

"Yes. How about you?"

"Yes."

"Well, let's get them going. And it's only for a week, right?"

"Right," Rose Marie agreed. "What could it hurt?"

So I called Bill Loeb back.

"Listen, I don't want any problems with material. I'll do 'Moonlight in Vermont,' of course, and a medley of my father's songs, and I have a ballad, 'A Song For You.' "

He cut me off. "Don't worry about it. I got Frankie Ortega and a fourteen-piece band."

Now *that* was a non sequitur.

"And about the closing?"

"Nothing too hard," he said. "Barbara isn't coming in from Vegas until opening night."

The whole show was slapped together. Two days before opening I found myself coming down the aisle of the Beverly Doheny, and there was Rosemary Clooney onstage, rehearsing with the band, and she was singing "A Song for You."

"What is that?" I asked.

Rosie grinned. "'A Song for You.'"

"I know that," I said. "I use it in my act. It's my big ballad. My second number."

"I've been using it as a closer for years," Rosie said.

"But I cleared this material with Bill before I came out. I sent him a list."

"Bill *knows* it's my closer."

I looked around. "Well now, what do we do?"

At that moment Rose Marie came sauntering down the aisle. She looked at me.

"You got another ballad?"

"Yes."

"Sing it."

From then on, she was Rose Marie the Peacemaker. And I was the Organizer. I had suggested to Bill that we alternate billing, change the marquee every day, and also rotate the order of appearance with each performance. The girls had agreed. They had literally picked numbers out of a hat.

"Who's opening?" I inquired.

"I am," Rose Marie said. "Comedy is opening the bill."

"Yeah, but only for one night," Rosie said. "Next night I open."

"And who's second?" I wanted to know.

"You are," they told me. Fine. Okay. "Where are the dressing rooms?"

Two trailers in the parking lot outside the theater had been provided. What were we? Valley Girls before our time?

"Oh well, what difference does it make? It's only for a week." I shrugged and started to rehearse.

We weren't exactly overprepared for this engagement. There were no pictures of the four of us together, and there was no time for publicity. Frankie Ortega and the band ran through our numbers. The musicians were wonderful, the way musicians usually are when they're having a good time. We were getting a kick out of performing because the show harked back to the days of band singers and the big bands. And after the revolution of the sixties, maybe audiences were ready for this kind of entertainment. We really didn't care. We were having fun; we were, to put it kindly, relaxed.

Barbara McNair flew in on the day of opening night, and she was so relaxed she almost wasn't there. Usually Barbara is bubbly and enthusiastic, but she had just gone through a lot of marital trouble: her husband had been implicated in a drug connection and her name had been spread all over the papers. She was working hard and she was tired. But she was a good sport and a pro, and she rehearsed the closing with us. There wasn't one of us who could remember the special lyrics to "Side by Side," so we had them written out on enormous cue cards.

Opening night hit us. There were a couple of minor problems. Barbara had trouble with the band because her orchestrations were especially intricate and she hadn't had time to rehearse. But there was nothing that could spoil the mood. Just working was a tonic for all of us, for there was not one of the four who hadn't been knocked around a bit by life: Clooney had had her emotional problems, Rose Marie had lost her husband, Barbara's marriage was a mess, and nobody was exactly offering me Las Vegas. But none of that mattered. We just had the best time, coming out and performing. And if we had a good time, the audience had a better one. We were totally unprepared for the reaction. When we reached the finale, the four of us came barreling out, grinning and singing:

"Oh! we ain't got a barrel of money,
Maybe we're ragged and funny,
But we'll travel along,
Singin' a song,
Side by side . . ."

and the audience roared its approval. We forgot those special lyrics. They didn't care. At the end, the entire crowd rushed down to the stage. I could see arms outstretched and hands reaching for us. They

Nat Cole, Margaret Whiting,
and disc jockey Alex Cooper meeting
at a party

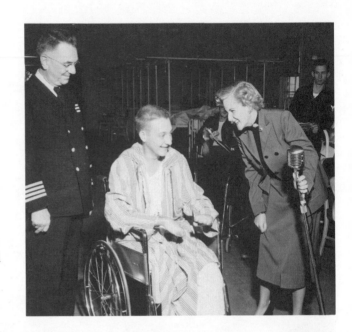

Victor Borge, Danny Thomas,
Margaret Whiting, and an NBC vice-president about
to entertain for an NBC banquet
COURTESY OF NBC

The Whiting Girls,
Margaret and Barbara Whiting.
I always gestured too much.

Mabel Albertson,
Margaret Whiting, and
Eleanore Whiting. That Whiting
Girl with her TV mother
and her real one.

Scenes from
Those Whiting Girls,
Margaret and Barbara

From
Those Whiting Girls

Margaret and Barbara Whiting—those
Whiting Girls at it again

Daughter Debbie, Lou Busch,
and Margaret Whiting. Just Louie and me
and Debbie make three. Or four,
counting the giant deer.

Carl Betz, Joy Garret,
and Margaret Whiting doing a song and
dance from *Plain & Fancy* at
Milwaukee Melody Top

Hugh O'Brian and Margaret Whiting
at a Hollywood premiere doing their
"We're so happy to be here" bit

Aunt Maggie, Richard Moore,
Margaret Whiting, Debbie, and an unidentified waiter
at our wedding. Who ever said the third
time around was the lucky one?

Debbie Reynolds, Margaret Whiting,
Art Linkletter, and friend at opening day of Thalian Clinic.
Apparently that key was very heavy.
STANART PHOTO

Johnny Mercer
and Margaret Whiting.
God, I loved him.

Margaret Whiting
sings for her supper in Sandusky, Ohio—and,
believe me, it wasn't easy that night.

Rosemary Clooney, Helen O'Connell,
Margaret Whiting, and Rose Marie in *4 Girls 4*.
This could be the start of something.
JOHN ENGSTEAD

My opening night at
Studio One in Hollywood, California. Mabel Mercer,
Johnnie Ray, and Helen O'Connell
came to wish me luck.

Jim Lowe and Margaret Whiting
congratulating Harold Arlen on his award at a
Songwriters' Hall of Fame dinner.

RITA K. KATZ

Helen Hayes and Margaret Whiting
at New York Mayor Ed Koch's house, both
wondering, "Where's the beef?"
New York Post

Production shot from *Taking My Turn:*
Tiger Haynes, Margaret Whiting, Marni Nixon,
Cissy Houston, Mace Barrett

John Wrangler, Margaret Whiting,
and daughter Debbie. Yes, I'm an Ivory Girl
—and so is my family.

The night I met
Baroness Maria von Trapp in Stowe, Vermont
MICHAEL CLARK PHOTO

Margaret Whiting and Jack Wrangler
together again for the very first time
ERIC STEVEN JACOBS

just wanted to touch us, to hold on to us. It had never happened to me before. In fact, I had never seen that kind of overwhelming approval.

The next day, that approval was echoed in the press. By curtain time that night, you couldn't get a seat in the theater. The entire week was sold out. We were immediately offered three weeks at the Huntington Hartford Theater in Hollywood during Thanksgiving.

"Would you believe that?" Clooney crowed.

"Of course. We have just been ahead of our time," Rose Marie counseled.

"Do we take it?"

"Of course we take it," said Margaret, the Organizer. "This is very crazy, this kind of success, but it's going to make us big money."

"Then we take it," Rosemary Clooney agreed.

Only Barbara didn't want to continue. Truthfully, she was not quite right for the act. Her material was more contemporary and she stayed a bit apart. One matinee, we looked for her and she wasn't around. When she strolled back, all three of us said, "Where have you been?"

"Out front, watching you," Barbara explained.

We thought she'd been in some kind of accident.

At the end of the week, she went her way, and we went ours, each with the other's blessing.

But now we had to find a fourth. We talked with Connie Haines, Jo Stafford, and Kay Starr. And then Helen O'Connell came into our lives. Here was a true representative of the big-band era. She had become famous as the vocalist with the Jimmy Dorsey Band. I think we chose Helen because she said, "Gee, if I had known I was going to be part of an era, I would have paid more attention." How can you resist someone like that?

Since we had a month or so before the Huntington Hartford engagement, I returned to New York. Riding high, feeling good about the success of *4 Girls 4*, feeling even better about the future, I was ready to celebrate.

One night in November, just before returning to Los Angeles, I went with Dr. Jody Wemberly, a friend of mine, to Ted Hook's Backstage. It was the kind of place I love, where someone is always playing good piano. Both the stars and the gypsies hung out there after the theater. Ted made sure that a lampshade with your name on it miraculously appeared at your table before you sat down. He made you feel you were the most important person in the world. The trick of it was, he made everyone feel that way, by introducing everyone from the floor.

On this particular night, after he had made some very flattering remarks about me on mike, he said some words I didn't hear about a young good-looking blond man sitting across the room from me. I heard the name Jack Wrangler. The young man stood up, smiled, and bowed. I applauded and thought, My, he's attractive, and thought no more about it. Then he started to wave to me from across the room. I waved back. I thought, Do I know him? I think I would have remembered him. Yes, I definitely would have remembered him. But then he came across to my table.

"Hi," he began. "I thought, since Ted introduced us both . . ."

"Sit down," I said grandly.

"I've been sitting across the room, listening to that wonderful voice of yours and watching you—and you are everything New York should be."

"Just what do you do?" I asked. It wasn't enough that he was young, good-looking, evidently funny, but he also had a way with words. At least, he got right to this 1 Girl 1.

"I'm an actor," he said. "Jack Wrangler. . . ."

The name didn't mean anything to me, but it sounded as though it should.

"Where are you playing now? Or are you?"

"Oh, yes. I'm on Fourteenth Street."

It seemed an odd place for a theater. But then New York is full of odd places.

"I'd love to come to see you."

He seemed amazed. "You would? If you could tell me when you're coming, I'll have the stage manager set aside some tickets."

"Well, how about Friday?"

Friday would be fine. My friend, Dr. Wemberly, and I would be going on Friday. At this point Ted Hook came by.

"We're going to see Jack's show Friday night," I announced. Ted seemed a trifle taken aback, but he soon recovered.

"I wouldn't miss this for the world," he said to Jack. "How about two more seats?"

Jack wrote the names on a piece of paper, and we said good-night. After Jack left, Ted looked at me.

"You do know who he is, don't you? He's one of the leading gay porn stars in the country. I hope you know what you're getting into."

"Well, in that case, maybe I should bring a girl friend," I said. Now, that made absolutely no sense at all, and to tell you the truth, I didn't know what I was getting into. I had only seen two pornographic movies, one of them written by a friend, neither one of them gay. But I didn't care. I was having a wonderful time. And I pride myself on being inquisitive about everything. And so it was that we ventured (a girl friend, Susie McKusker, having joined us) down to the Jewel Theater on Fourteenth Street to see Jack Wrangler's performance.

The theater was all by itself; the neighborhood was quite murky and deserted at night. Ah yes, but this was Adventure. The marquee was lit and the lobby was filled with men. Young men in jeans and older men in business suits. Several nodded to me; several more stared. But I'm used to that. Lots of people know me. I have a reputation for going everywhere—to art-gallery openings, restaurants, nightclubs. Why not to the Jewel Theater?

We were ushered inside. The theater was small, and it was not attractive. We were shown our seats, an island of couples in a sea of gentlemen. The lights went down and Jack appeared onstage, dressed in jeans and a lumberjack shirt. He looked very boyish. I got the impression of Huck Finn describing the vicissitudes of making pornographic films. I was right. He did have a terrific sense of humor.

"He's very funny, he should be on the stage," I whispered to Ted Hook.

"Margaret, he is on the stage," Ted reminded me.

"No. You know what I mean. Not this stage. A *stage* stage."

At that moment, music that sounded like *Daphnis and Chloé* (and later proved to be) wafted out from the wings. Jack began to describe being in the great out-of-doors and how it turned him on. As he talked, he began very slowly to take off his clothes. Mentioning the heat of the sun on his body, he began to move slowly, sinuously. The effect was like a slow-motion ballet. The music pulsated and so did he. Hypnotically, rhythmically, he doffed shirt, pants. Then, as the music crescendoed, he turned his back to the audience and, simulating an orgasm, ended with a great sexual cry.

I am never at a loss for words. But this time, it was close.

"My word," I said. "He's very good, but what is he doing here?"

Perhaps Jack was wondering the same about me. Dressed in a burgundy robe, he stepped to the front of the stage and, smiling, announced to the audience, "There's someone I want you to meet. I would like to present a lady with more balls than I have—Miss Margaret Whiting."

I rose to acknowledge the applause. To my amazement, the audience rose with me. A standing ovation! And all I had done was just *be* there.

Afterward, outside the theater, Jack asked if he could see me again. I gave him my number, which he promptly lost, so he had to ask Ted Hook for it. A week later, I found myself sitting, a bit bemused, in the library of my apartment with Jack stretched out on the floor by my feet, relating his early childhood in Los Angeles.

His name was originally Stillman. I knew his family; his father, Robert Stillman, was a well-known TV and movie producer. Both Jack and I had attended Elisa Ryan Dancing School—at different times, I might add—and we had both gone to the El Rodeo School. We were both progeny of show business, both California kids. And Jack made me laugh. He told funny stories. He knew a great deal about the theater. So how had he gotten where he was, performing porno on Fourteenth Street? What had happened?

The afternoon passed. I do believe the shadows lengthened, and we continued to talk. I found myself very attracted to him. There was a sweetness, almost a naïveté, that touched me. And then, when things got a shade serious, he would cut any sentiment with a funny remark. Oh Margaret, I said to myself. Don't get caught up with this one. It is going to be very painful. You don't need that. Keep it light, keep it funny, and don't get involved.

"When are you leaving for L.A.?" he asked me.

"Tomorrow."

"Can we have dinner Tuesday night?"

"Where?"

"There."

"Of course. If you want. I didn't know you were leaving New York."

"I was only here for this one engagement. It's been very successful, and now I'm going home."

We did have dinner in Los Angeles on Tuesday.

There were three of us—Jack, Margaret, and Jack's manager, Bob Meyer. Meyer and I instantly disliked each other. He was wondering what I was doing. Was I taking away his meal ticket? He obviously had big plans for Jack. But what kind of plans? Jack's future was something I did not care to contemplate. At the moment he was young, even devil-may-care. But porn? Gay porn? No one had ever succeeded in rising above that. Sylvester Stallone had been in some porn films, straight ones, and not a star, and he had overcome that. There were other examples. But Bob Meyer was grooming his client for porn stardom, whatever that might mean. I really didn't want to get involved.

Jack took me home, and asked to take me out after the *4 Girls 4* opening on Thursday. I said yes. He kissed me. It was a man kissing me, a sexy, passionate man. And a sweet man. I didn't want to get involved, I didn't want to get involved. I resolved I wouldn't get involved. I got involved.

"You know I'm in love with you," Jack said to me, between kisses.

"No, I hadn't a clue," I managed to say, between kisses.

I really didn't understand any of this. Wasn't this boy supposed to be gay? What was he doing being attracted to a woman? What was he doing with his manager? What was *I* doing, being attracted to Jack? I said to myself, Let it happen. Whatever happens will be all right. Go with the flow. Time takes care of everything. A lot of truisms to cover up my confusion.

On my opening day, he sent a picture of himself to my dressing room, accompanied by a huge can of Magic Nuts. In the photograph, Jack was standing bare-chested, his hand deep in his jeans pocket, a come-hither expression on his face.

As I was contemplating his pose, Helen O'Connell came into the dressing room and, spying the can, said, "Where did those nuts come from?"

I dropped the photo. She glanced at it and then made things worse.

"Oh, I meant *those* nuts," she said, pointing to the table. And that made us laugh, and the laughter drew the other two, so that it was like being in a sorority house: Who is he? What kind of fella? Is he sweet? He certainly is good-looking. How did you meet him? What's he like? . . ."

"He's nice," I said. "He's sweet," I added. "You'll meet him tonight. He's taking me out after the show."

"The show!" we all said in unison. This was opening night, and we were behaving like kids at a pajama party. Everyone fled to their own quarters.

Overture time. Frankie Ortega had put together our signature tunes: "Tangerine" for Helen, "Come on-a My House" for Rosie, "Rose-Marie" for Rose Marie, and—what else?—"Moonlight in Vermont" for me. Audience enthusiasm mounted with each moment of recognition; word had got around town that *4 Girls 4* was something special. Lucille Ball was out there, as were Milton Berle, the Bob Hopes, and Danny and Marlo Thomas. They were ready for us.

And boy, were we ready for them. We just swung into everything. Frankie's band was behind us, and each one of us had something special to offer, a particular style, a way with a ballad, a voice that conjured up memories, a kind of excitement that brings the audience to the immediate moment. That night, we had it all. We clowned, we ad-libbed. We had almost fourscore and ten years of professional experience behind us, and we used every bit of it. We just reveled in the moment, and the audience showed its appreciation. Nothing beats the moment when you step forward for bows and the roar of the audience is like a tangible thing, a force. It surrounds you, envelops you, carries you with it. There is nothing like it in television, or in the movies. It comes from live performance. It is a totally personal kind of communication.

Afterward, four stunned, sweating prima donnas looked at one another in amazement, wondering what had happened.

Success had happened. We were an act. We were deluged with offers. The timing was right for *4 Girls 4*. We had survived the war. We had survived the sixties. We had survived rock 'n' roll. We caught the public's imagination. There was a whole audience out there, wondering what had happened to their lives, wondering indeed what had happened to ours. They came to see us and said, "Look at them up there, still having fun, still being crazy and romantic. If they can do it, so can we." We were a tonic for them and, oh, were they a tonic for us. It was a love affair and it was success.

And there was Jack. We were having a nutty, wonderful relationship, cockeyed as only relationships in Hollywood can be. We were often photographed together—Margaret Whiting and Jack Wrangler (sometimes they would add "singer and porn star"). "Older Woman. Younger Man." These weren't always the captions. Indeed most of the time they weren't. But of course, everyone was wondering.

Yes, we were making love, and I want to tell you about it because it was so special. Because Jack was so caring, so gentle, and so strong. Because he really did love me. Of course he was an expert lover. Of course he had a terrific body. An awful lot of people had seen that body on the screen, in action. That had nothing to do with it. The man who made love to me was a different person. He was tender and beautiful and caring, and he needed me, and that made all the difference.

But it was not perfect. The situation was confusing to me. Jack insisted on having dinner every night with his manager. He felt he owed it to Bob. Why? I wondered. What was going on? I asked myself. What was this hold that Bob Meyer had on Jack? I couldn't answer it, and for the time being I couldn't ask Jack. I just accepted it. I was staying at my mother's. Jack would come by after the show. We slept together. Eleanore, having gone through three marriages with me, was very understanding. She liked Jack and thought he had good manners, but questioned his jeans and leather jacket.

Mostly, I questioned nothing; I was having too good a time. We were invited to Paramount to a special screening of *Saturday Night Fever*, the film that catapulted John Travolta to stardom. The movie didn't impress me half as much as a ride, a special tour given Jack and me by one of the studio heads, who drove us around the back lot in an electrified cart, pointing out the spot where Jack's father had produced *Bonanza* and where my father had written "Louise." There we were, Jack and I, whirling around the back lot under the stars, seeing the places where our fathers had worked and succeeded. After that, we went back to the Hartford. I was on fourth that night. And then, after the show, Jack and I walked past a store near Musso and Frank's restaurant where Jack stopped to admire a huge teddy bear in the window. The next day, I had it delivered to his apartment. Okay, that was Hollywood. And so what? *Hooray for Hollywood!*

And yet . . .

And yet . . . Jack and I were together every night. And yet Jack had dinner every night with Bob Meyer. Jack and I were close, very close. And yet he never let me see his apartment. Jack and I were very happy, and were making each other happy.

And yet . . .

It concerned me what was to become of him. I already knew he couldn't get a job, a straight acting job, in Los Angeles. He had gone to see about a couple of them, had been hired, in fact, until they found out about his past. In New York, perhaps, it would be different. In New York, perhaps, he could work in the theater. New York was less a company town, it was more accepting. It was obvious that Jack had no future in Los Angeles, no future as anything but a porn-star stud, and that kind of success lasted maybe twenty minutes. Jack was too good for that, too talented. And I cared too much. Jack could have been anything he wanted to be. I knew what was good about him. I could also see the cracks, the insecurity. He said he had a wonderful family, but somebody had sure kicked him around. Why would anyone as attractive and as talented as he feel so insecure? And it was true Jack was full of insecurities, full of rebellion. And yet . . . he could make me so happy.

And yet . . .

When *4 Girls 4* ended its run at the Hartford, I decided to stay in California for the holidays. New Year's Eve was coming up and I wanted to be with Jack. During Christmas we had a grand time going to all the parties. Then, the night before New Year's Eve, at a party in Malibu, he told me he planned to spend New Year's Eve with Bob Meyer.

I was very quiet.

"I don't think this is going to work out for us," I said.

"I love you," he protested.

"Yes. Well . . . love. That is a word. But when people are in love, they want to be together. And maybe I'm sentimental, but New Year's Eve is an occasion. It's a time I want to share with you. I would think you would want to share it with me."

Jack was looking very little-boyish. Sheepish. I was right. It wouldn't work out. I'd better protect myself.

"I *want* to be with you," he said.

"But you're going to be with him. I am not prepared to understand that, Jack."

"Let's take some champagne out on the beach," he suggested.

Sure, I thought. Sure, but it isn't going to change anything. And it didn't. We walked on the beach. It was a beautiful night. He toasted me with champagne. I drank, but I don't believe I toasted him back. I wished him well, of course. Why not? I loved him. But I was not prepared for the pain. Maybe it was better this way. Again, time had a way of healing all things, yes? I told him I was booked on a cruise for January. I would be flying back from Acapulco to Los Angeles in February.

"I'll meet you at the airport," he promised.

I said nothing. I thought it was better to get away clean. I thought perhaps I had. We left the beach, left the champagne. I spent New Year's Eve packing and thought, Well it was fun. And it only hurt a little.

16

4 Girls 4
(Continued)

Four crazy dames on the road.

Was it fun?

You bet!

Was it a strain?

You bet!

Was it worth it?

You bet!

May 1978. *4 Girls 4* had been booked into the Blue Room at the Fairmont Hotel in New Orleans, our first nightclub booking after the sensational appearance at the Huntington Hartford. It was the first time all four of us were available.

Looking back on it now, I wonder how we ever made it work. We were four such different individuals. Actually, that was one of the attractions of the act. Clooney was Mother Earth, a fantastic cook and a marvelous mother. She had five children, fathered by

José Ferrer—Miguel, Montcita, Maria, Gabriel (now married to Debbie Boone), and Raphael, but life had crowded in on Rosemary. It was a case of too much, too fast. She was trying to take care of the children while balancing two careers, artist and mother. Ferrer suffered from that common Latin disease—*mucho macho infidelito*. In other words, she caught him playing around. Rosie was also devoted to the Kennedy cause. She was (as who wasn't?) greatly upset when John Kennedy was assassinated. She then concentrated on aiding the Robert Kennedy campaign, and was at the Ambassador Hotel the night Kennedy was assassinated. It became too much for her and she cracked. After her breakdown, Bing Crosby persuaded her to accompany him on tour. He literally brought her back to music. She adored him, adored working with him. She was well on the road to recovery when he died, and that was another setback. His death shook her severely. But Rosemary is a very strong woman and she knew, as many of us do, that work was the answer. On the rare occasions when she would refer to that part of her past, she would simply laugh and say, "For several years, just consider that I was under water. . . ." But I knew that demons had pursued her. Some still did. She could act . . . well, strange.

Once, when we were rehearsing a television segment, she walked off and wouldn't talk to me. I said to the stage manager, "What gives? Find out for me." He returned to report that Rosie was angry. Well, even I could see that. I asked her to come into my dressing room. "You're not sincere," Clooney told me. "You wrinkle your nose at me when you sing."

I looked in the mirror. "Well, I don't know what to do about that," I said. "If I wrinkle my nose, I guess I wrinkle my nose. I never thought about it. And I'm not *going* to think about it."

Then, the ridiculousness of the situation became apparent to both of us and we ended up throwing our arms around each other.

If Rosie was Mother Earth, Rose Marie was the salt of the earth, a breezy wonderful woman who had been a child star, who had been performing all her life, who loved going out and having a good time. Very disciplined when it came to her work, socially she seemed to have a very vague sense of time. After the show we would agree to meet for what she called "night lunch." But then she'd start talking to her mother or her agent on the phone. She loved to talk on phones. Hours would pass. Then, at four in the morning, she would breeze into the lobby, where I had been waiting for a couple of hours, smile, and say, "Ready?"

Helen was more difficult for me. She was . . . well I would have called her the Ice Princess, except she had a divine sense of humor. She was a loner, a survivor. In the early days when she was singing with the Jimmy Dorsey Band, she had sent all her money home to support her family. In those days of one-night stands, the band would play until midnight and then get on the bus and sleep till the next stop. Helen would pray that she could sleep late on the bus, because she didn't have the money to pay for breakfast. It was difficult being the only woman on a bus full of men. Clooney had had her sister to travel with her. But Helen had always been alone.

She had gone through two marriages, both of them bad. Her second husband (who subsequently burned to death) evidently beat her. But her first husband, by all accounts, was a nice enough chap, though hardly memorable.

One night, after our show, a man came up to her and said, "Hi, Helen. How are you?"

"Fine, thank you," she said, smiling politely and moving on.

Somebody said, "Helen, isn't that your ex-husband?"

She claims she didn't have her contact lenses in, and that's why she didn't recognize him. Well, it's a possibility. . . .

I don't mean to imply that Helen didn't have a heart. She was devoted to Bob Eberly, her *confrère* in the Dorsey band, and when he was dying, she called constantly and took care of him when she could. She also brought up four fine children. But to me she was reserved, and before the tour was over, Helen and I had lots of problems.

And I—I was the Shopper. There is no counter in any department store, mall, or boutique in these United States that has not felt the weight of the Whiting pocketbook. Also, the other part of my personality began to emerge. I soon became the Resident Pain in the Ass.

The New Orleans engagement was very exciting. The four of us were raring to go, but the experience was semichaotic. "You girls are on your own," Bill Loeb had warned us. We didn't have a stage manager, which meant that each one of us was responsible for getting there on time. It was obvious somebody had to act as stage manager. We met. I volunteered to go on first. Eleanor's daughter, Margaret, would always be punctual. It had been drilled into me from infancy. The Blue Room's maître d' would then phone each of us, so that we would be prepared. Then we got to the second problem, the rest of the order of appearance.

We figured Helen would follow me. Then Rose Marie's comedy (you can't force a comic to go on first; it's like feeding her to the lions). And then we would wow them with Clooney and a sock finale. But Helen wanted to close. To me, it made much better show-business sense for Clooney to close. Helen was a surprise, going on second. She was very funny, and no one expected that. We could use the humor early in the show. For her to follow Rose Marie, the comic, was not nearly so satisfying. By that time, the audience wanted someone who just sang. And Rosemary Clooney just sang. And how she sang! During the New Orleans run, Helen and Clooney alternated closing, but finally, Helen realized the show worked better with Clooney going on last.

Business was fantastic for the two weeks, the engagement ending with an onstage birthday celebration for Clooney and Helen. There is a picture of the four of us around a huge cake, singing "Happy Birthday." We look like four girls away at summer camp.

The mood of euphoria was contagious, as evidenced by a sample of our first press interview. I had just been shopping and had had my wallet stolen. I flew into the press conference in a dither and the dialogue went like this:

MARGARET: . . . and there I am standing on Royal Street, and my wallet is lifted right out of my purse. Can you imagine? I had no money.

ROSE MARIE: . . . All right, all right. I'll loan you a few bucks.

CLOONEY (TO MARGARET): Hey, Helen.

MARGARET: The name is Margaret.

CLOONEY: You lost your wallet. You got no identity. You could be Helen O'Connell.

MARGARET (SINGING): "Pennies in a stream . . ." *That* should tell you who I am.

ROSE MARIE: This press conference is like a marketplace at high noon.

And so on.

But the success of that interview just pointed up what the Resident Pain in the Ass kept saying: "We need a real press agent to call ahead and coordinate interviews. To get us TV coverage. To make up a press book. We need to *work* on this act." (I could hear Eleanore whispering, "This is some wonderful opportunity, don't blow it.")

And the rest of the girls would look at the Pain in the Ass and say, "Yes, Margaret, that is a wonderful, *wonderful* idea. Did you know there was a sale on at Neiman-Marcus?"

Still, I kept thinking: The audience is saying, "We love you. We love the camaraderie. We love you four separate women. We love the fact that you sing together." But sooner or later, I could see we would need better publicity pictures, new costumes, some new routines, some material. We had the opportunity to be *extraordinary*. Maybe even go to Broadway.

When I expressed this opinion to Bill Loeb, who not only had created the idea but was also one of the partners, he agreed. But the others felt it was up to Loeb and his partner Bill Weems, or the theaters, to make the investment in publicity. These ladies were very practical. They had been in show business a long time, and I had to respect their common sense. It wasn't as though we were four millionaire playgirls. In fact, that was part of the charm of the act. We were all coming back. We were all working women. We had all had down times, and were headed back up.

Still, the Resident Pain in the Ass persisted.

"We need costumes! Press! Pictures!" I cried.

Clooney fixed me with her eye.

"Margaret, the act is fine."

"Yes," I retorted. "For summer stock."

It was hard to argue with success, and that we were having. So, no press agent. Still, the Resident Pain in the Ass didn't give up.

During the run in New Orleans, *New York* magazine sent down a writer, Sidney Zion, to interview us. Sidney arrived and started to go to work; he did a story on Helen, on me, on Rose Marie, and on Clooney. He was mad for Clooney. And we were all mad for him. This was to be a marvelous press break. After the completion of the run in New Orleans, we were supposed to go to Houston for an engagement. However, the theater folded, and we were left with two open days.

I had been approached by the Savannah Civic Center to perform at the dedication of the Johnny Mercer Theater. I suggested that *4 Girls 4* go. We all had some link to Johnny. Clooney had sung all of his songs, and had a big hit with "Come Rain or Come Shine." Rose Marie had appeared in his musical *Top Banana*. Helen had sung "Tangerine" in Johnny's movie *The Fleet's In*. We all thought it was a great idea.

We hit Savannah like a hurricane. Sidney Zion came along with the photographer. We had a great time, seeing the sights, and performing on Sunday night. The mayor of Savannah made the introductions. Gerald Marks, from ASCAP, and Hollywood scriptwriter Hal Kanter, who was originally from Savannah, put the whole thing together. We were joined by songwriter Sammy Fain and we made a memorable dedication. The order was: Helen, Rose Marie, and intermission, followed by Rosemary. They put me on last, because I had known him the best. Helen was very sweet then. She relinquished "I Remember You" so I could sing it in my reminiscence of the man I had met when I was seven, whose advice to me had been "Grow up, kid."

Of course, in the back of my mind was the idea that Sidney Zion's story would be a terrific press break. But Zion left *New York* magazine for the *New York Times*, and by the time the story appeared, there was a picture of Frank Sinatra on the cover and the story was about bringing back the big bands. It was two years later and it was a good story, but it wasn't *our* story.

Jimmy Nederlander, who owned a string of theaters across the country, had booked us into his Fox Theater in San Diego. It was suggested to us that this was kind of a trial booking. If business warranted, he might be interested in booking us for a Broadway run. This, of course, I found very exciting. I immediately thought of directors—Tommy Tune, Joe Layton, Michael Bennett—who could take a look at us and tell us how to shape the material into a theatrical production, as opposed to an "act." Shirley MacLaine had just wowed them on Broadway with an absolutely exciting presentation, which had all the show-business savvy that was Broadway at its best. My Lord, there were so many possibilities with our four basic characters. A television series. Broadway. I dreamed on happily.

San Diego was a bit of a shock. We did not do so well there. The reviews were fine, but the people did not flock to see us. This time, the publicity work was handled as a routine job through the theater and was not effective. It seemed to prove my point, that we needed our own staff, mainly a publicist, somebody to work for *us*. However, we didn't have time to dwell on the lack of business. We were headed for the Fairmont in San Francisco. The only damage done in San Diego was that we never heard from Jimmy Nederlander again.

But San Francisco was another story. In all immodesty, we *owned* that town. We were contracted to perform two shows a night. But the response to us was so great that we responded in turn, and that second show didn't let out until three in the morning. Rose Marie's "night lunch" turned into "dawn dinner." I still remember leaving the hotel one morning about 5:00 A.M. and watching the sun hit the peaks across the Bay, watching the fog rolling in, and smelling the air that has such a pungent mixture of salt, eucalyptus, and flowers. Herb Caen, the columnist, noted that he caught us one morning, "Rosemary Clooney and Margaret Whiting, walking arm-in-arm, singing 'It's Delightful, It's Delovely.' "

And it was. The hotel had to hire extra waiters to take care of all the customers. Busboys sent their kids through college from the money they made on that one engagement. And we lived in a state of total euphoria. Or almost.

There were disagreements. Before the opening, television cameras had come in to film our rehearsals. Helen was adamant.

"No pictures during rehearsals," she said. "I thought we agreed on that."

"What difference does it make?" we asked.

"I've got my hair in curlers," she said.

"So?"

"I don't have my lenses in. I'm here to make sure the band knows the charts."

"Well, we're all here for that."

"It's no good for the image," she said, shaking her head. "People shouldn't see us in any light but the best." And she was probably right. But, at the time, I just saw it as another missed press opportunity.

At this point, that Resident Pain in the Ass was in very good form.

"We need a number," I kept saying. "We need some kind of number that explains who each one of us is, and what we're doing together."

"You're right," the other three agreed hastily. "Take care of it." So, while we were in San Francisco, I had Bill Loeb contact Billy Barnes (at Clooney's suggestion, because Billy was a friend) to see the show and write us a number. He was responsible for the long-running and very funny Billy Barnes Revues. Billy met with the four of us and said, "I know exactly what you need" and returned to Los Angeles. About a week later, he came back with the material. We read it excitedly and then with growing disappointment. We could tell it wasn't right. He hadn't caught the spirit of us. Maybe we hadn't explained fully what we wanted. We asked him if he would rewrite it, and he seemed willing. However, a day or so later, we got a call from his agent, who put it on a "take it or leave it" basis. So, unfortunately, we had to leave it.

Undaunted, I had dinner one evening with a friend of mine, Tom Hatton, and broached the subject.

"That's true," I agreed. "Do you think maybe . . . ?"

"What? I could write you a piece of material?"

"Well, I wouldn't want to offend Billy."

"I'll call him up. I don't think there'll be any problem. Maybe he just couldn't get a handle on it. So, what are you doing about costumes?" he asked, changing the subject.

"Well, we each bring our own in. . . ."

"Mmm," he said. "You need some definition. Organization.

Someone to coordinate your four styles. But all in the same color."

"Like green," I said.

"Or red," he suggested. "Why don't you get a designer—"

"Pete Menefee," I said.

"He's very good."

The girls were agreeable. "Take care of it," they said. So I called Pete. Oh, Eleanore's daughter was *functioning* like crazy. Before the end of the engagement, Tom came up with a nice set of lyrics that did exactly what was wanted. Since I was leaving to go back to New York, I decided to take it to John Meyer to set musically. And Menefee had sketched some outfits for me, including a red sequined gown that I thought was exquisite. Before leaving, I showed the girls the sketches.

"This is what Pete designed for me," I explained to Helen. "But he could do something for each one of us. I just think there should be some color coordination. Like red."

"Perfect," said Helen. "I can get something just like it."

"I mean, you don't have to use Pete," I explained, unnecessarily.

Rose Marie was just as amenable. "I know just what you mean," she said, examining the sketches. "And I know just where to pick one up."

Rosie, I remember, was in the hospital, and I went there to show her the designs. She was surrounded by her whole family; it was a very crowded hospital room. The whole family responded with enthusiasm, as did Rosie.

"Of course, you don't have to use Pete," I repeated. "Edith Head or Jean Louis—"

Rosie cut me off. "Wonderful!" The family was thrilled.

I left for New York, feeling triumphant. I had really accomplished something. Oh, Eleanore, as always, your advice was right. Stick to it, and you will succeed! I called Pete and told him to run me up my little finale number, and it came out a gorgeous affair. I felt glamorous and loved and wanted. I couldn't wait until I could see the four of us, triumphant in our gowns, performing our wonderful finale.

And when the time came, the first night that we all appeared—it was in Phoenix, as I recall—it was a stunning moment! Mere words cannot describe the effect.

Picture the Marx Brothers in drag.

I looked at my three colleagues, my friends, my pals. Actually, Rosie's gown, designed by Jean Louis, was beautiful. But Rose Marie! Rose Marie looked like she had grabbed something off the rack. It was red, all right, and with sequins. However, it was the wrong red, a tomato red. Then I spied Helen. She was wearing a pants suit. There's nothing wrong with a pants suit, but it looked so informal against our gowns. And it looked practically orange. To the audience, I suppose it looked all right, but compared to my expectations . . .

This cannot be, I thought, as we smiled and clowned our way through the finale. And thank heavens, it was not to be. Whatever our differences, we certainly did realize when something was not right. Helen finally got herself an organza confection from Jimmy Galanos that looked superb. And Rose Marie abandoned her tomato-red number. Now that I look back at pictures taken at the time, we ended up looking terribly fashionable, and terribly attractive. But not without a struggle.

In the beginning of November, we were booked into the Music Hall in my home town, Detroit. I was thrilled. It gave me a chance to visit with my sister, Barbara, and her husband, Gail. We were going to be royally entertained during our stay. Johnny Meyer phoned to say he had finished the special number. I was delighted and arranged for Tex Arnold, my regular accompanist, to bring it out with him when he came to Detroit to substitute for Frankie Ortega, who had a booking conflict.

So, *4 Girls 4* arrived in Detroit, where we proceeded to break every house record. Every night was New Year's Eve. Every night, the limousines waited at the stage door, purring with luxury, ready to take us to yet another party. After the opening show, we had a party onstage, with marvelous food, particularly some magnificent honey hams. Both the great cooks in the group, Rose Marie and Rosie Clooney, raved about the hams, so much so that Barbara offered to find out where they came from. Rosie thanked her gratefully.

Two or three days later, Tex arrived in town. That evening, Frankie conducted while Tex played the show in the pit, so he could get the feel of things. Afterward, I made an announcement.

"Listen, everybody. Tex has brought out the new number. *The* number. Before we all go out, I'd like you all to listen to it."

"But the limousines are waiting," somebody said.

"Let them wait," I said grandly. "This has been a long time coming."

So, while the limos throbbed outside, everyone, including Barbara and her husband, stood onstage while Tex and I performed the number.

The response was deafening.

CLOONEY: Nice. . . . It'll work. . . . Terrific. . . . Barbara, did you ever find out where I can get those hams?

ROSE MARIE: The number needs more laughs.

HELEN: There should be some harmony. We got to sing harmony.

FRANKIE ORTEGA: Don't worry. I'll fix it when I get back.

After which, they all swept out to those throbbing limos. To say I was crushed was to tell the truth. I found myself standing onstage crying terrible tears of frustration. I was mad and I was tired. And I had worked *so* hard. And to get this kind of dismissal?

It sounds silly now, and maybe I picked a bad time to present the material, but I thought their reaction was unthinking and callous. So I stood there and cried my eyes out. That was so unlike me. And then, never one to spoil a party, I put on my party face and went to join them.

We did try the number in Dallas. We did it once, and then a second time. We broke it in and added our own bits and pieces until it developed into a first-rate piece of material.

We performed together for the next couple of years. Fortunately, we had our separate careers, so we weren't spending all that time together on the road. The time we did spend was exciting. In a way, we were like a circus family. Friends, children, lovers, agents, musicians—everyone passed through. And as I said, just being a celebrity makes the whole world a small town. Everybody knows who you are, what you have done, what you are doing, who you're involved with romantically. So there's no such thing as being a stranger in a strange town, not for long anyway.

But it seemed to me that somewhere we had passed up the chance for greatness. There was a time, with the first inspiration that brought us together, when we could have gone anywhere. But, after a year or two, we had become a very good nightclub act, a wonderful attraction for the tents and the tonier hotel rooms. There were worlds we had not conquered yet. One was the legitimate theater. The second was television. And the third, surprisingly enough, was the gambling circuit. We never did play Vegas, which was a most lucrative market. We did play Tahoe, however, and an engagement in Reno, obtained by a friend of Rose Marie's, which, ironically, resulted in one of several spats that became more and more frequent as time went on.

The cardinal rule in working a gambling casino is Don't interfere with the action. Therefore, all shows were cut to the absolute minimum. We were instructed, in Reno, to shorten each one of our acts to twenty minutes. And we all agreed.

That night, Helen and I were both good little girls and did exactly twenty minutes each. But Rose Marie was the comic. And, as sometimes happens, she got on a roll. The laughs were coming thick and furious, and nothing would have gotten her off that stage. Finally, she did make her exit, flushed with success and smiling, to be greeted by a furious Clooney, waiting to go on, who snapped, "What's the matter? Did you lose your watch? You were on twenty-*nine* minutes!" Poor Rose Marie was totally crushed. Of course, Rosemary was right. We had agreed. And it made Clooney's job all the tougher because she had to cut more.

Yet Rosie was also the first one to stand backstage and rub Rose Marie's neck when she was suffering one of her migraines. There would be times when I would come offstage and see both Helen and

Rosie standing with ice and rubdowns for Rose Marie who, in typical trouper fashion, would sail out onstage when she was introduced, smiling as though nothing were the matter.

Helen and I had minor difficulties. She sometimes seemed oblivious to other people—for instance, during the Terrible Television Trauma: Since I opened the show, I often would wait in the green-room while the other acts went on. And I would watch television. Helen would come in and switch the channel. The first few times this happened, I didn't say anything. But inwardly, I began to seethe. Finally, I had had it. One night, she came in and switched channels. I got up and started screaming, "Ask! Ask!" She looked at me as though I had lost my mind. But she didn't touch the television set again—until the next time.

Before the nightmare began, one episode did cause serious friction between us. Helen was going out with a charming man named Ken. For a time he accompanied us on tour and became friendly with all 4 Girls 4. And then he wasn't with us. I didn't pay much attention.

We were performing in Kansas City that summer, and as sometimes happens when you're appearing at an outdoor theater, we were rained out for a number of performances. There is little enough to do when you are not working, and when it is raining in Kansas City in the summertime, you must make do with what you can. Both Helen and I had worked a club there called Eddie's, an important club on the circuit. A fellow who had been a bartender there now owned his own club. He came backstage and we all went out. He was somebody who was fun to pal around with, and again, it was *raining* that week. As I have said, Helen was a loner, and I never bothered to know whom she was seeing or not seeing. So, one night, I was surprised when Ken called me and wanted to know Rose Marie's birthday, because he was going to send her flowers. I told him, and I was doing my nails, and he continued talking and asked what we were doing. And I did mention that it was *raining* and that we had all been having drinks with this man that both Helen and I had known in the past. Suddenly, he said, "I really love Helen."

"Oh," I said, putting the polish on carefully.

"But it's not working out," he added.

"That's too bad," I replied, perhaps with not too much feeling.

It really wasn't any of my business, and I didn't know anything about it anyway.

Either it stopped raining in Kansas City or we finally left town. Either way, 3 Girls 3 went to Phoenix to prepare for our next engagement, while Helen flew to the Coast on business.

I was out by the pool taking some sun (and probably doing my nails again—that seems to be a major activity on the road) when they brought a phone poolside. I said, "Hello," and this charming Ken was on the other end of the line. We probably talked about the weather, how it *wasn't* raining in Phoenix, and, yes, hadn't it rained in Kansas City, and no, Helen wasn't here, she was in Los Angeles, but, yes, she would be back the following day, and here was Rose Marie, who would like to say hello! I handed the phone to Rose Marie and said, "It's Ken. He wants to talk to you." Then I went back to doing my nails or taking the sun.

The next night, when Helen returned, she brought with her all the frost from the Andes. I had never felt such a chill. She wouldn't even speak to me. She just glared, except when we were onstage. Not being one to let these things pass, I asked Helen what was wrong.

"You're trying to take Ken away!" she said, accusingly. "He called me in Los Angeles. He said you had been calling him all the time."

"Please believe me," I said, "I never called him. I don't even know his last *name*."

"He says you called him. Here and in Kansas City."

"He called *me* in Kansas City, wanting to know Rose Marie's birthday."

Helen countered with a great deal of jealous logic. "Oh? If he wanted to know Rose Marie's birthday, why didn't he call *Her*?" I didn't have an answer for that one. It was obvious Ken had felt this was a way of securing Helen's affections, by making her jealous. I tried explaining this to Helen, but she was having none of it. In desperation, I snatched Rose Marie, who was passing by. "Here, ask her. She'll tell you the truth."

"What? Who?" Rose Marie said. "Oh, yeah. Ken. He sent me flowers. Wasn't that *sweet*?"

Well, it all got ironed out. It was one of those spats that happen when one has been on the road too long.

Nothing really went wrong until Tom Hatton called me.

"What do you think of *Four Boys Four?*" he asked.

"Not much," I replied. "What is this, a joke?"

Tom sounded surprised. "No. Bill Loeb called me up. He wants me to write some material for Gordon MacRae and Billy Daniels—"

"Just hold it right there!" I said. "I got to talk to the girls." I hung up. This news did not make me a happy person, to say the least. First of all, *4 Girls 4* had not come close to achieving its potential. I certainly didn't want to see Loeb and Weems dissipating their energies on a rival group until they had done all they could for us.

During the past year or so, Bill Loeb and Bill Weems, unable to get the best bookings themselves, had hired Marty Kummer, formerly an agent with MCA. This meant that we were paying the two Bills their share, as equal partners in the group, and also paying the booking fees. Either Loeb and Weems should pay the booking fees from their share or get the bookings themselves. We also thought we were an obvious bet for television, but we had had very little television exposure, and we had to put some of that blame on management. Now, with the idea of another group called *4 Boys 4*, it was time to act.

But it was also very difficult. First, the idea of the group had been Bill Loeb's. Second, he had been involved with all of us. He had been Rose Marie's manager, had seen her through the trauma of her husband's death. He remained Rosemary Clooney's manager. She was very loyal to him, since he had stuck by her through all *her* problems. And, wouldn't you know it, Bill and I had been romantically involved many years ago. At this point, the reader may well ask, "Was there *anybody* that Margaret was not involved with at one time or another?" And the answer is yes, Mickey Rooney. And Artie Shaw. We were just Good Friends.

So we 4 Girls 4 held a meeting and decided, after a great deal of discussion, that we would have to confront and perhaps replace Bill Loeb. The next day, however, Clooney had misgivings. She suggested that maybe we should replace *her*, but that made no sense.

I decided to talk to Rosemary. She was sitting under the hair dryer. It was not the best place to hold a conversation. Certainly not the one that followed.

ME: Rosie, I certainly can understand your feelings.

ROSIE: What?

ME: Your feelings.

ROSIE: What about them?

ME: I can understand why you feel a loyalty to Bill. After all, he did stay with you then.

ROSIE: What do you mean "*then*"?

ME: Well, after your breakdown.

ROSIE: Why are you bringing *that* up?

ME: I didn't mean to bring it up. I just wanted to say I understood.

ROSIE: You don't understand anything. And you have no right to . . .

And so it went. Not well. I left her under the dryer. That night backstage she turned her back on me. Rose Marie sprang to my defense. After the show, we all met again. "Rosemary," I said, "I wouldn't hurt you for the world. In fact, I think it's such a crazy idea, replacing you. You are the act. We are. Nothing should get in the way of that. It's just that something has to be done about Bill. . . ." The situation was straightened out, as always. We threw our arms around each other.

And so, Loeb and Bill Weems agreed to do the bookings themselves. And that was the last that was ever heard of *4 Boys 4*. But it was the beginning of a very ugly situation, one that was to get much worse in the months to come.

17

Jack
(Continued)

I have never been one to sit around feeling sorry for myself. I just can't do it. I have to keep working, that's my nature. Thank heavens I had a very full schedule after Jack and I said good-bye.

A friend of mine, Nanci Eisner, had booked me on the *Rotterdam* for a cruise, leaving New York January 7, that went around the world. Actually, I wasn't going that far. I would do two shows for two weeks, get off at Acapulco, fly up to Los Angeles for one day before leaving on the *Q.E. 2* for *another* cruise to Tahiti. If you're going to nurse a broken heart, what better way to do it than in romantic places like Tahiti, Mooréa, Aruba, and the Panama Canal? (Well, maybe not the Panama Canal.) Actually, my heart wasn't broken—oh well, yes it *was*, but I was not about to admit that. So, just say I was hurt, and I was confused. Jack had promised he would meet me at the airport in Los Angeles when I flew back from Acapulco. I wondered if he would. It was terrible. I found I wasn't trusting him. I wasn't trusting his word. With the people I've loved, I've always counted on their telling me the truth. I didn't care what they did, so long as they didn't lie. I can't bear lies.

Nanci was going on the cruise with me. She, Tex Arnold, and I arrived at the *Rotterdam* on an incredibly cold day in January. The wind whistled off the Hudson River right through the drafty pier and right through us. We were bundled up against the weather and supervising the loading of our luggage when a voice cried out, "Miss Moonlight in Vermont! Oh, I'll take special care of you. Where is your music?"

I said to Tex, "This is wonderful. We won't have a worry in the world."

"That's right," the man said. "You just go right on board ship and leave everything to me. *You* get the *special treatment*."

With this kind of welcome, I confided to Nanci, "I'm going to enjoy this."

It got better. They sent champagne. Tex had a bottle, and Nanci and I had a bottle. We cried "bon voyage" to Manhattan, and drank the champagne. Nothing happened. We did not leave port. So we drank some more champagne while still nothing happened. There we stood, gazing at Manhattan, which gazed back at us frostily as we looked out the porthole. After a little *more* champagne, we asked what the problem was.

"Why aren't we leaving?" I asked someone in uniform.

"The oil," he answered.

"Oh," I said. It didn't make sense. "What oil?"

"It is so cold the oil has thickened." The man tipped his hat and left before I could ask him what that meant. I assumed it had something to do with the engine. We were safe in New York harbor, and I figured either the oil would loosen up or we would get off the ship and go home. Either way, it wasn't like being marooned on a desert island. Tex went to his room; Nanci and I stood on the glassed-in aft deck staring out at the city. I found myself telling her about Jack.

"I really don't know what to make of him," I said when I had finished.

"I think he loves you," Nanci said, "and I think it's wonderful."

"Well, he said he'd meet me at the airport."

Nanci nodded. "I know he'll be there."

I wasn't nearly so sure. "I don't even want to think about it," I said. "Listen, out of sight, out of mind. Meanwhile, onward!"

At that moment, we felt the ship lurch. Whatever had happened to the oil had been fixed. We were leaving port.

Onward was right.

I met the cruise director, who gave us a great welcome and then said parenthetically, "Oh and there's a separate table in the dining room for the entertainers and the rest of the crew." *This* was how they were going to treat Miss Moonlight in Vermont? We went down to our staterooms.

"I'm getting off right now," I told Nanci. By now, we were somewhat south of the Statue of Liberty. "I'm not going to be segregated like that."

"They don't mean you," Nanci said.

"And Tex?"

"They don't mean any of us. We have our own table. We can invite anyone we like. The other thing is just a convenience so that you can eat anytime you want, and you can get away from people if you have to." How silly, I thought. There was no one I wished to avoid. . . .

I discovered a kind of desperation on shipboard, based on the chilling realization that one was going to spend a lot of meals dining with people one might end up loathing. That first night out, there was a great jockeying for tables and sittings. Right in front of me, a man, waving a big cigar and wearing a golf cap announced, "This is my ninth trip. I been everywhere. Who are you?" he asked, already emceeing the occasion. Then he squinted at me. "I know you." He pointed with his cigar. "Don't tell me. Just a minute. I've got it." The cigar waved in indecision. "You're . . . *famous!*"

"Evidently not enough," I replied. "I'm Margaret Whiting."

"Of course you are!" he said as if he'd thought of it. "So," he said to us all, "are you having any fun? Are you making any money? Whatcha gonna do?"

What I was going to do was get as far away as possible from him. This proved to be trickier than I thought. There was nothing wrong with this man, but he was the kind you keep dodging. You would go to deck C if you saw him going toward B. You would head to the lounge, but wherever you went, there was no escaping him. And invariably, he would say, "Having any fun? Making any money? Whatcha gonna do?"

I arranged to be at the second sitting, since he was at the first, but that did not mean we had seen the last of each other. The next person I met was a friend, Stanley Geller, who owned a men's shop in New York. We knew each other from Ted Hook's Backstage.

"Come join our table," I said convivially.

"I wish I could," he answered, "but I already promised this other group."

He spent one meal with them and then came over. "Can I join you for the rest of the time?" He sounded desperate.

"Of course," I said. "The more the merrier."

I was growing jollier by the moment. I had good friends, good companions. Then Tex came back to the table and said, "I've been looking for the music. I can't find it anywhere."

"Isn't it with the rest of our things?" I asked with slight panic in my voice. Slight, but controlled. "That man said he would take special care."

"I can't find it," Tex said.

"Well, it has to be on board ship," I said with slightly more panic in my voice. "Doesn't it?"

Tex is always calm in crises. And reassuring. He shrugged doubtfully. "I guess so."

"We *must* find it."

It wasn't a question of just finding the music. First we had to find the man who had taken the music. In uniforms, they all looked alike to me. Nanci, Tex, and I went downstairs and searched through our luggage. No charts. No orchestrations. It looked as if Miss Moonlight in Vermont might be singing whatever Tex could remember. "Oh please, *please*, let the music be here!" I cried.

Suddenly, I saw the man.

"Remember me—Miss Moonlight in Vermont?" I said desperately. He smiled. "Of course."

"Where's my music? You said you'd take special care of it!"

"And I have. It's right under the piano in the theater."

Of course. Why would we have bothered to look in the logical place? The three of us gave a sigh of relief.

One word of advice to all you girl singers out there: Comes a crisis, an emergency—a fire, for instance—grab your gowns, your orchestrations, and your musical conductor—not necessarily in that order—and head for the nearest exit. All three are indispensable.

After that excitement, we were ready for a nightcap.

"Who else is going to entertain?" I asked, and was told there was a duo called Jackie and Roy.

"I love them! They're good friends!" I cried, thinking of the very gifted husband-and-wife singing jazz duo.

This Jackie and Roy, however, turned out to be two very show-bizzy English male singer-hoofers who owned a hotel three hours outside of London. They were very popular on these cruises, and when I met them, I could see why. Roy had a wonderful singing voice and the kind of blond hair that looked as though he had spent the summer sailing his own yacht. Jackie had a divine sense of humor, a great set of teeth, and wonderful sweaters. They were accompanied by their manager, Colin, a fussbudget who wrote their arrangements and played piano for them. He was rather portly and solemn. Colin had taken Jackie out of the coal mines, had put him on stage, teamed him up with Roy, and written their act. It was the kind of act that was perfect for shipboard. It was terribly ingratiating, an English music-hall turn at sea. The boys would be announced and bounce out, singing, "Ain't We Got Fun," and Jackie would flash those thousand teeth, and then they would dance some of those horrible routines with a cane and top hat—but funny—and then they would tell some jokes that were simply *awful*—but funny—and then they would sing to the women in the audience.

The audience adored Jackie and Roy. They had a following who would go on cruises just to be with them. And they knew everybody from Ginger Rogers to Ruby Keeler to Barbara Stanwyck. They had made friends with all the leading ladies. They promptly did so with me. I took one look at those thousand flashing teeth of Jackie's and said to myself, Onward! We had a shipboard romance, or would have, except for Cape Hatteras.

Cruises are wonderfully relaxing, but there is the inevitable storm that occurs as you round Cape Hatteras. It must be the equivalent of going around the South Pole or the Cape of Good Hope, or wherever the *Bounty* went through that caused that mutiny. When it happens, the conditions are simply awful. Furniture slides from one side of the deck to the other. So do the passengers. The bravest of us came down to dinner dressed in evening gowns and sneakers. Ropes were put up everywhere, and it was common to see people inching their way down the corridor as though they were scaling the Matterhorn.

It was on such an evening that Jackie invited me for a drink. First we were in the Lido Bar, where people lurched forward to say hello, and we had a drink or two. The wind rose and the waves rose and the rain fell. And the people disappeared. The crew was busily securing everything that could be secured. From time to time one heard the crash of silver falling, or dishes. But Jackie and I merely chatted through that.

"It seems a bit empty up here. Care to see my digs?" he asked me.

I would care to indeed. We staggered down the corridor, holding on to ropes and then to each other and laughing. We laughed as we watched others trying to keep their dignity and their balance at the same time. We laughed as we tried to navigate the stairs. We kept laughing, and then there I was in his stateroom, just the two of us against the storm. It was very cozy and he kissed me. He almost missed because the ship suddenly pitched to one side, but that was just another giggle. We had another drink and he became more and more romantic. Those teeth, I thought. Has anyone ever been hypnotized by teeth? Seduced dentally? Well, why not? Jackie did seem like fun. We staggered over toward the bed. The ship lurched again and Jackie hit his head.

"Oh dear, are you hurt?" I asked, clutching the sides of the bed.

"No, no, think nothing of it," he said. I lay down as seductively as was possible under the circumstances, my hands still gripping the sides of the bed. Jackie approached. Those teeth. Those divine teeth, urging me on to be bad. Oh Margaret, you little fool. I was breathing heavily. He leaned over. We were as close as two people can get, when he suddenly reared back. I looked at his face. It was ashen.

"What is it?" I asked.

"Oh, it's nothing. Think nothing of it," he said.

"You don't look well," I observed.

"Don't *say* that," he said, heaving, I thought from passion. The ship rose, and *sank* again, tossing me out of the bed. I heaved in turn.

"I'll be right back," he said, vanishing into the bathroom. I found the room spinning around. He returned.

"Where were we?" he asked in a dazed voice. He had loosened his collar. He looked like a man getting over a two-week binge.

"We were on the bed," I reminded him, "but that was long ago."

"I was about to make love to you," he said weakly.

"Don't *say* that!" I repeated his words. Love was the last thing on my mind now.

"I never get sick," he said to me.

"Nor I," I said. "I think I'm a wonderful sailor." We got sick simultaneously then, and, as one, we desperately raced to the bathroom, where we spent the night throwing up and laughing and throwing up again. That was the end of any real romance for that night.

We formed our own clique. The members varied, but essentially we all were interested in the same things and in each other.

What was fascinating to me about ships was that I thought I couldn't stand them. There I was, saying, "What am I going to do all day and all night on this ship except be bored on board?," when suddenly I realized I had a schedule. Everything was done for me. I got up at ten o'clock in the morning, was served my morning coffee, went out on deck, met Jackie and Roy, met Stan, met Nanci and Tex, dodged the Little Old Man, and suddenly it was lunchtime or teatime. And then it was cocktail time. Dinnertime. Showtime. And another day had whizzed by. It was perfect for me, because I really didn't want to think. I certainly didn't want to feel. It was terrific to be occupied with pleasant people. And it was just what I needed.

There was a stop at Aruba.

Nanci, Tex, and I had all been to Aruba many times, so we thought we would stay on board ship while the rest of the passengers made the obligatory tour. Suddenly the little man, sporting his golf cap and a cigar, hurtled around the corner.

"Well, *Margaret*," he cried. "Are you having any fun? Are you making any money? Whatcha gonna *do*?"

"We thought," I said, trying to outguess him, "we'd . . . take a tour around the island. We hired a private little car."

"Wonderful!" he cried, smiling and brandishing the cigar. "We're planning to go ashore ourselves. Except we've seen everything. And been everywhere."

"Oh." I improvised. "But then we discovered we had to rehearse, so we're just going to have lunch on the island and come right back."

"When you gotta work, you gotta work," he said cheerily. "If you want to make your money. See you around the ship."

We thought we had eluded him, but as luck would have it, as we sat down to eat, who should come in and sit down at the next table but You Know Who and his cigar. We smiled wanly, ate up, and hurried back to the ship after lunch, which was just as well. A boatload of native dancers came on board and entertained us, and I'm sure they were more exciting than the duty-free shops. And that comes from your Inveterate Shopper.

The days passed, the nights passed. We went from port to port. In Cartagena, Nanci jokingly said, "Oh, good. Here is where we can bring back some good Colombian pot."

"Don't even joke about it," Jackie warned us.

That was how I discovered there were agents on board ship. They were nice men—I got to meet them later—but customs agents have the right to search your cabin, confiscate any drugs.

"Cartagena! *That's where the sloths come from!*" I cried, dredging up this information from somewhere. And indeed, it was true. We went on shore, and had our pictures taken in front of the grand cathedral with a couple of sloths hanging upside down on sticks. It occurred to me that perhaps they had been smoking a little of the native product.

Colombia was the first country I had visited where one could see armed soldiers in the streets. It was not a comfortable feeling, being in the middle of all that unrest. I was glad to get back to the unreality of shipboard. There I felt relaxed, peaceful. We passed through the Panama Canal and steamed up the Mexican coast, surrounded by sparkling water, dazzling sun, pleasant company.

I avoided thinking about Jack. I had made no effort to contact him, and had given him no way to contact me, although, if he had wanted to, if he had really wanted to, he knew which ship we were on. He could have called. The closer we got to Acapulco (and therefore to Los Angeles and reality), the closer I was to dismissing the entire relationship as a case of delayed adolescence.

In place of real feeling, I substituted a kind of dreamy curiosity about my fellow passengers.

One night I saw the Little Old Man, dressed in yet another dinner jacket. He'd never worn the same one twice. They were Liberace jackets without the fur, just the sequins. And each one was in a different color. There was red. There was a delicate yellow. There was pink.

I went up to the Little Old Man.

"Hello, *Margaret!*" he cried.

"Say, what are you? In show business? I've never seen so many dinner jackets. How many do you have?"

He beamed. "A stateroomful. Come on down and see."

So Nanci and I went. It was true. He had an entire stateroom for his clothes. Thirty-three different evening jackets. One for every night of the month, with a couple left over in case of seasickness. Racks of slacks. He was a floating Saks Fifth Avenue. But only that one golf hat.

I did my shows. Shipboard audiences can be tricky. They have seen everything, and they are neither the youngest crowd in the world nor the most demonstrative. But I had no problems. I sang in two different spots, the last being in front of a giant staircase where I expected Gloria Swanson to descend at any moment.

The response to my shows was good. But the response to Jackie and Roy's shows was ecstatic. I figured, if they're this good on shipboard, they should be sensational on land. So I arranged for Loeb and Weems to present them to a regular audience. But an off-cruise audience looked at them as though they had descended from Mars. "Oh Margaret," Bill Loeb said to me later, "those boys are good. But the material is so dated. They're so *English*. I mean, if they had other material, other songs . . ." He didn't have to go on. The boys were wonderful fun on ship, successful enough to have, in addition to their hotel outside of London, an apartment in Marbella. They are welcomed wherever they go. And Jackie still has the best sweaters and the greatest teeth I have ever seen. But I guess, like some wines, they just didn't travel well. In this case, from ship to shore.

We reached Acapulco, where Nanci, Tex, and I were getting off. Jackie and Roy said good-bye to us. I waved farewell to the man in the golf cap. And he waved his cigar at me. He was going around the world again. But this time he never made it. I heard that he died on board ship later in the cruise. I was sorry to hear that. (But it does bring up a fascinating piece of information. Cruise ships carry twenty or thirty coffins with them—just in case. Now, *that's* something you'll never find out from watching *Love Boat*.)

I was very nervous on the flight to Los Angeles. I looked down. Sapphire swimming pools winked back at me. Hello, Beverly Hills. Will he be there? Why should he be there? He won't be there. We landed and taxied along the airstrip. It seemed to take forever. We disembarked. Walked. It seemed to take forever.

There was a crowd of people waiting for the arriving passengers. Even so, I could have picked him out anywhere, because of all the flowers. He looked like an ambulatory get-well card.

"You're here!" I shouted. I could have been heard in San Francisco very easily.

"I said I would be." He grinned and threw his arms around me.

"I know what you said." I stopped and took inventory. "These are really a *lot* of flowers."

"I always believe in the subtle gesture," he said, and we went off into the sunset, so to speak. For the moment I forgot about Nanci, I forgot about Tex. I forgot about my resolve (if I had any). I only knew Jack had promised to meet me, and he had met me. He did care. I could see that. As long as I could see that, I could take almost anything.

And, I discovered, I was going to have to.

We only had one day before my other luxury cruise, but it was heavenly. We all had a wonderful dinner together—Eleanore, Jack, Tex, Nanci, and I. Then Jack and I had a chance to talk.

"You didn't write," I said.

"I never write. I'm no good at writing," he said. "And . . . I really did have a lot of thinking to do. You're asking a lot of me."

"What am I asking?" I did ask.

"You want me to give up what I'm doing," he said, reading my mind.

"Jack, I just don't see any future in it."

"No future?" He grinned crookedly. "Don't you know there are Jack Wrangler sweatshirts, socks, towels? I am practically a commodity."

"I can't wait to wrap myself in a Wrangler towel," I said.

"This is the only way I can make money," he said more seriously.

"Out here, yes," I agreed. "That's why I think you should come to New York. Look, Jack, you are very talented. You've been a successful director in stock. You can write. You can act. But I know this town. They're not going to give you a chance. New York is different. And I can get Nanci started on getting you auditions. . . ."

"You'll be gone for a week. During that time, I'll make up my mind," he said.

Which was how I took off for Tahiti. Maybe it was my mood, or maybe it was Tahiti, but I found it a cold place. It was colonial French, not romantic, concretized. The romantic island was Mooréa, which was the Pacific paradise it was cracked up to be.

And all this time, in one paradise after another, I found myself thinking, I really love Jack. Perhaps it isn't everything I would want in a relationship, but what is? He needs a lot of understanding, a lot of caring. And I've got to have somebody who fits in with my life, too. I'm not going to marry a shoe salesman and move to San Antonio, Texas. I'm not going to marry. Period. I'm going to do what I want.

We flew back from Tahiti. In the airport in Los Angeles I saw a woman with three small children. I thought, Fifty thousand dollars for this one, fifty thousand for that one. It's a tremendous adjustment to have a child and it takes so much time. I had my child. Thank God I had Debbie. But I didn't want another child. And I felt, I really am a modern woman. Nowadays, I think a lot of women don't want to be bothered by convention for convention's sake. They don't feel they have to have husband, house, children to feel successful about their lives. It takes such a lot of one's life. Such an investment. I think women are happier now that they can adjust their life the way a man can, and I think it's been very tough for men to realize this. But it's going to be much better. We say, "Look, we're partners. I have my space, you have yours. When we're together, it's beautiful. When we're apart, I'm part of you and you of me. That doesn't mean every night when I come home, we have to sit here at dinner, or go away on a two-week vacation with the kids"—that kind of rigidity people have felt. I think it's going to be an easier age for living.

So this was what I thought about when I was away from Jack. And what he thought about was, yes, it was time to experiment. To take the next step. To try for some straight roles. He had some commitments in L.A. that he had to meet. I had the New Orleans engagement of *4 Girls 4.*

But then he would come to New York.

And guess what? We'd take a cruise—Jack, Debbie, and I.

This is hard to write about—it's hard even to think about—because it tends to put either Jack or me in a strange light. But I swore I would tell everything the way I saw it, so I will.

Part of this is funny and part of it is painful. But I guess that's true with every relationship.

This one starts out funny. Funny for me, painful (in fact, excruciating) for Jack.

Before coming to New York, Jack was scheduled to film on location at Lake Shasta. A few days before we were to leave on the cruise, he called me. There was tension in his voice.

"I don't think I can make that cruise with you," he said.

"Why?" I inquired, the frost in my voice chilling the telephone wires for three thousand miles.

"Problems with the picture," he said. I was thinking, What excuse is he going to come up with?

"What kind of problems?" I asked, fascinated.

"It really has to do with the mountain people," he explained.

"What mountain people?"

"Do you know what this movie is about?" he asked, in turn.

"I haven't the foggiest."

"It's called *Summer Heat*."

"Mmm," I said.

"And I am this senator who's crusading to have the water level in the lake raised. . . ."

"Go on," I said. And he did.

"Now, raising the water level is good for the conservation people, but bad for the farmers—the mountain people."

"Aah . . ." I said, wondering what kind of pornographic movie this was. Then I found out.

"So they string me up and then they rape me. You see, symbolically I have raped their lands by raising the water."

"Uh-huh."

"Then, I escape and have to roll down this hill, which is what I did today."

I interrupted him. "Jack, I still don't know why you can't go to Bermuda."

"I have this problem," he said faintly.

"I can't hear you," I said. "You'll have to talk up."

"I have this *problem!*" he fairly shouted over the phone. "The hill I had to roll down—Margaret, you see, I had to roll over and over . . ."

"Yes . . ."

"Naked . . ."

"Yes . . ."

"And the hill was . . . Margaret, I have this terrible rash all over my body. The hill was covered with poison oak."

I tried not to laugh. I mean, an itch is no fun. But in my heart of hearts, I thought, God wants you to stop making these movies.

"Listen, Jack. You come to New York. We'll take care of you."

"We?" he said.

"Debbie and I," I said. "Debbie is coming on the cruise with us."

"Oh. Well, I look awful."

"Never mind," I said blithely. "You come to New York."

He did. And Debbie, Nanci, and I went to the airport to meet him with a banner. Welcome to New York—Jack Wrangler Fan Club!

He looked fine, as long as he kept his clothes on. His face had not rolled down the hill, only his body.

"Jack, this is my daughter, Debbie. Debbie, this is Jack."

"Hi."

"Hi."

Things are off to a *wonderful* start, I thought. Nanci and Jack embraced, and we all went back to my apartment, where Jack was going to live.

I showed him around. "This is the study . . . this is the living room . . . this is our bedroom . . . and this is where Debbie's staying . . ." I said cheerily.

"Debbie is living here?" he asked.

"Well, yes. She broke up with her husband. So she's staying here."

His face was solemn. I thought I ought to give him all the news at once.

"With Carol," I added. Carol was a friend who had just broken up with her boyfriend. The two of them were commiserating with one another in my guest room.

"Ah . . . well . . ." I could see that Jack wished he was back rolling down a hill of poison oak.

"It's not forever," I said. "And tomorrow we're going on a cruise."

That is exactly what we did. The three of us—Jack, Debbie, and I—met Tex Arnold at the pier. The ship was Dutch—the *Rotterdam* again—and very clean.

"This is going to be fun!" I said exuberantly as we walked up the gangplank. This was just a short cruise to Bermuda, not the elegant round-the-world cruise I had just taken. But a cruise is a cruise, I thought then.

I introduced myself to the cruise director. "I'm Margaret Whiting."

"Oh yes, the *entertainer*." He nodded sourly, making me feel that I had stepped up from the wrong side of Forty-second Street.

Not to be daunted, I added, "And *troupe!*," gesturing to Tex, Debbie, and Jack. The cruise director looked at us grimly and left.

"This is going to be *fun!*" I repeated.

"Call for Jack Wrangler. Call for Jack Wrangler . . ." I heard over the ship's loudspeaker.

"A ship-to-shore call already!" I said to Jack. He didn't seem too amused. He went to take the call. I knew who it was from. It had to be Bob Meyer, Jack's manager.

Bob had been Jack's manager (he actually had known the Stillman family for years), but he had also been much more than that. He had fallen in love with Jack, which was frustrating because Jack refused—right from the beginning—to have any physical relationship with him. But Bob had lived an entire fantasy life through Jack. Jack was the attractive man Bob had never been. Bob lived with a great deal of style and he knew every maître d' in California. He had introduced style to the male porn scene, if such a thing is possible. And he had made Jack a star who even had his own line of merchandise—Jack Wrangler gym shorts, towels, sweatshirts. There were photos of Jack in magazines posed with a Rolls-Royce, the "choice of Jack Wrangler." And last, but not least, there were guided tours to San Francisco's netherworld, hosted by Jack Wrangler. Bob had made Jack into a very profitable commodity and he didn't want to lose that. But he also loved Jack, indeed was very possessive of him, and he was determined not to lose that either. So determined, in fact, that he would make this "gangplank" call.

I wondered whether Jack would return on board. In the back of my mind, I knew this scene must have been impossible. Supposing things didn't work out between us, what then? Was he right to burn all his bridges? Probably not. And Jack was caught in the middle of a situation. Early in our relationship, when we had been in Hollywood, Bob had entertained lavishly, one restaurant after another, demonstrating to Jack, and I suppose to me, how well known he was. And then one night, I took them out. I was picking up the check. We went to a very expensive restaurant, and it was "Welcome, Miss Whiting," and "Right this way, Miss Whiting," and there were a number of producers who came over and greeted me. In the middle of the evening, I said to Jack, "Tomorrow we have to go to—"

Bob said to me, "What is this? Fun and games?"

Well, it wasn't going to be that. It wasn't going to be a battle over who was going to pick up the check for Jack, since I knew Jack wanted to pick up his own check in life. And I wasn't going to tell him whom he should be with, or what he should do. He was going to have to come to that decision himself.

So I wondered whether he would come back on board ship.

He did.

"You're here," I said.

"I am," he replied. "It was Bob Meyer. He had a movie for me. I turned it down. I said it was important for me to stay in New York now."

"Oh? He can't have liked that."

"He didn't."

We went to our stateroom. Debbie had her own, Tex had his, and Jack and I had ours. Nice. Neat. Clean.

We were due to have cocktails on deck at seven-thirty. Dinner was at eight-thirty, the second sitting.

At eight o'clock, Jack was still getting ready.

"You look fine," I said, as he gazed in the mirror.

"No, I don't. I want to look perfect."

"We'll miss the cocktail hour."

"Oh, Margaret, nothing starts on time."

Little did he know. Those schedules on shipboard are followed like clockwork.

At eight-twenty, I reassured him. "You really look okay."

I wouldn't have minded if he was gazing at himself in the mirror with admiration, but he was looking with such concern.

"You go on up. I'll be right there."

He arrived at nine-thirty. Dinner was almost over. He had missed it, but it didn't seem to bother him. When he was with the group, he was wonderful—charming and witty. Nobody noticed any insecurity.

The next morning we got up.

"I hope there's a gym on board," he said. "I can feel myself getting out of shape."

"I'm sure there is," I said, getting ready to go out on deck. "Ask the cruise director."

"I will, as soon as I get dressed." And there he was again, in front of the mirror, adjusting his hair. *Fluff, fluff, fluff.* I thought, Somebody must have kicked him really hard for him to feel this way.

"No gym," he said when he met me on deck.

"That's impossible. There's always a gym on a ship."

"It's not really adequate. It's just a couple of machines and a sauna."

I found that wasn't the only thing that didn't work. It was time to rehearse with the band. I remembered the superslick English band that had been on the *Q.E. 2* a few months before. What a pleasure they had been. It was like singing with velvet behind me. I was anticipating such enjoyment.

"When do I rehearse with the band?" I asked the cruise director, who was to coordinate such matters.

"I haven't the slightest idea," he replied, pure English frost. I felt helpless. Jack didn't.

"She's got to rehearse. Get them together."

The cruise director actually pouted, but he did call a rehearsal. Tex, who had already run down the charts with the band, looked a little pale. But perhaps it was due to the difference in color. This band was 100 percent Filipino.

"Iwakuni," I mumbled to myself under my breath.

"What?" Jack said.

"Nothing." What had come to my mind was a tour for the troops I had taken just after the war. It was the kind of tour, from base to base and up and down river, where you never knew what to expect, either from audience or orchestra. At Iwakuni, I started to sing, finished the song, and heard a kind of *thump, thump, thump* behind me. The band, not accustomed to reading music, had mistaken the repeat signs, and had just started over. There was nothing for me to do but sit down and wait for them to finish. I suspected such might be the case here.

We started the rehearsal. The cacophony was incredible.

"Could you ask them to tune up?" I asked Tex.

"How do I ask them?" he replied.

"Well, don't they speak English?"

"Very little."

"Well, what do they speak?" I wanted to know.

It seemed they spoke Tagalog. Nobody in our group spoke Tagalog. Jack jumped in as interpreter. He somehow managed to have them all hit the same note at the same time. They thought that was a nice game. The variances in pitch were exquisite. We pushed onward.

It seemed none of them could read music either, but they were terribly eager to play. We stripped their work down to a few chords for openings and closings, beginnings and endings.

The sound was so curious I looked at the instruments. They were regular instruments such as saxophones and brass. But they *sounded* like gamelans. They *sounded* like Chinese New Year. It was most extraordinary.

Then I discovered that the cruise director was going to run the lights.

"What will this performance be like?" I whispered to Jack.

"Don't worry. It'll be all right. I'll be right with him, and if he doesn't do it right, I'll run the lights myself." That did make me feel more secure. Jack had had experience both as actor and director. That stood him in good stead now. He smiled an engaging smile at the cruise director, who looked at him frostily.

Meanwhile, we were speeding south. The show was announced. I prepared for the evening, got dressed, met Tex. Jack stationed himself by the spotlight. The houselights dimmed to black. I was announced. The Filipino band struck up its overture. I say "its" because it was surely nothing I had ever heard before. I walked out to applause, saw to my relief that Tex was at the piano. He played a reassuring chord, and I began the first song, which, as it happened, was "Here I Go Again." I had gotten no further than the first phrase when I felt an irresistible desire to move all the way to the right. I did just that. Fortunately, the microphone slid right along with me. The spotlight did not. I continued singing. Then I felt an irresistible desire to move left, I did that too. By this time, the spotlight had found me on the right. Somehow it followed me in my trip to the left.

"Here I go again . . ."

Shift right . . .

"Here I go again . . ."

Shift left . . .

The entire ship was rolling. Just my luck. We had reached Cape Hatteras again. I continued singing, sliding from side to side, accompanied by my Filipino band, whose crashing coincided with the crashing of glassware and cutlery. And during all of this, I was aware that the spotlight followed me wherever I happened to slide.

After the performance was over, I lurched along to congratulate the cruise director, whom I had badly misjudged. He was phenomenal, not to have missed me once! Instead, I found Smiling Jack.

"Pretty good for a first time around, right?" he said.

"Incredible! Let me thank the man."

"Oh, well, he got a little seasick. He's gone to his cabin."

Jack never admitted it, but I am sure he was the one running the lights.

We would allow nothing to mar our fun. Debbie caught her hand in a door and we had to go to the ship's physician, but that became an experience too. We all had a good time, and then, when we arrived in Bermuda, we all went our separate ways, using the ship as our hotel.

Terry Brennan and his wife, friends of mine who lived in Bermuda, were anxious for Debbie to meet their son. That took care of her. Tex had his own friends. That took care of him. And Jack found a gym in a renovated church. So that took care of his mornings. I took my exercise in shopping. Then Jack and I would spend the afternoons on the beach. Bermuda is lovely and mild—an English countryside, but with good weather—and a sweetness in the air that is a mixture of roses and the sea. It is very conducive to romance.

Jack and I made love in the stateroom one balmy afternoon, where I made the discovery.

"So that's Love in the Afternoon," I said. "It's better than the movie."

And after three days it was back to the salt mines. Another day-and-a-half sail. Another performance with the Filipino band and the glowering British cruise director. One more Cape Hatteras. And then we were home.

That was a very happy summer for me. I had bookings with *4 Girls 4* that stretched from New England to San Francisco. Jack visited me on weekends when we were out of town. In the meantime, he was concentrating on getting work in New York. Nanci, as promised, got him several interviews and arranged for him to become a member of the Meat and Potatoes Group, which performed theatrical workshops. All this was great. The idea was for Jack to get an agent, and this was a good way to be seen. He stayed in the apartment with Debbie and Carol, and I thought everything was wonderful.

By now, it must be obvious that I believe everything is wonderful until catastrophe occurs. I was so wrapped up in my own work that I was not aware of the friction between Jack and Debbie. And Jack went out of his way not to let me know. Evidently, Debbie had decided that Jack was no good for me (the wonderful things kids do to protect their parents!), and she didn't hesitate to tell him that I had many men in my life, that he was just another one, and the moment I was bored with him, out he would go. Tell this to a man who already spends an hour in front of the mirror before he goes out, and you do not have a secure male. Since he had so many doubts already about our relationship working out, this kind of information sent him right to the telephone to call Bob Meyer. So while I was humming away through a happy summer, this is what Jack was facing. He had moved to a new city (*the* city for great rejection), he was trying to advance a career as an actor (never easy under the best of circumstances), he was trying to make new friends, he was being told that the relationship he had chosen would never work out, and he wasn't making any money. He was, shall we say, very, very nervous.

I came back after the summer, and things were humming in our apartment. We were all humming. There was a great deal of humming going on. Margaret humming happily, Jack nervously, and Debbie humming like a hornet.

MARGARET: Jack, what shall we do tonight? Hum Hum Hum?
JACK: We could take in a movie. . . . Hmmm, hmm, ahem . . .
DEBBIE: Oh, X-rated? . . . Hmmmmmmmmmmmmmmmmmm.

So I remained oblivious and Jack hid things from me. I knew, however, how difficult it was to make money in the acting business. I knew that Nanci, who was trying to erase Jack's image as a male porn star, had set up appointments for him to make straight adult movies, just so that he could make some money. Due to her efforts, he had just completed one called *Misbehaving*, where he played a maître d' in a restaurant who meets a waitress—*boom*, instant attraction—and they make love on a butcher block in the kitchen. *That* made me a little nervous, but only because I eat out a lot. Therefore, it did not surprise me, at the end of October, when Jack announced that he was going on a photo call for a magazine the last three nights of October.

"What kind of shoot?" I asked him.

"It's two guys and two girls taking in the sights of New York. Central Park. The kitchen of some restaurant. A club in the Village. They're late-night things. I won't be home until early in the morning."

"Well, that's terrific. I hope you're making good money."

"Yes, the money's fine."

I made plans for those three evenings. On the last one, which was Halloween, I went out with Nanci Eisner and my friend Stanley Geller (from the first *Rotterdam* cruise), and his partner, Herb Gray. During the evening, Stanley asked about Jack. I told them he was out on a photo call for a spread in some magazine.

Nanci said, "Gee, I had the funniest thing happen. Somebody called up and told me Jack was appearing at a gay nightclub. You know, that made me very upset, because I've been trying to change that image."

"Well, he's not at a nightclub," I said.

"They even said it was advertised," Nanci continued. She wouldn't let it alone. Finally, she looked in the ads of some Village paper. There was some place, The Loft or the Nest, that carried Jack's name.

"I'm going to call up," Nanci said. She left me sitting with Stan and Herb. I started collecting all the crumbs of bread on the table with a knife, very carefully.

"There's a very good explanation . . . ." Herb started to say.

". . . or a good reason," Stan finished for him.

"Oh, I know, I know," I said, hastily, concentrating on the crumbs and the knife. "Nanci gets upset. . . ."

Nanci came back and sat down.

"Well, what happened?" I said.

"Whoever answered the phone was Greek. I said, 'Is Jack Wrangler appearing there?' And he said, 'Who wants to know?' and I said, 'I do.' And he said, 'Well, I won't tell you.' And I said, 'Why?' and *he* said, 'Because I was told that if a woman called up I shouldn't tell you.' "

Nanci stopped, then looked at me. "You're so calm about this," she commented.

"Yes, I am. If it's true, it's true, and I'll have to talk to him about it. But I'm not going to scream and carry on."

"Well, I *am*. He promised me he wouldn't do this anymore! I've been trying to line things up for him! I'm acting as his agent. How does that make me look?"

Stan hoped to put things in perspective. "Margaret, stay calm."

"I *am* calm."

"I know he loves you very much, whatever he was doing. Be very careful how you approach this . . ."

"I *will*, I will."

When Jack got home that night, I asked him, "How was the photo session?" And when he said, "Fine," I said, "We have to talk."

Jack claims that I had his bags packed and at the door when he came in. He claims that I was very sweet and I had packed *everything* he owned, including the gifts I had given him, and put them all tidily by the door. I don't remember this, perhaps I did. I do remember saying, "You don't have to lie to me. . . ."

"I don't want to lie to you."

"You told me you were leaving tomorrow for Washington. To appear in a theater. What kind of theater?"

"All right. Yes, it's a porn house. And from there I'm supposed to go to Pittsburgh to a nightclub and from there to the Coast to do a movie. . . ."

"And Bob Meyer set these all up?"

"Yes. I told him I needed the money."

"You could have told me."

"I didn't know how. But, look, now you know, I'm going to call Bob. I'm going to tell him I'm not going to the Coast."

He went into the bedroom and picked up the phone. I could hear him talking to Meyer.

". . . and Margaret knows everything about the theater. She knows about the nightclub. She's not very happy, but I love her and I'm going to stay here, after I honor these commitments. . . . I'm leaving tomorrow morning on the ten o'clock train. . . ."

When he hung up the phone, I said to Jack, "You have to do what you do. I don't like it. But don't hide anything from me. Tell me the truth from now on."

Jack went to Washington the next day. That afternoon Bob Meyer called to ask when Jack was leaving.

"He's already gone. He told you last night on the phone that he was taking the ten o'clock train."

"I didn't talk to him last night."

"I was right here in the room when he called you and said he wasn't going to Los Angeles."

"He never called me."

I felt my face flush. Meyer could have been lying. But what good would it have done? It wasn't Meyer who was lying.

"Margaret, Jack's a very sick boy," Meyer said, and then hung up. I stood there for some time, feeling nothing. I didn't feel anger, I didn't feel the hurt. I was mostly dazed. I walked around like that all day, and that evening I was to have dinner with Marvin Poons of Actors Equity, a friend of Jack's. He asked how we were. I didn't tell him everything, but I said, "We're having some problems. I've wanted Jack to get out of that male porn business."

"Well, he should," Poons agreed. "He's a talented actor, a talented director. But this is so stupid. It's just his goddamned ego. He just got knocked around somewhere in his youth, and now he's using this. It's some kind of gratification, but it's so silly. He's not showing what he can do. He's directed for me."

"I can't take the lying," I said.

"I know that he loves you," Marvin declared. "And I know that he wouldn't do anything to hurt you. But he's caught in a bind."

"If it doesn't work out, then it won't work out," I said.

"It'll work out. Maybe when he comes back, he should have a place of his own. He may need some time. He's forming a new life."

"Maybe you're right," I said dully.

Jack called that night. He had made no attempt to cover his tracks. He could have called Bob Meyer and said what he had done. He could have done anything, but he wanted to be found out. I confronted him with this.

"I had dinner with Marvin," I told him, "and he made me see things more objectively. But Jack, that was an unconscionable thing to do. I'm not going to hang up the phone and say this is the end, because I care for you too much, and I think you care for me. But I can't have any rest. I can't ever believe you."

"I love you."

"Yes. Well, you're going to have to earn my trust again."

"Well, I've got something terrible to tell you. They asked me to extend the engagement in Pittsburgh over the weekend. . . ."

"And you said you would. Well, I won't try to stop you. And I'm glad you could tell me the truth about that."

"I really want this to work out for us," he said, "and I'm very scared."

"Funny how we can talk better on the phone," I said.

"I *do* love you," he said.

"Oh yes, we have love," I agreed.

Jack came back on a Monday. He rang the doorbell and I answered it. He was standing with his bags out there, looking rather sheepish.

"How are you?" I said.

"Fine."

We stood there for a moment. Then I said, "Won't you come in and unpack your bags?"

"Do you want me to?" he countered.

"Oh, Jack, come in. You're *home*. But we have a lot of talking to do."

Well, we didn't talk right off. We made love. We both needed each other. I needed the comfort of his arms around me. He needed to feel my warmth. We both cried some. Jack was doing a lot of crying during that period. And a lot of drinking. I didn't drink. He was drinking to feel no pain. It didn't work.

"Jack, you can do whatever you want to do. Be whatever you want to be. Just don't lie to me."

"I want to be able to support myself."

"You can do that. I understand. Hopefully, you'll phase yourself out of this porn business. You'll have to. Someday you'll be too *old*."

He laughed. "Thanks, Margaret. You're so damned *honest*."

"Well, yes, I am."

So he unpacked his bags.

"Come on," he said. "I've got money. Let's go out. Let's go to the Rainbow Room. Everything will look better from there."

He was right, of course. At the Rainbow Room, you are eighty-four stories above reality. The city in the setting sun stretches out like a golden glistening series of diamonds, strands of diamonds leading out to the luminous water surrounding Manhattan. In the last rays of the sun and the coming of evening, everyone looks gorgeous, and there's something about the music, the railings, the architecture, the dance floor, that makes you think you're back in the thirties, maybe the forties, when penthouses were really the thing, and people dressed for dinner. The orchestra played, and we danced, and night fell over Manhattan and the city continued to glow below us.

We were happy, of course, and in love, of course. And we were terribly aware of the pain at the same time. It gave an added intensity to our feelings.

"I'm off to Detroit," I said.

"I'll be in L.A.," he said.

"Then, we'll meet here the day before Thanksgiving and have a few days before we go off to London." I had promised Ted Hook that I would help him host a tour of London named after his restaurant, Backstage. Backstage in London with Margaret Whiting. It was some package. Jack was going to go along with me.

Jack smiled. And I smiled. "Isn't this wonderful!" he exclaimed. And we danced away from the Rainbow Room and even further away from reality. Jack, you see, had *his* tour, Jack Wrangler's Fraternity, where he was to play host to some travelers hoping for a glimpse of the wild side of life in California. And he also had a film to shoot on the Coast. Before she had walked away, Nanci had gotten him another straight porn film for filmmaker Chuck Vincent. Jack was a star. A porn *star*.

I came back from Detroit on a Sunday, the day before we were scheduled to leave for London. The phone rang. It was Jack.

"I can't go to London with you," he said. "I'm still filming. But give my love to Ted, and have a good time." He sounded like someone who was a rather good friend. He didn't sound like a man who was in love.

"Fine," I said. "Yes, and *you* have a good time."

So perhaps that was it. Perhaps we were going to be friends, good friends.

I flew to London the next day with Ted and all those Backstagers making the theatrical pilgrimage to London, then Concorded back to New York, and went to work in Florida, Cleveland, and Chicago with the girls. When Jack called, and he called almost every day, we chatted. And then like *good* friends but not intimate friends. And then he said he would be back in New York for Christmas to shoot a film, *Navy Blue*, a male porn film about Christmas in New York with a bunch of sailors.

The ornaments were up all over town and the trees were lit along Park Avenue, when Debbie said to me, "Jack called. He's in town at Marvin Poon's apartment." We didn't look at each other. I went in to the bedroom and called. He answered.

"You're at Marvin's."

"Yes," Jack replied. "He's away and so I'm here." His voice sounded a little thick and foggy. Obviously his bags had been packed. I mean, he wasn't at my apartment.

"Funny that you called. I had forgotten. We ordered tickets for *Ballroom* a couple of months ago. It's this Thursday."

"I'm supposed to—" he began, then interrupted himself. "Yeah, let's go. I'll meet you at Ted Hook's before."

He was there when I came in, sitting at a little table for two by the piano. Christmas conviviality surrounded us. It was cold outside and warm in Ted's place. Everyone's face was flushed. Jack and I looked at each other. He was pale.

"You look terrible!" I observed.

"Do you know how much I love you?" he blurted out. "I've been sitting here. This was where we met. You remember the night we met? And I was sitting here, and I started to cry. Because I can't see my life without you . . . and I love you. . . ." And he started to cry again. Fortunately, it was Christmas season and lots of people cry then, so no one took any notice.

"I need a drink," he said.

I nodded. "I think we both do." And so we had a drink.

"I've been so afraid of screwing things up," he said, "and, of course, I have."

I didn't deny it. We finished our drinks and went to the theater.

He didn't fall apart again until intermission. Part of it was *Ballroom,* which we both found very moving. Part of it was our predicament. I handed him a Kleenex.

"There are so many things I want to say to you, and I don't know how. You know I love you, and believe me, I understand you only want the best for me. . . ."

"I hate to watch you throw your talent down the drain."

"I know. And I'm so sorry. I wanted to please you, and yet I knew I had to continue making personal appearances. That's how I make my money. Not from the films. I promise that in the future I will be up front with you about every decision I make, but please don't let's throw this relationship down the tubes. I just don't think I could deal with that. Can't we try again?"

We were alone in the lobby. The second act had started.

I borrowed his Kleenex, and wiped my eyes. "I guess we'd better, otherwise we'll miss the whole second act."

That night he came back to the apartment, and unpacked his bags. Again.

Shouldn't that have been it? Wasn't that the perfect ending?

Well, it almost was.

18

4 Girls 4:
The End

When did the good feelings start to go wrong? Conflict over Salt Lake City? Brouhaha in Omaha? Hard to tell.

4 Girls 4 had always had a few problems, which we also managed to solve. The problem with Bill Loeb we patched up; we were doing okay. Sometimes there were personality clashes. After all, we were four strong-willed ladies. And sometimes there were just personal problems.

We had a lot of bookings, which made us all very happy. There was Dallas, there was Omaha, there was Long Beach. The month of May was packed with dates around the East Coast. We couldn't complain that Loeb and Weems weren't keeping us working. There was a week free, it seemed, in the first part of June. And then, steady work all through the summer.

I was on the Coast in February when I got an emergency call from Jack. He had injured himself in a fall. That was really bad luck. He had just managed to get a good role in a play with Carrie Nye and Anne Francine at the PAF Playhouse in Huntington, Long Island. One day, returning to New York like a regular commuter, he jumped off the train to buy a paper and fell down some cement steps, aggravating an injury from the previous year and resulting in traumatic arthritis. The other actors managed to get him back on the train. At Penn Station the cops carried him out. When he finally got to the apartment, he found he couldn't move. Debbie supervised the hospital, the doctors, everything.

Now, he told me, he was facing an operation.

"Margaret," he said, "they want to replace my hip."

I didn't understand any of this, but it sounded serious.

"They'll put in a prosthesis, an artificial joint. The socket is plastic, the ball is metal. They say there's very little risk. I should end up with ninety percent mobility."

I should have said, it sounded *very* serious.

"When do they want to do the operation?"

"The first of June. They've already scheduled it."

"Well, I'll be sure I'm not working."

"You don't have to do that."

"Yes, I do."

It was fortunate that nothing was booked for the first week of June. But almost immediately, a booking came up in Salt Lake City. Some other act had canceled. It was a split week. The money wasn't that terrific, but the girls wanted to take it. It wasn't just my decision; there were four incomes here. We were 4 Girls 4.

Jack called the doctor. The hospital was able to reschedule Jack's operation for the fourth of June.

"Now, that's it," I said to Bill Loeb. "I am going to be there for Jack's operation. I want the rest of that first week in June free. He has nobody to take care of him."

"You got it."

Then, about the first of May, Bill Weems called me. A week in Cleveland. Great money.

"When?" I asked.

"Right after Salt Lake City. Before Chautauqua."

I kept my voice very steady. "Bill, I told you, I am not going to work that first week in June. I've already had Jack reschedule the surgery once. He can't do it again. It's not like show business, you know."

"The money is great. . . ."

"Bill, it's not the point. I promised Jack I would be with him. . . ."

"Okay, Margaret."

I had an afterthought. "Oh, Bill, please don't tell anybody about this booking offer."

He said he wouldn't. But he did.

The first clue I had that there was any trouble came from Rose Marie, who called me about two-thirty in the morning. She sounded like a kid in school. "Oh, boy, are you in trouble. Are *they* mad at you!" she said. We were going down to Painter Mills, outside of Baltimore, heading for a very heavily scheduled two weeks coming into the end of May.

"What's the matter?" I asked.

"You turned down that booking . . ." Rose Marie said.

"Now, *look*!" I said. "First of all, we agreed months ago. I was going to have that week off. And secondly, this came up at the last minute. We would have had to cancel some of the Chautauqua bookings. . . ."

"Yeah . . . well, you're really gonna get it!"

I don't know what I expected, but I didn't expect what I got, which was a barrage in Baltimore, the Second Night of the Knives, I called it afterward. It was also Mother's Day. Rosemary and Helen were furious.

"You canceled a whole week's booking!" they said accusingly.

"That's right."

"Without consulting us."

"That's right."

"We would never have done that."

"Rosemary, you *did* do that." She had canceled the whole Japanese tour when her boyfriend Dante hurt his back. "Musicians, crew, everything. They were already on the plane! And that Japanese booker couldn't even speak English," I added irrelevantly.

"But I didn't do it to this act!" she shouted. "I didn't do it to the *girls*."

Helen pointed a finger at me. "Don't you *ever* let your love life interfere with *my* career!"

"I told you all months ago!" I shouted back. "I gave the boys enough notice!"

"Yeah, but you don't know the money we gave up!"

"I don't *care!*"

Voices reached a decibel level visited only by operatic sopranos. Rose Marie didn't say anything, while we three glared at one another. Then we went out and did a show as if nothing had happened.

In New York, Greg Dawson threw a big press party for us gratis at his club, the Ballroom. This was wonderful for us, since we didn't have a press agent. Greg knew that we probably wouldn't be covered by the reviewers because we weren't in New York itself, but out in Westbury, on Long Island, so he saw to it that John S. Wilson from the *Times* and most of the other important critics came to the party. The mayor came. The reporters popped their questions, photographers snapped photos, and we cracked wise. It was all very professional, and good publicity. I thought that maybe the Second Night of the Knives had been forgotten.

On the next night came a birthday party for Rosemary and Helen. It had become a little tradition; Rose Marie and I would give a party for Rosie and Helen in May, and they would give one for us around the end of August. Rose Marie and I had planned to hold this one at Ted Hook's Backstage. Greg Dawson, Jack, and Debbie went along with me. Ted met us at the door.

"We decided to break the party up into two groups," he said, slightly nervously.

"Why?" Jack wanted to know.

"It's a little unwieldy at one table," Ted extemporized.

In we went.

The room wasn't very big, granted. But there was this one long table, and there sat Rosemary with Dante, Helen, Rose Marie (who looked as though she wanted to die), Bill Loeb, and a few other functionaries. They waved to me as Ted ushered us to a little table on the opposite side. We sat down.

"Hello, girls," I said.

"Hullo," came the unenthusiastic reply. Nobody spoke a word to

Jack. Jack, Greg, Debbie, and I sat down. They sat at the big table and made conversation. I could hear every clink of glass and every scrape of knife and fork against plate, that's how much conversation there was. I never saw Ted Hook so busy. He moved back and forth like a hummingbird. He never hovered, though. He just darted in. And out. And then back in again. I guess to make sure we hadn't killed one another. Even the flowers on the tables looked a little droopy. Rose Marie came over to our table, but she didn't sit down. She cracked a few lines and laughed hoarsely, and when we didn't really laugh that much, she went back to the other table and sat down beside the unopened presents, ours included. Incidentally, I was paying for half of this Inquisition.

Then came the cake.

"Happy birthday to you . . ."

Helen and Rosemary blew out the candles. Everyone applauded. Jack had already gone to the bar.

"I think it's time to go home," I said, smiling.

"All right," Greg said. Debbie was right with us. We were making a grand exit.

"Good night, Helen. Good night, Rosie. Happy birthday. Hope you enjoy the party!" I said, smiling my way right past them.

I heard silence at my back as the Whiting party swept out.

I was furious. How dare they? What right had they? I had planned so carefully. How dare they take revenge this way? And what did they have to take revenge about? But I think I was maddest because neither Clooney nor O'Connell had even acknowledged Jack. They hadn't even spoken to him. They were blaming him for everything! It was insulting. Jack, of course, was angry too. He was angry on my behalf. Oh, it was going to be a lovely weekend at Westbury.

The following day, Bill Loeb called up. "The girls want to have a meeting."

"I don't."

"I think there should be a meeting to clear the air."

"The air couldn't be clearer. It's pure frost. And you want to know something else? I don't care if I ever see the girls again. That behavior last night was the most disgusting display of poor taste I have ever come across."

"Yeah, honey," he began. "You know how the girls are."

"Yes, I know how the girls are. I just learned. There's nothing else to say."

I couldn't believe how detached I was.

Just before all this occurred, I had been to see a psychiatrist for the first time in my life. It wasn't just about 4 Girls 4. I was having a lot of confused feelings about Eleanore, who was aging and seemed to be failing. Life with Jack was not all smiles either. The first thing the doctor asked me, obviously used to more of a Beverly Hills type, was "Are you on any pills?" I thought maybe he would be a little disappointed when I said no, but he didn't seem to be. A little later, when we were talking about destructive feelings, I said, "Doctor, if you ever hear that I committed suicide, you'll know it was a very well-planned murder. I am just not the type." I described the situation between the girls and myself.

"I think these women are all very talented. I have enormous respect for them. We are all pros. But I realize they are all capable of hurting me. They *have* hurt me. And I don't know how to deal with it."

The doctor regarded me. "Just look at them as dollar signs," he said. I thought about that, and it did take the emotional edge off. It was true, we were a very successful combination. Every time we went out on the stage, it meant money. In a way, Helen was right —only it wasn't my sex life, it was the women's emotional tension that was getting in the way.

"Let me work on that," I said to the doctor.

"I plan to see you perform at Westbury," he said. "I think I ought to know more about this situation."

Westbury was a theater on Long Island; 4 Girls 4 had always done well there. I had looked forward to playing the engagement, but I didn't look forward to it now. We arrived in separate limousines. We went to our separate dressing rooms without a hello and then went out onstage and performed a hell of a show.

That Sunday we had a matinee and another show to do that evening.

After the matinee, there was a knock on my dressing-room door. It was the doctor. He was shaking his head.

"I don't know how you all do it," he said. "You looked like you were having the greatest time up there—all four of you."

I shrugged. "Listen, we've done that all our lives. Perform. That's what we were trained for, from the time we were kids."

"I don't think I'll ever understand completely the actor's mentality," the doctor said.

"We're just dollar signs," I reminded him cheerily.

We were interrupted by Rose Marie.

"We've got to get together. . . ." she began.

"Oh, he*llo*," I said. Rose Marie brushed past that.

"Margaret this is *serious*. The boys have been fooling around with the money."

The doctor knew when to make an exit. I joined the three other girls. They were already in high operatic dudgeon.

"Can you imagine!" Helen said to me as I came into the room. "Bill has been making out double contracts!" It was as though there had never been any unpleasantness between us.

"We get one contract and the theater gets another!" Clooney echoed.

"We told Loeb we weren't going to pay to have Marty Kummer book us! We told him the bookings had to come out of his share! We saw a contract. Bill couldn't get the bookings. So he hired Marty Kummer and paid him out of the difference between what we were getting and what Loeb *said* we were getting."

"How did you find out?" I want to know.

"We happened to look at the contract here." Helen waved it in front of me.

"Believe me, we are not going on until Kummer and Loeb come out and *explain* this!"

"Are they coming out?" I asked.

"You bet," Rosie said. "We phoned. They're on their way."

"You know *I* never liked Loeb," Helen reminded Clooney.

"He owes me money," Rose Marie said.

I looked at them. We were all like children. The previous anger had vanished. I was part of the group again. Now it was Bill's turn.

There was not too much time between the Sunday matinee and the evening performance, which is traditionally earlier than most night shows. Loeb and Kummer sped out to Westbury from the city. When they got to the theater, they were greeted by high-octane outrage. The papers flew. The voices raised. Hands gestured. Loeb and Kummer were helpless.

"I don't know anything about this," Marty said, throwing up his hands. "I just got paid by Bill Loeb, that's all." Thus leaving Bill Loeb alone to be surrounded by us Apaches. There was nothing that dishonest about the affair, only underhanded.

"It happens all the time," Loeb cried out.

"Oh, yeah? Well, it isn't going to happen to *us*."

In the midst of this, the poor stage manager kept calling time.

"Half-hour," he announced meekly.

"*What* half-hour? There will be *no* show tonight!"

He crept off and the battle continued. We had Bill Loeb surrounded. It was like the last wagon train. He was in the center and we were circling, tomahawks drawn, and giving out with the war whoops. He didn't have a chance.

"Five minutes . . ." the stage manager said wishfully.

"Never!" somebody answered him. Possibly Helen. She was really splendid in her anger. We all had arias of outrage, rivaling Rigoletto. Bill was spared nothing.

Suddenly I heard the overture. I drew myself up. It was *my* turn.

"There is the music," I announced dramatically. "I am going out and *perform*! The show must go on. Give me two minutes. I, for one, am not going to be *docked*," I said to the panicky stage manager.

I left very grandly, expecting applause on my exit. I didn't get any. Only on my entrance *on*stage.

I did my twenty minutes. I must say, I was wonderful. Full of bounce, tender with the ballads. My voice was certainly warmed up. In the back of my mind I kept wondering if anyone was going to follow me or was this a case of *1 Girl 1*?

I finished my last number, took my bows (*lots* of bows!), and looked up to see Helen O'Connell, smiling, radiant, entering from the wings to greet the audience. Our eyes met. I started to laugh. Helen chuckled. And the show did go on.

It was one of the best performances we ever gave. Maybe we were pumped up with extra adrenaline. If the poor doctor had stayed, it might have convinced him to give up his practice altogether. Performers are unfathomable.

There was a serious side to this contretemps. We called in lawyers. Bill Loeb called in lawyers. Helen contacted a West Coast lawyer. We split that consulting bill. I contacted a West Coast lawyer. Clooney, Rose Marie, and I listened to his advice. I got stuck with that bill.

In the meantime, Jack had his operation, and it was successful. The following week *4 Girls 4,* a bit battered by all these events, started the summer tour at Chautauqua.

Loeb finally settled with us and we looked for other management. For a while, *4 Girls 4* had four managers four. And for one dizzy moment, one of Rosemary Clooney's daughter's friends took our careers in hand until he left us with the hotel bill in Norfolk, Virginia.

This man had promised us a television deal, which was how we met him. Before the big blowup with Bill Loeb, Clooney had introduced us to this entrepreneur who was as eager as we were to get us into television. We arranged a meeting with Loeb, who liked the idea. When Loeb left the room for a minute, Clooney, his loyal supporter, said, "Oh, by the way, Bill Loeb doesn't get any percent of this idea. . . ."

In Atlantic City (another one of those gambling casinos), Clooney blew up at Rose Marie for staying on too long again when we had been asked to cut the act. And Rose Marie fell apart. She retreated to her room, got one of her migraines, and couldn't do the second show; it was the only time I can remember when she couldn't perform. That's when she made her decision to leave.

I had already announced some time before that I thought five years with *4 Girls 4* was enough, but after Rose Marie's decision, I agreed to stay through the summer until they found a replacement. I didn't think it looked right for two of us to leave at the same time. Martha Raye took over Rose Marie's spot, and she was fine. We were lucky to get Kay Starr as my replacement. We had wanted Katie from the beginning, when Barbara McNair hadn't worked out. So this was a wonderful way to close that chapter in my life.

I gave my last performance in Latham, New York, in September 1981. Clooney cried. Martha said good-bye. Helen didn't.

Come to think of it, I'm not sure *why* Clooney was crying. Greg Dawson had booked the two of us into the Ballroom the first two weeks of October, so that certainly was not a long good-bye.

Helen and I made up our differences later in Cincinnati, a good place for that sort of thing. Cincinnati puts life in perspective. We were booked on a jazz concert. We met onstage and said a strained hello. Then Helen looked at me.

"Couldn't we just take it from the top?" she asked. I knew what she meant. Let's forget all the trouble we had, and start all over again, feeling the way we had in the beginning. I nodded. We threw our arms around each other. The two of us had seen too many good times and bad times, gone through too much. We were just too old for all that *enemy* jazz.

To sum it up, my feelings about *4 Girls 4*—and about Bill Loeb —are that if a phone call came from any one of them, I'd be on the next plane. I know each one of them would do the same for me.

19

My Funny Valentine

Easter in St. Paul! What could have been nicer?

Nothing. I had everything. Jack and Debbie had given up fighting and now were friends, so much so that when I came back to New York, I found that the two of them had gone to Macy's over Easter and bought a rabbit! They had already named the rabbit Jump-Jump and Jump-Jump was doing what all bunny rabbits do. Just when I thought I had everything.

Jack had always loved rabbits. It goes back to his childhood and a party for his seventh birthday, but that's another book. His. *The Jack Wrangler Story*. He wrote it and it certainly does make lively reading. I watched him play on the floor with Jump-Jump. Jack had a lot of love to give. He had been scared and Jump-Jump was scared too. Jack sensed this. He was giving Jump-Jump a home. It was absurd. It was real. Whatever it was, it was us. Now we had a rabbit, we had a family, we had a full schedule, and a happy life.

Part of the reason we were happy was that I had been able to adjust to Jack's work. This sounds as though I had taken a course in porn 101 at New York University, but that is not the case. I did go to some of the movies, and in the three years that Jack and I had been together, that whole industry had changed. No longer were the movie houses being raided and closed every night. Now it was even possible to see X-rated films on television. I do admit I was a bit naïve about going to these movie houses. Nanci Eisner (now reconciled with Jack) and I went to see *Seven into Snowie*, about You Know Who and seven bad dwarfs. We went because Tony Pastor, the son of the bandleader and a friend of mine, had directed it. Tony had written a topnotch score, which he performed with his brothers, and I was very impressed with the quality of the production.

"Oh, Nanci, look at that color!" I exclaimed as naked bodies drifted and draped themselves through scenes. "Look at that *set*! Isn't that music marvelous!" A man behind us finally said, "Lady, would you shut *up* and let us enjoy this?"

During these years, Jack made only straight porn films. I was introduced to the people he worked with. I even accompanied him to an Adult Film Convention in San Francisco, where we all wore identification badges just like the Shriners. And we looked like the Shriners, come to think of it. The people who owned the theaters looked like Mom and Pop, and the people who made the movies looked like Bud and Sis.

Also, more of my friends had found their way into this business. Rose Marie's boyfriend, Vince Maranda, who had been the head of the Variety Club in Los Angeles, and the most generous, sweet man alive, operated a string of theaters called the Pussycat theaters. When we were in San Francisco, Vince asked a cab driver for the best adult film theaters in town. The cab driver did *not* say the Pussycats.

"What's wrong with the Pussycat theaters?" Vince wanted to know.

"Not clean enough," the cab driver informed him. That was all Vince had to hear. At six the next morning, he was on the phone, calling all the managers. He was going to make an inspection tour. Needless to say, by eleven that morning, every Pussycat was gleaming. Vince was running a business and he intended to run it right.

So this business was moving up at the same time that Jack was branching out. He was again proving himself to be a very able director with a very good eye for detail and a wonderful imagination.

But the main reason we were happy was that we were honest with each other.

We were approaching another Thanksgiving. A lot of things seem to happen to us around that time. We both had very heavy schedules. I was due in London to record an album for *Reader's Digest* in a serious called Great Ladies of American Song. Jack was due in Hollywood to make a movie titled, I believe, *Palace of Pleasure*. This was a gay porn film. I wasn't too happy about it, but, as I said, I had made my adjustment. I thought. Before I went to London, I was due in Las Vegas for a television special with Rosemary Clooney, Helen Forrest, Debbie Reynolds, and others. Jack was supposed to meet me there. We would come back to New York, and then fly to London. Sound familiar?

So did the call.

I was just leaving for the airport when the phone rang. It was Jack.

"Jack? Honey, I'm just rushing to the airport."

"I know. We were robbed and almost killed."

"What? Who was?"

"Me and Bob and Lee. It was horrible. Last night we had just come back from dinner . . ."

I listened. Bob was Bob Meyer; Lee was Jack's step-grandmother. (Jack is in the illustrious Hollywood tradition.) I knew they had planned some celebration.

". . . These five men dragged us into the bedroom and tied us up with rope and put these guns to our heads. . . . I thought I was going to die."

Why was he concocting such an elaborate fabrication? Was this another way of avoiding something? He was lying again! And such a huge crazy lie!

". . . And, oh God, my wallet's been stolen and, Margaret, I'm so frightened. I just want to come home."

I heard myself saying, "Then you're not meeting me in Vegas?"

"I thought I'd catch a red-eye flight so that . . . Oh, Margaret, I'm a mess. I just want to come home."

"Okay."

"I'll call you from New York."

"Okay."

"God, I love you so much."

"Okay."

I was not feeling much compassion as I flew to Vegas. Just when I thought everything was fine, he starts acting up again. He knows what I hate is the lying. . . .

I arrived in Vegas, went to the hotel, checked in, bought the local papers, which in Vegas means the L.A. papers, went upstairs, kicked off my shoes, opened the *Los Angeles Times*, and saw the headline BEL-AIR ROBBERY and Jack's name, mentioned very prominently. And an exact duplication of everything he had told me. Five men had held them at gunpoint, forced them to lie on the floor, held guns to their heads, and threatened to kill them. It could have been another Manson murder, and here I had thought it was all a lie. . . . I wanted to call him, but it was no use. He was in the air. I met Clooney in the coffee shop. She had already read the papers. She asked how Jack was, and I mumbled, "Fine." We went out to do the show.

I got back to New York as fast as possible. To my enormous relief, Jack didn't look too bad. One eye was puffed up and discolored and his cheek was black-and-blue. His ear was a bit frayed. But he was safe!

"I am so sorry," I began. He stopped me with a wave. His grin reassured me. Everything was okay.

We left for London.

Everything was *not* okay.

We checked into the Grosvenor House and settled down to watch the presidential election on television. Reagan won so handily that the BBC filled in with some dreadful old programs. Jack kept opening up the little refrigerator that had been stocked with miniature bottles of every imaginable liquor and liqueur. He kept downing the little bottles and tossing them away like bonbons, with no visible effect, except that he kept complaining of a pain in his ear. He had worked his way through to the last Maitai, when I suggested maybe he would feel better lying down. He did not. I suggested he call the house physician. *He* suggested Jack go to a hospital. I went with him, and that was the last I saw of Jack for twenty-four hours. He had disappeared into the maze of socialized medicine.

I was frantic. I was on the phone, and then waiting by the phone. There was no word. In the afternoon, I was scheduled to record the first session. I hadn't slept. I wasn't worried about my voice—nothing ever happens to those pipes; I just open up and sing. I was worried about Jack.

The phone rang. It was long-distance for Jack.

"He's not here," I told the overseas operator.

I heard a man's voice break in. "That's all right. I'll speak to the lady."

"Yes?"

"This is Jim Rogers. Has Jack told you about me?"

"No."

"Well, we were making a movie together in L.A.—and I know about the robbery and his getting beaten up—and I wondered if he was all right."

"He's fine," I said, not wanting to involve anyone else. There was a pause.

"You know, Jack and I are very much in love," he said.

"Oh?" I heard myself say. Then, after another pause, I said: "Well, I'll tell him you called."

I hung up. I think, actually what I did was let the receiver drop on the phone. Just . . . let . . . it . . . go.

Jack returned, maybe an hour later. I didn't give him the message. He told me that his eardrum had been punctured and infected. The doctors had patched him up. He related his escapades with the British medical profession; I prepared for the afternoon's session, and we left for the recording studio.

There was a forty-piece orchestra backing me up, conducted by David Whitaker, an absolutely charming man who conducted everything from the groin up. Or out. It was heaven on rhythm tunes, but a little strange on ballads. We started rehearsals. Jack stayed up in the booth, which was on a second level, reached by a long flight of stairs.

"Where or When" was the first number. We ran it down. David had written a gorgeous orchestration, and I was just getting in the mood for Rodgers and Hart when I saw Jack limping down the stairs from the booth. He came into the studio waving his arms. All forty men and a girl stopped.

"That's not the right lyric," he said to me. "You're not singing the right lyric."

"Wasn't I singing

" 'And so it seems that we have met before,
And laughed before, and loved before . . .'?"

"Yes," he said, "and that's not right."

"Not right? I've been singing it that way for twenty years."

"No," he insisted. "You don't have the right lyric."

In my state of mind, I considered it possible to have made a mistake.

"Well, what is the right lyric?"

"I'm not sure. I'm just sure that isn't it."

It was important. This was a very prestigious recording, and these were prestigious songwriters. I always wanted the lyrics to be correct. We ended up calling the publisher in London.

Word was brought back by a very elegant Englishman, who said in his clipped voice, "The *correct* lyric is:

" 'And so it seems that we have met before,
And laughed before, and loved before,
But who knows where or when!' "

"Oh," said Jack, and limped out of the studio and climbed those stairs—I counted twenty-five steps—back into the booth. David Whitaker tapped his baton and said, "May we begin again, please?" And we did.

My state of mind? What about his state of mind? I thought while I was singing. There he is, black-and-blue from a beating, just out of the hospital, and I should take *his* word on a lyric? He's punch-drunk.

The next song was "My Funny Valentine." Jack *was* my funny valentine. He *did* make me "smile with my heart." I loved him a lot, and God, was he putting me through hell. It was hard for me to sing, but I was damned if I was going to break down in front of forty musicians. So Margaret kept singing.

At the end of the session, we went out to dinner at an Italian restaurant I liked. Jack ordered a double Scotch. I ordered . . . I don't remember what.

"There's something I want to tell you," he began.

"Oh? Yes. I had something to tell you, too. Jim called. He said he's very much in love with you. I said I'd give you the message."

We looked at each other. It was very noisy in the restaurant, difficult to communicate. Waiters were yelling orders. People were standing next to our table, talking. There was a lot of noise. Jack was shaking his head and saying something I couldn't hear.

"What?" I said.

"I'm a *fucking faggot!*" he said. This time everybody heard. If he had wanted to get attention, he had succeeded. In the silence, I said, "Only around the edges."

That made him laugh. The situation—this ridiculous situation in this ridiculous restaurant—made *me* laugh. Then a curtain of chatter surrounded us again. We could talk.

"I think you better tell me about Jim."

"I met him during a picture last time on the Coast. But I'm telling you, nothing happened. And I mean nothing happened."

I said, "Jack, come on. Tell me the truth."

"No. He was a bartender. And some producer saw him one night and thought he'd be great playing the second lead in the picture I was doing. But he couldn't get it up, he was so new at this. He was embarrassed. He just couldn't make it. They had to fluff him up. . . ."

I sighed into my wine.

"They had to fake it. The poor guy was so embarrassed, I had a drink with him. He was very emotional and very upset. He probably got drunk and called. There's nothing to it."

"I don't think you want that gay life-style, or you'd have gone for it. But, listen, if that is what you want, I'd respect that too. That wouldn't make me stop loving you. But I can't stand the confusion. I'm a very tidy person. Everything in its place. I don't know what our place is."

"I love you."

"That's a start."

We looked at each other. We giggled.

My Funny Valentine and I wandered out of the restaurant and into the London night.

"A week in Phoenix would be good," I suggested.

"We could see who we are," he said.

"We could just rest a bit," I said.

"Sounds good," he said. "I've got a week before I have to be in L.A."

"Thanksgiving's coming up."

"It'll be good to get away."

However, it was *not* good. Neither one of us liked to be idle. There we were with time on our hands. We were there to see who we were, and what did we see? Two people who were bored silly just sitting out in the sun. We did a little work on a new show of mine that eventually became *Maggie & Friends*. We went out to dinner. We bickered.

"You're going to see him in L.A., aren't you?"

"I don't think so."

"I think you are."

"Well, maybe I will."

"I think maybe you should."

We left each other at the Phoenix airport, Jack flying to L.A., me to New York.

It was gray and cold in New York after all the sun in Phoenix. Thank God!

Greg Dawson invited me to his place for Thanksgiving dinner. He was going to cook all day. His aunts had been invited. It would be a splendid feast. It would warm me up.

"I can't wait!" I said.

Debbie came over the night before Thanksgiving.

"You don't look so hot," she said after she kissed me.

"Oh, I'm all right," I said bravely. She came into the living room, where the rabbit was lying in his box. She went over to the rabbit and knelt down.

"Jump-Jump doesn't look so hot either," she said.

"Would you stop!" I said. "You imagine we're all sick. We're *fine*."

"No," she said, "Jump-Jump really doesn't look well."

"I think he misses Jack," I said. Debbie and I sat down to talk. At the end of the evening, she glanced again at Jump-Jump, and gave me the number of the Animal Medical Center.

"If Jump-Jump isn't jumping by morning, you better give them a call."

The next day he wasn't. So I phoned Greg.

"I don't know a thing about animals," I said to him. "I have to take the rabbit to the hospital. . . ."

"I'm just putting the turkey on," he said.

"Well, I'll probably be late for dinner," I said in my abandoned voice.

"All right," he sighed. "I'll be right over."

So we bundled up Jump-Jump, put him in his cage, and took him to the Animal Medical Center. The one thing lonelier than a hospital on holidays is an animal hospital. The waiting room was heavy with drooping leashes and sad faces. It was about ten o'clock in the morning. We delivered Jump-Jump to the people in their white uniforms.

"Just have a seat," the nurse behind the desk told us.

We joined the others in the waiting room. Noontime came.

"Greg, your turkey . . ." I said.

"It'll be okay," he said glumly.

"This is not right," I said.

"Don't think about it."

A nurse called us. "Miss Whiting?"

"Yes."

"We have to do more tests on Jump-Jump."

I said, "Greg, you *must* go home."

At three, he did go home to his turkey, and I continued to sit. At four, the doctor joined the nurse and they approached me.

"Jump-Jump is quite ill," the doctor said solemnly, "and I don't know what it is, but he should stay overnight."

"We'll fix the bill and you can pay for overnight," the nurse suggested. I said, "Yes, yes, whatever you think best."

The doctor disappeared and the nurse went to adjust the bill. While I was waiting by the desk, I thought, What am I doing here? I never even really liked animals. Why am I spending my Thanksgiving Day here? I could have been watching the parade. I could be sleeping. I never cared for animals. All the animals I had . . . Eleanore took away the dachshund on Christmas Eve. And then we lost Debbie's dog.

Suddenly the nurse returned.

"I have bad news for you. Jump-Jump just had cardiac arrest. And died. I'm terribly sorry."

I just stood there. I began to cry. What the hell, the nurse must be used to that. After a few minutes, I started to leave.

"Do you want to take the body?" the nurse inquired.

"No! No!" I cried, and started to run.

"Don't forget Jump-Jump's cage!" she called out.

"I don't *want* the cage!" I shouted and fled like Little Nell, into the open air. It was dark now and snowing. It was snowing and I was crying. The doctor ran after me.

"You forgot the cage!" he said.

"I don't *want* the cage, doctor!" I said. "I don't want to be reminded of his death." But he gave it to me anyway, and I slung it in the trash can on the corner. I thought, How am I going to tell Jack? He's going to be heartbroken.

I went home and called Greg and told him.

"I'll be down in a few minutes," I said. "I have to pull myself together." It was now seven o'clock. Dinner had been planned for five.

When I arrived, Greg introduced me to the two aunts. Then he said, "How are you?"

"Fine," I answered, and immediately burst into tears again.

"Let's eat," Greg suggested. There wasn't much conversation at the table. I would sniff from time to time.

"The turkey seems a little dry this year," one of the aunts commented. Greg just nodded. It was an early evening.

I called Jack later that night, resolved to be brave. When I heard his voice, I just burst out, "Jump-Jump is dead!" And he said, "Oh my God!"

And then I heard him consoling me. And I didn't even like animals. But, amid my sniffles, and crying, I realized something different was happening here. Jack was taking care of *me*.

"You come out here . . ." he was saying. "Margaret, I'll meet you. Don't worry. Just come."

I did. I went with Greg. Jack met us at the airport. We were staying in a hotel suite and he had filled it with flowers. I watched Jack. He looked as though he had been through a hell of a time. But he was standing there and he was smiling. He seemed stronger.

"How are you?" I asked him.

"I'm . . . okay now," he said.

"Yes, you look okay," I agreed. And he grinned.

"It's about *time*."

Rose Marie decided we needed more rabbits. We found two, and named them Groucho and The Kid. They were small and gray, and would gang up on us.

It was hell trying to persuade the chambermaid they weren't rats.

20

She's Funny
That Way

I never had nothin', no one to care,
That's why I seem to have more than my share,
I got a woman, crazy for me,
She's funny that way . . .

Daddy wrote the lyrics of that song about Eleanore. He usually didn't write lyrics. But he wrote this one. And she *was* funny. Eleanore was a truly funny, stylish, rather outrageous woman. A born manager. But not a born mother, at least not in the usual sense of the word.

I found myself thinking about my mother a good deal. She was alone now in the apartment on Spalding. Aunt Mag had died in 1968. They had been together since my father's death in 1937. Sisters, two of a kind. Barbara remembers that when the parties, those Saturday nights at the Whitings, started, she was allowed to sit on the top step and look down until she had to go to bed. Each year she got one step lower, until she finally joined the rest of the Whiting women.

The parties continued because both Eleanore and Aunt Mag loved the gaiety of it all. They had always loved a good time. When it was *their* day, they had had fun in vaudeville. During my father's heyday, there had been fun just being around the celebrities. After my father's death, there were a number of their friends who stopped coming around. I think Eleanore resented that. I know it hurt her. But the parties were a perfect antidote for gloom. As I have said, my mother was a fabulous cook, as well as being a wit. And Aunt Mag was a good-time girl. The fact that I was emerging as a recording star and that Barbara was playing *Junior Miss* didn't hurt either. The combination of fun, food, and some kind of celebrity fed Eleanore and Aunt Mag through those years.

When we moved to the house on Loring and Comstock, the parties continued. They didn't really stop until Eleanore moved to the place on Thayer, but after the war, they lost a bit of their joyousness perhaps. Part of that was due to Aunt Mag's being so political. When she had her drinks in her, she could go on for hours haranguing everyone within earshot, and with her belter's voice, that included most of Beverly Hills. Both Eleanore and Aunt Mag were fiercely anti-Communist, and pro-McCarthy. They both hated communism so that they would go with anybody. They were both sure that somewhere, *someone* was warming up in the bullpen, ready to take over the country and destroy our way of life.

In truth, something was changing *their* way of life, and it wasn't communism. It was time. And fashion. Aunt Mag, the coon shouter, was an anachronism. And Eleanore, who had such vitality, had always had to live vicariously through other people's careers—first Aunt Mag's, then Daddy's, and now mine.

They were hooked on show business. Barbara wasn't. One day, when she was on the point of signing for a television comedy series, she looked around at her life and decided show business wasn't worth it. She wanted to be with Gail Smith, and so she married him, and moved back to Detroit, the city my mother had struggled so hard to leave. Barbara's leaving had nothing to do with talent. She had plenty of talent. She was a great actress. I once saw her do Tennessee Williams's *This Property Is Condemned* and she was brilliant. But she wasn't hooked.

I was. Eleanore was. Aunt Mag was.

Aunt Mag would take midnight sojourns in the car, when she had been drinking. She wasn't drunk. She just needed to get out, to get away. We would wait up for her until two or three in the morning. The house on Loring and Comstock had a very short steep driveway, and Aunt Mag, who closed up many a bar in her time, would have some struggle making her way up it. So Eleanore built an iron railing just for Aunt Mag to hold on to as she came back to the house, weaving a bit, and singing a lot.

Eleanore and Mag would go to the Beverly Wilshire Hotel. There was a wonderful restaurant there and they would walk in, make an entrance, and have dinner. Eleanore wore her turban and long ropes of pearls. People would stop her in the lobby. "You remind me of Bea Lillie," they would say. She would be thrilled. After dinner, every night they would go into the drugstore. They loved it because they would see everybody they had worked with in vaudeville— Milton Berle, the Ritz Brothers, the Marx Brothers. It kept them in show business. When they closed the pharmacy at the Beverly Wilshire, it was a calamity.

"They closed the goddamned drugstore!" Eleanore exclaimed, dismayed. "Now, what are we gonna do?" Like most show people, they would stay up until three or four o'clock in the morning and sleep until eleven.

In 1968, Aunt Mag had to go into the hospital. She wasn't really ill. She was lively and full of complaints. "Vociferously vocal," someone put down on the hospital chart. She was there for about two weeks on a low-salt diet. She had high blood pressure and was retaining liquid, which is why she was on the diet. One day, while Eleanore was there, Aunt Mag got out of bed and paced the room, complaining. "Goddamned place. They never put any salt in the food." And then—*boom*. She went down on the floor. That was it. She was dead.

That almost killed Eleanore. They had been together their entire *lives*. She wasn't too rational about that. In fact, she accused Barbara, who was separated from Gail Smith at the time, of being responsible for Aunt Mag's death. They had all adored Gail—and why not? He was, *is*, an adorable man. But Gail and Barbara were having problems. Divorce was in the offing. Eleanore was a very strict Catholic. (God knows what she thought about my many marriages. She never said a word about them.) Like everything else in our family, Catholicism got very complicated. Barbara had married Gail out of the Church, because he had been divorced. And when he was dating Jane Wyman, before Barbara, that had posed another problem. Jane was a convert to Catholicism and very big with heavy crosses and all that. So they never got married. When Barbara, who later divorced Gail, married him *again*, it was in Eleanore's apartment. Unfortunately, however, too late for Aunt Mag.

I don't mean this to sound irreverent. I guess I have always been a little rebellious. I slip into church from time to time, but I keep my distance. Both Eleanore and Aunt Mag were very strict, if a bit unorthodox. My mother truly venerated the Holy Mother. She would constantly say the rosary during mass. When Barbara asked her about that, she said, "You just worship *your* way. I'll worship *mine*." When mass was no longer said in Latin, Eleanore threw up her hands. "Well, there goes the Mystery of it all," she said in the same tones she used to describe the Beatles taking over the country. "Now you can *understand* everything."

Eleanore revived after Aunt Mag's death. She had a social schedule. Stanley Adams, the president of ASCAP, would escort her and Grace Kahn to the ASCAP meetings, and they would lunch afterward. I was busy and living in New York, and Barbara was raising a family in Detroit. Every time *4 Girls 4* played anywhere close to Los Angeles, Eleanore would come to watch us perform. She had a wonderful time and got along great with the girls when she visited the dressing rooms afterward. We would have gossip sessions. Maybe it was almost as good as those days in the Beverly Wilshire drugstore.

But she had difficulty with her legs. She had tried a brace. Her knee had become arthritic. After Jack's operation, when they replaced his hip socket, I went to see Eleanore and saw her with the brace. I couldn't bear to think of her spending the rest of her life wearing it. I could see she was still in great pain.

"You must have an operation," I told her. "Like the one that Jack had."

"I don't know. I don't think it would work."

"It will work. I've checked with the doctors."

Suddenly, I was managing, and she was taking my advice. The roles had changed. She went into the hospital. Thank God, the operation was a success. Eleanore was thrilled and I was relieved. Suppose it hadn't worked? I would never have heard the end of that. But it did, and Eleanore resumed her activities.

Barbara and I were in a quandary, however. Should Eleanore come and live with me in New York? I was on the road a great deal of the time. Should she live in Detroit? That would have been a fate worse than death. There were plenty of relatives to take care of her in Los Angeles. But that didn't relieve our feelings. We both were concerned about where Eleanore called *home*. It seemed to be L.A. And there she stayed. We could see, when we visited, that she was failing. We didn't want to put her in a nursing home, but we couldn't leave our lives.

Eleanore understood. The woman who never put her arms around me to comfort me, in turn did not demand to be comforted. She was very aware of her life and ours. She welcomed our visits. Jack and I spent an afternoon with her.

"You know, sometimes things get a little hazy for me," she told Jack. "I see a window. It's a window that opens *out*, and it is open. The view is very beautiful, but I know if I ever go through that window, I'll never come back." She smiled. Jack nodded. I smiled.

As she weakened, she had nurses who came in to take care of her. Eleanore confided to Barbara, "I would like to be buried with your father." Daddy was in Forest Lawn.

Barbara called Forest Lawn. She suggested their being buried side by side. But there was not another gravesite there. What about on top? Forest Lawn flatly refused that. They offered to find yet another plot, or . . . It all sounded too complicated.

Eleanore was philosophical about it. "Never mind. I'll go with Aunt Mag," who was buried in a Catholic cemetery on the other side of town.

"Don't worry, Eleanore," Barbara told her. "I'll think of something."

Eleanore nodded. Barbara had given her word.

Debbie went out to visit her. Eleanore was sitting up, the turban on her head, wavering back and forth between the past and the present.

"It's Debbie, your granddaughter," the nurse prompted Eleanore. Eleanore looked piercingly at Debbie.

"I'm glad you're here," she said. "I've sent for the car. I've sent Barbara for the car to go to Detroit. But she's taking so long. I've been waiting so *long*."

She looked away and then back, and said, "Whatever happened to Margaret?"

Eleanore died in August 1981, just as *4 Girls 4* was to set out on what was to be my final tour. I flew out to L.A. to help Barbara with the arrangements. I wondered whether I should cancel the tour. It would knock out a lot of work for the other girls, and I was thinking of what had happened at the time of Jack's surgery. I didn't want a repeat of that situation. Barbara was very practical. "Of course you're going out on tour. Eleanore would have insisted. And when you get back, then we'll have a memorial. We'll have time to prepare."

I met the girls at the airport. We had had our ups and downs, but at this point, they were so genuine and compassionate, I was terribly moved. Each one of them came up to me separately and talked about Eleanore. Clooney whispered to me, "You're going to have a memorial? I'd very much like to sing. I really did love that lady."

The memorial was at Saint Paul's in Westwood, where I had received my first communion. The church was filled. All the family was there. Such an extended family we had, and we had all loved each other in our own way. Janet Blair came. Helen, Rose Marie, Rosie, Martha Raye. Milton Berle.

Donald Kahn, Gus and Grace's son, gave the eulogy. He talked about Eleanore, the Duchess. He had always called her that.

Rosie sang "She's Funny That Way." The ceremony was simple, and touching. And loving. At the end, Frankie Ortega, who had been playing the organ, came down and played the piano.

I looked around. There were Debbie and Richard (Barbara and Gail's son), sitting together. There were Barbara and Gail, and Jack and I. I listened to the piano. Frankie was playing "Till We Meet Again," the song the boy from Detroit had written just before the two Youngblood sisters embarked on their show business career. Look how far it had carried them—carried us all: to this California church.

The next day, we set out on our mission to Forest Lawn. Barbara had promised Eleanore she and Daddy would be together. After Eleanore's death, Barbara went to the Pierce Brothers Funeral Parlor, carrying two urns. One was an ordinary urn and one was small and made of sterling silver.

"Could you divide up the ashes into these two urns?" she inquired. They looked stunned. They had never had such a request.

"Separate the ashes?" they asked.

"That's right," replied the girl who might have made it into Tehachapi at age twelve.

They wavered. "Well, I guess so."

For a month after Eleanore's death, Barbara had lived in the apartment with the two urns. Then one day we went to the cemetery where Aunt Mag was buried, and placed one urn in a plot the cemetery had prepared beside her.

Then, Forest Lawn.

Barbara and I, Gail and Jack, and Debbie. We were nervous.

"What we are committing is *grave robbery*," Barbara said.

"Oh, I don't think so," Gail said coolly. "Grave robbery is when you're taking something *out*. We're putting something *in*."

That made Barbara feel better.

We couldn't find Daddy's grave.

"It's got to be here," Barbara said, clutching the urn.

"Of course it's here," I said. "I think we better go back for directions."

"Whispering Pines?" the attendant said. "Follow this path for twelve garbage cans, and then turn to the right. You can't miss it."

That remark released the hysteria and tension we were all feeling.

I remembered Eleanore at Laird Cregar's funeral. She had been very close to him—we all had—when he died suddenly. Ralph Blane, Hugh Martin, Eleanore, and I went out to visit his grave. On the way, Eleanore stopped at Daddy's plot to place some flowers she had brought for him. I think this unsettled her. She didn't like deep emotional moments, didn't know how to handle them the way that most people do. She became positively giddy. On the path toward Cregar's grave, we passed an enormous reproduction of Michelangelo's *David*, naked except for that fig leaf. Eleanore remarked, "Now, you *know* Laird had to sit up for *that!*" And then she started to sing, to relieve her tension. We watched her wending her way among the grave sites, her pearls swinging.

"There goes the Bea Lillie of Forest Lawn," I remarked.

I told them the story now. In the manic moment of the time, we, too, began to sing. It did help relieve the tension. We found Daddy's grave. Jack had the clippers and began to clean up the area. Barbara and Gail knelt down to pray. Barbara was clutching the silver urn. Gail was furtively digging with a trowel while Debbie and I kept lookout. We sang, they dug. Finally, Gail nodded. Barbara took the urn and emptied the ashes into the hole over Daddy's grave. They were together, as Barbara had promised.

We got up, brushed off our clothes. I glanced down.

I'm not sure I ever loved Eleanore. You don't *have* to love your mother. I had very complicated feelings about her. She did what she could, certainly, the best way she knew how. Jule Styne was very touched by her. She was the one who gave him the encouragement to go on. And there are a thousand people who can tell you of her kindnesses and her exploits. She was flamboyant and witty and enterprising and always theatrical.

In the end, I realized, without my even knowing it, she was the one who made me go on, keep going on. She was the strength. She gave me the strength.

In the end, thank heavens, we came to terms.

And so, exit Eleanore.

21

Moonlight in Vermont: Forty Years Later

When I got the phone call, I couldn't believe it. After forty years of long-distance romance with Vermont, the state had finally invited me to come visit! Among my friends, it had become a joke. Forty years of singing about moonlight in Vermont and I had never found an agent, lawyer, manager, or hot boyfriend to take me there even for a quick weekend. In my act, I used to ask audiences if any of them came from Vermont, but I never found anyone who did. The only Vermonter I had ever met was the former governor who had given me the key to the state while he and I were both visiting the governor of Massachusetts. But I had never gone north of the border.

So I was terrifically excited when the Vermont Travel Division asked if I could visit the state in early February so they could photograph me skiing, sleigh riding, and doing other things when the moon was full. I told them I would do everything (even skiing), but only if I got a chance to meet the governor. They laughed and asked me why. And I explained that just two days before their call, the new governor-elect, Madalyn Kunin, had invited me to sing at her inaugural ball on January 10, but I had been unable to do so, because I was working elsewhere. So now I could make up for it.

When the plane landed and I stepped on Vermont ground, I started to laugh. I told everybody that it was about time I saw Vermont since it had supported me for such a long time. The staff had made arrangements for me to stay at the Edson Hill Manor in Stowe. There was a fireplace in every room, including the bedroom, and a beautiful view of the Green Mountains. The whole place was full of warm lovely people on their way to or from the ski run. Of course, the first question asked of me when I arrived was how well did I ski. I dodged that one by saying I was terrific at *après*-skiing by the fireside.

For the four days I was there, I was doing something every minute, usually to the strains of "Moonlight in Vermont." I went to the lodge at the bottom of the ski run for luncheon, and as I walked in, the pianist started playing the song and I kept thinking, This is just like a movie. I mean, when does Doris Day make that bright entrance, chirping, "Slopes, anyone?" For lunch I had a beautiful salad and they asked if I wanted maple-syrup dressing. I said, "Why not?" And when I tasted it, I almost went crazy. I had never tasted any real maple syrup before—it had always been Log Cabin or Aunt Jemima's. But the real stuff was thick, gooey, and wonderful! But not exactly my idea of a salad dressing.

After lunch I was taken up in a gondola, where I was to lean out and wave at the skiers. Quite a feat when the wind is blowing and the gondola is swinging. At the top, I stood with the skiers and watched them take off while I was being photographed. As a final lovely gesture, they showed me what a ski tow looked like. I wondered for a moment if it would have altered the success of the song if I had sung "ski tows on a mountainside."

Then I was taken through a cider mill and shown where the apples were ground and pressed and the liquid converted and bottled. After *that* I was given some Vermont cheddar cheese. I told my host, Russell Smith, that I had read about Ben and Jerry's ice cream in *New York* magazine, where it had been voted number one in a poll of ice creams. Russ said there were several stores and restaurants in the state that served it and he would see to it that I could sample some.

Then I was whisked away to do a radio show on WJOY in Burlington. After I had talked to the disc jockey for a while, they opened up their phone lines so I could chat with people who called in. I was really thrilled. One man said he had been stationed in Okinawa forty years ago and he and his buddies used to sit around their radio station at eleven-thirty at night to listen to "Moonlight in Vermont." He wanted to thank me for bringing back old memories. Another Vermonter told me he had been in the service down South where many people had never heard of Vermont before, but thought it must be a beautiful place—all because of me and my recording! A lady called and told me the record had brought her together with her husband, in Palm Beach, Florida. He said he was from Vermont and she had asked, "What state is that in?" And soon after that my record came out, and that helped sell her on the fact that when he went back to Vermont, she should marry him and go back there with him. It constantly amazes me the impression records have on people's lives.

That evening I had dinner with Maria Von Trapp and her family, including her son Johannes and his wife. Stowe was where the baroness had decided to move after having been forced to flee Europe. Her lodge had been burned a couple of years before my visit, and this was the first year they were in the new lodge. I was so charmed at meeting Maria, a lovely lady of great breeding and gentleness, and was delighted when we went into the dining room and saw over a hundred people seated at tables drinking wine and eating beautiful food. Everywhere there were flowers that had been grown in Maria's own greenhouse. I kept searching each table, looking for edelweiss. I have seen *The Sound of Music* several times, and sometime during the evening I expected the baroness to pick up her skirt and burst into "the hills are alive with the sound of music."

The following day, in Montpelier, I sang for the state legislature and was introduced as "the woman who made Vermont famous." There was a standing ovation as I walked to the piano, and before I started to sing the song I had done over five thousand times, the only thing I could think of to say was "I'm scared!"

Earlier that morning, one of the press people had told me how funny it was that the lyric mentioned sycamore trees, because they couldn't think of one place in Vermont where there were sycamores. Maples everywhere. In my four-day trip I had seen nothing but maples. He whispered to me, "Why don't you change the lyric?" I thought, Dare I? Just before I got to the line "falling leaves and a sycamore," I decided, Why not? and sang "falling leaves and —a maple tree." The entire legislature roared its approval, and when I was through I heard many bravos and everyone jumped to their feet again.

Governor Kunin and I shared a press conference and we had a chance to speak for a few minutes. She signed a proclamation declaring February 5, 1985, Moonlight in Vermont Day. She told me she had danced to the song at the inaugural ball, and then she whispered an aside: "You can't say now that you've never been here, so you'll have to change your story!"

I had the four most wonderful days of my life in Vermont. There's a sense of identity there that I don't always find in big cities. People are kind and giving and make you feel at home. I know I will return. In fact, I want to experience spring, summer, and fall there. Even though I've been singing "Moonlight in Vermont" for over forty years, I know I will sing it with greater feeling now. And in my act, when I speak of the song about Vermont, I can tell everybody I've finally been there, and the state is even better than the song!

22

Taking My
Turn

—

Sometimes it's just a question of waiting long
enough.

I had always wanted to be in the theater in New York, doing an
original show. Something I could help work on and help create as an
actor.

I had paid my dues. I had learned how to perform onstage. I had
grown as a real *performer* performer. As an actress. And I had waited.

Not alone. There was quite a bunch of us who had performed in
the forties and early fifties, had been discarded in the late fifties and
the sixties, and rediscovered in the seventies. ("Discarded" may be
too brutal a word, but what else do you say when Frank Sinatra had
to plead with Columbia Pictures to allow him to play Maggio in
From Here to Eternity and Bette Davis put an ad in *The Hollywood
Reporter*: THREE-TIME OSCAR WINNER NEEDS JOB?)

Maybe it was easier on us singer types—the ones who weren't

making movies. We always *worked*. But it wasn't the same. I look at Mel Torme, Kay Starr, Jack Jones, Keely Smith, Tony Bennett. Clooney. Peggy Lee. We were the survivors, and because we had survived, we were suddenly considered a sort of show-business royalty—or perhaps more precisely, elder statesmen. Not only because we had survived, but because we had all grown as performers. Things we couldn't have sung or understood when we were kids now made deep emotional sense. It's one of the benefits of getting older. You really can get better.

Which brings me to *Taking My Turn*.

I got a call from my agent, Eddie Robbins, at the Morris office, about a musical show off-Broadway.

My friend Ted Hook had seen the show during a workshop production, and had found it delightful.

"Of course, it's about aging," Eddie continued, sounding tentative.

"Great!" I said. "It's about time somebody spoke up about that."

Of course, I knew about the Gray Panthers and other organizations that were fighting for the rights of the elderly. But there had been nothing in the *theater*.

"You have to audition," Eddie added.

"I don't mind."

I was further encouraged because I knew two of the people connected with the show. Maurice Levine, one of the producers, had also been the man behind the very successful Lyrics and Lyricists series at the 92nd Street Y in New York, and I had appeared in the series many times. He was a very dear man, a musical conductor with fine taste. And I knew Will Holt, the lyricist, who had collaborated with the Sherman brothers on a wonderful musical about the home-front activities during World War II called *Over Here!*, starring the Andrews Sisters. I took over Patti's role in 1976 and appeared with Maxene. During that time I had gotten to know Will and his wife, Dolly, quite well.

So I went to audition. To my surprise, Barry Levitt, who sometimes worked as my accompanist, had been hired as musical director of the show.

"Listen," I announced as I came out to audition for what seemed like an entire roomful of people—most of them the producers, I found out later. "I got a friend here—your conductor. So when it comes to voting, his vote doesn't count."

I sang a couple of songs. They seemed to like that, and the director, Robert Livingston, handed me a poem to read.

This was an audition?

I wasn't sure what to *do* with a poem. But I thought of Johnny Meyer's advice. Take it moment to moment. The poem was called "In April," and its voice was that of a woman who had lost her only son in April, and was amazed that, grieving as she was, nature continued to burst into bloom around her.

I took my time, and read it simply.

I guess that worked, because they were very quiet after I finished. Then Livingston got up, shook my hand, and thanked me. There were murmurs of thanks all around and I left.

It was the Christmas season. Barry Levitt came to a party and said, "They're very interested in you."

"I'm very interested in *them*," I replied. "When does this interest develop into a little action?"

I found out soon enough. They called me back. The creative people wanted to see how the different combinations of characters worked. This was, as they explained to us, an ensemble piece, and the only way that it would work was if every character was separate and distinct, so that the combination formed a forceful total.

"Uh-huh," I said. In other words, they wanted another audition. But it seems they were right. I found there was a kind of chemistry at work. My character, Dorothy, was outspoken, funny, happily married, and devoted to marching for good causes. Another character, Janet, was totally repressed and wounded by the death of her husband. We had to work together. We had not only to act, we had to interact. I started understanding the process. So, in various combinations, we actors sang a little, danced a little. The creative team looked us over. Then we left. Later that afternoon, Eddie Robbins called. The part was mine if I wanted it. I did.

We couldn't get into rehearsal until April. There wasn't a theater available off-Broadway at the time. Perhaps it was just as well. By the time we started rehearsals, everybody was eager to get going.

The little group that was to be a family for the next few weeks of rehearsal gathered together at the Entermedia Theater on Second Avenue and Twelfth Street at ten o'clock on a cold gray spring morning.

The first order of business was that the composer, Gary Friedman, and Will Holt, the lyricist, were going to perform the score of the show. It was a terrific moment. I have found over the years that nobody performs music better than the people who write it. Mercer and Arlen knew exactly what they were doing. So did Will and Gary, I found out. We sat there onstage, and they sang in front of the work light. The second thing I found out was that nobody likes to waste anything in the theater. Like electricity. Or heat. So you got used to a work light, and rehearsing with your coat on.

The next week was devoted to learning the score. I was not prepared for the enormous amount of music we had to sing. Neither was anybody else. This was not a usual musical, where you came out and did a couple of numbers solo, and maybe had a trio number, and then during the finale the chorus sang most of the tune and you only had to come in with your arms up and your voice out for the last few lines. No, this was singing, from beginning to end. An *ensemble* piece, with the emphasis on the ensemble. It meant that nobody ever left the stage from the moment the lights went up until the end of the act. Ditto for the second act.

We had to learn songs. We had to learn harmony. Parts. This was a seasoned bunch of pros I was working with. Marni Nixon, who had dubbed everybody's voice in the movies, including Audrey Hepburn's in *My Fair Lady*. Tiger Haynes, a marvelous performer and guitarist I had seen many times at the Bon Soir nightclub. Victor Griffin, who had been so moving when Jack and I saw him in *Ballroom*. Cissy Houston, a jazz and soul singer with a great reputation among musicians. Ted Thurston and Sheila Smith, both veterans of many Broadway musicals. And Mace Barrett, whom I had never met but who was in essence going to be the interlocutor of the piece.

After three days, all of us began to look at each other cross-eyed. What had we gotten ourselves into? The music kept coming on and on. Okay, the songs were brilliant, but did we have to learn *all* these harmony parts? Yes, Gary Friedman said firmly, we did. And so we sat. And learned.

But a new musical is not the same as one that has been polished and performed. We would sing. And Gary would listen. And then Gary would change things. Harmonies we had memorized, we had to relearn. It was all part of the process, but it did make for a *little* tension. Something akin to the peasants just before the French Revolution. On Day Five, I think it was, Gary and Barry had an argument. Or rather, Gary blew up at Barry. I don't recall the reason, maybe I never knew it. Strangely enough, it broke the tension. Gary very gracefully came back and apologized to all of us for putting Barry on the spot, and from that moment, we all really started acting like a family.

Which was terrific, except for the family squabbles that ensued. Marni was, to put it kindly, inquiring. She had to know a reason for everything. Why should she do this? What was the purpose of *that*? Sometimes Bob explained it patiently and to her satisfaction. Other times, not.

"Marni," we would say, "for Christ's sake, let's get *on* with it! We've got a whole *show* to get through."

Bit by bit, we did get through it. Like little babies, first learning to crawl, and then, "Let's get it up on its feet."

By this time, Bob had made us into a group, and he discussed, or rather, made us discuss, what everybody's purpose was. Why did the character, Janet, react that way? Why was Eric afraid of death? And so on. Personally, I have always thought it okay to leave a little of the *mystery* intact, but I wasn't going to quibble. Bob was very definite about the way he wanted to work. In his mind, we could all, if necessary, perform each other's roles—we would understand each other that well. Since he had also gathered the material and put it together (it came from poems, essays, and other pieces that people "of age," as he put it, had submitted to him), Bob had a very clear intent of a group's expression as well as an individual's.

So we worked, and discussed, and lurched through a run-through. And it came time to perform it for a very select group of people: the producers, the creative staff, and the people that they had invited. That moment has to come sometime. We felt totally unprepared.

We were being tossed to the lions. This wasn't even a public performance, just a run-through in a rehearsal studio. But I found my
hands sweating. There were so many moves. When you're onstage
the whole time, and you have to keep moving, and they give you
these moves, and you're supposed to get them into your head, along
with fifty million lyrics. . . .

The stage manager called "Places, please," and away we went.
We did pull through the opening song together. I don't think we
were even aware of the reaction to the piece. Nothing hit me until
Marni, Cissy, and I did a trio called "Fine for the Shape I'm in,"
which catalogued all the illnesses we fall prey to. It had a jaunty
country-western flavor to it, and at the end, Marni gave her coloratura
all, Cissy spiraled up and down four or five octaves of soul, and I
gave the girl singer's trumpet tones. We did sound pretty damn good
together. And the reaction was terrific. Hey, I suddenly decided, this
is going to be *fun*. And so it was. It was fun, and it was joyous. And
it was also very moving.

We all felt very confident after that run-through. We had gotten
the show up on its feet. It had "legs," as they say in Hollywood. In
other words, it could run.

Then we weren't quite so sure. We had to deal with the stage set,
which was a series of risers, supposed to represent a park. The risers
were there so that we could sit on different levels. However, for us,
it was the equivalent of climbing up and down the Matterhorn, or
at least five flights of stairs a night. You say your line, go up three
stairs, turn, say another line, sing your song, move down two steps,
and so forth.

Bob gave us one whole day just to move around on the set. First
the men. Men *first*. The pioneers! Then us fragile women. We tried
to get comfortable. It was not easy. From the balcony, the set looked
gorgeous, for it had been designed for another theater with more
stadium-like rows of seats, so that the audience would be looking
down on the set. However, the producers had not been able to obtain
that theater. Here, the audience was looking at the set at eye level.
And to most, it was extraordinarily ugly.

But we clambered up and down, and from that moment, we
rehearsed *on* the set. That made things easier.

My next crisis came with my costume. Judith Dolan, the designer, had instructions from Bob as to the look of each character. I had only one caution.

"Oh God, don't dress me in purple," I said. "I look lousy in purple."

They didn't. They brought out an orange skirt and a beige sweater. And a jacket that looked like a horse blanket.

"What is this?"

"It's Dorothy's costume."

"I don't understand. I am a fairly wealthy woman. I am married to a very successful lawyer. I have taste. I have a sense of humor."

"You also march for worthy causes," Bob reminded me.

"Yes, but not in sackcloth!" I said. "I'm not a sweater-and-skirt type."

"Dorothy is," Bob said. He could be very stubborn. He had in his mind that Dorothy was the last of the old-time radicals, and she would never get dressed up. I, on the other hand, wanted to go the other way with this show. I thought it was a beautiful show, but missing something. Missing a kind of joy of . . . well, fantasy, say. I remembered when *4 Girls 4* opened, and we four women, all over fifty, came out, dressed to the nines. People reached out for us. "The way you look. You really gave us an inspiration. If you can do it, why can't we?" they said.

In *Taking My Turn*, I thought there should be a moment—yes, hell, call it a musical-comedy moment—when we all come out, kick up our heels, and show what we as *performers* can really do. That magical moment, true or not, when we are dressed up, doing a great number of moving and dancing. In other words, saying, "Hey, what's the alternative? Let's go with what we've got, for as long as we've got."

Maybe performers *are* different from other people. People question performers. "Why aren't you retired?" The thought of retiring doesn't enter any performer's mind. *Taking My Turn* presented one view of looking at people who do what everybody has to do, which is to age. But for me, there wasn't enough *joy* in the show. I wanted to say, "Let's take those joyful moments. Let's go!" I wanted something like that in this show.

And I didn't want to wear a skirt and sweater. And horse blanket. Fortunately, one of the producers agreed with me. Joanne Cummings looked at me grimly and said, "I won't have *my* star wearing that." She went out to Saks, Bonwit's, wherever she had an account, and must have selected thirty or forty different outfits. Then she came over to my apartment with Judy Dolan while I tried them on. I couldn't believe she had done that. I found it absolutely amazing and I was very grateful to her. We tried on outfit after outfit. Finally, there was one left. It was purple. To please Joanne, I tried it on. It looked wonderful on me.

"I thought you said you couldn't wear purple!" Judy Dolan cried.

"Well, I was wrong," I said, biting my lip. "I'm sorry."

I added a little pearl necklace, and I was happy. Joanne was happy. Judy was happy.

The next day all the producers—everybody—was happy. Except Bob. He wanted that proletariat look. Well, he didn't get it. He didn't get his proletariat look and I didn't get my high-kick number. Which is why people say, "Well, that's show business." What we got for an ensemble number was the *opposite* of high kicks. It was a song called "Taking My Turn" and the gist of it is summed up in the lyrics

Takin' my time,
Takin' a stroll.
Lookin' at life,
Seein' it whole.
Keepin' the beat
All of the while.
Always in step,
Always in style! . . .

Douglas Norwick, the choreographer, gave us the least amount of movement possible, the equivalent of Peggy Lee's finger snaps on a rhythm song. Very underplayed. And we all did these steps, or crossed our legs, synchronized and with great style. It proved to be very effective. But I always missed getting gussied up and doing the high kicks! I guess it's what Eleanore or Aunt Mag would have done.

For me, there was a special challenge in the show—a song Gary had set from the poem I read at the audition, about a grieving woman, "In April." In spite of her despair over losing her son and her astonishment that in April nature continues to bloom, finally, she goes on with her life.

I had never sung a song like that before. It was stark and bare in the first part, and rather a poignant cry in the second half. I really didn't trust myself. I always wanted to do more with it. I had gone through no such tragedy. I had never lost a child. Maybe I felt guilty about usurping feelings, although I felt it was my duty. And my duty to make it *honest*. Will kept saying, "Let it happen. Just tell the story and it will happen. Don't *make* it happen." It sounded like Johnny Meyer again. And then one night, I was tired. Something had gone wrong with the day. Just a little frustration. I don't even remember it. But I used that feeling. I found a whole mass of feelings welling up inside me as I sang.

Again, it was one of those times when everyone came backstage following the performance to say, "What happened? It was so different. So moving." I told Will, "I've got to keep whatever it was I did." He shook his head. "No, it'll be different every time. Don't try to repeat. Just discover it new each time."

While you're working on a project, you don't really see what's going on. From the actor's point of view, we were all onstage all the time and we really did have to *listen* to one another and react honestly. There was no fooling or deception, because we didn't have a book in the usual sense. We had thoughts, poems, songs; we spoke of dreams and fears. Sometimes we spoke to ourselves, to each other, to the audience. It became almost impossible to dissemble.

So, you don't really see what you have. But there is a magical moment when an audience *tells* you.

It was *not* a usual Broadway musical. First, the subject of aging was not one that any commercial show would touch. Too depressing. Second, the show was mostly music. And the score had an enormous range. From the happy nostalgia of "Do You Remember?," lamenting the loss of the amenities of yesteryear—and its counterpart,

"What Would Have Happened?," listing the loss to the world if Michelangelo, Bernard Shaw, Chagall, and George Burns had all been confined to retirement at sixty-five—to the almost psychotic rage of a widow's lament, "Two of Me," the Sousa-like triumph of "Sex After Sixty," and the incredible poignancy of the last ballad between the married couple, "It Still Isn't Over." It wasn't until we performed the show in its entirety that we were able to grasp what Gary, Will, and Bob had accomplished. They had broken new ground in the theater both in the subject matter and the way that they handled it.

Whatever doubts one might have had were dispelled when we saw what happened to audiences. They loved the show. They found their way downtown, they saw, and they were conquered. The producers came back after the first preview and smiled secret smiles, said they were very happy, and went off to a restaurant across the street to confer. Which is what producers are constantly doing. The creators corrected little things each night, but for the most part, the show we started with was the one we opened with.

The opening was on June 9. The first-night party was held at the Ballroom. I had suggested to the producers that Greg Dawson's place would be a marvelous spot for a party. He was renowned for his food, and the ambience was really elegant. I thought the opening night, the party, everything, was really terrific. Especially when the reviews came out. The *New York Times* was ecstatic. And so were we. The other papers followed. Unqualified raves! At least for that one night, the "family" was happy. We all hugged and kissed and drank and celebrated.

But the producers balked at paying for the party. It seems that Joanne Cummings's father didn't like the food. So she didn't want to pay. Another mystery! The woman was generous and very giving to me, and yet angry at Greg. Greg called his lawyers. The producers called their lawyers. Finally it was settled. All because Joanne's father didn't like the food. I still don't understand it.

But what I did understand was that success in a New York play gave me a lot of credentials. It gave me a Broadway profile, offers for other shows—and an Al Hirshfield drawing in the *New York*

Times. When *Taking My Turn* was selected by the Public Broadcasting System to be the opening show for its Great Performances series, I couldn't have been happier.

After the opening, the producers were confident enough to hire understudies. One of the people they hired was a young black woman named Carol Woods. I thought, Are they out of their *minds*? This isn't an *old* woman. Aging, yes; we are *all* aging. As they said in the show, "Ain't none of us getting any *younger*." But I wasn't sure what she could do.

I found out. Carol had to replace Cissy for a matinee. There is a gospel song in the show, "I Am Not Old!," that always set off a terrific reaction because of its combination of sentiment and gospel pyrotechnics. It always stopped the show.

At this matinee, Carol appeared for the first time. The rest of us veterans helpfully guided her through the first act, leading her to her place if she got confused. At the end of the act, we congratulated her. She was a real asset to this ensemble. Then, in the middle of the second act, Carol came to her number and she *sang* it. She tore through it. It was hair-raising. Spine-chilling. I think we all must have sat there with our mouths open. When she was finished, the audience screamed.

I thought, Hmm, I must remember *her*.

From that moment on, nobody had to help Carol. She did just fine, thank you.

Before *Taking My Turn* went into rehearsal, I had been contacted by a man named Geoff Parker in Atlanta. Georgia State University wanted to honor Johnny Mercer, and Geoff asked if I wouldn't put a show together for a specially invited audience. I thought it was a splendid idea. The only problem was, I had never really put a show together. While I was doing a concert in Charlotte, North Carolina, I discussed this with Loonis McGloohan, a brilliant musician who worked at the Jefferson Pilot Broadcasting Company. He suggested Julius La Rosa as a good choice to sing Mercer. I agreed. Then he came up with a very hip sparrow of a jazz singer named Marlene

VerPlanck. I thought, well he's batting a thousand so far. And then he mentioned Johnny Hartman, and I thought, That's it, we're in business. I thanked Loonis very much, went back to New York, contacted all three of them, and we started to work. The "we" turned out to be the four performers, Tex Arnold, and Jack. At first, Jack was more of an interested observer than a participant, but that changed rather quickly.

We were faced with an overwhelming field of songs. Which ones to pick? It started out as random choice.

"I'd like to do 'Old Black Magic,' " Hartman said. I wrote it down.

"I've always liked 'G.I. Jive,' " Julie murmured. I wrote *that* down.

" 'Skylark'!" Marlene said.

I nodded. "I'll do 'I Remember You.' And we'll *all* do 'Ac-Cent-Tchu-Ate the Positive.' " We were on our way.

Daddy and Johnny had written "Hooray for Hollywood." I thought of doing a medley of Hollywood songs using that one as the key. Julie came up with an idea for another medley. The songs—band themes, really—that Johnny had put lyrics to. There was "Early Autumn" and the Benny Goodman–Ziggy Elman special "And the Angels Sing." In a couple of sessions we had mapped out great segments of the program.

"Suppose we end with 'When the World Was Young'?" I suggested. "We each take a chorus and walk off, vanish . . . that's the end of the program." And that's what we did.

Jack sat and watched. After three or four sessions, he said to me quietly, "You're going to need a little humor in there. Some stories about Johnny."

A few days later, Geoff Parker called from Atlanta. He wanted to know what our light plan was going to be and wanted to know who our stage manager was going to be.

"Lights . . . stage manager?" I repeated in a dim-witted fashion. I had no idea about lights. Except to know when they weren't on me. I looked to Jack. He took the phone. And suddenly, Jack was involved.

Thank heavens he was. No matter how good you are, you still

need another "eye" to look objectively. Jack was that eye. The four of us were singers, not dancers. Jack gave us some movement, and suddenly the production had a flow to it. He was also aware of the pace of the piece. He started to shape it.

I was still performing my one-woman show, *Maggie and Friends*, with Tex Arnold and Barry Levitt. So in the late winter, we performed *that* piece in Indianapolis, hopped on a plane to Atlanta, and arrived for a run-through of the Mercer show before the presentation the following evening. This was the first time we had ever done the whole show from beginning to end. It worked very well. Suspiciously well, I thought. *Something* should go wrong.

The next day, we spent with the media, the CBS News show with Pat Collins, *Entertainment Tonight*, and *PM*, and then that night the show was on. Local television was covering it. They shot the whole thing with one camera. We sailed through the piece. Afterward, there was a flood of people backstage. Sammy Cahn had flown down from New York to make a presentation. Ervin Drake, the president of the American Guild of Authors and Composers, was there, as well as Hal David, the head of ASCAP.

"This is the best show we have ever seen!" they all cried. Well, sure, it was in Johnny's home state. "No," they insisted, "this show is terrific. Do something with it." Ginger Mercer, Johnny's widow, was by my side. She nodded agreement.

Why not?

When I got back to New York, I telephoned a friend of mine, Jack Sameth, at channel 13, New York's public television station. He was very interested and wanted to take a look at the tape we had made.

"That's terrific," my Jack said, "but I'd like to change things around a bit before he sees the tape." Jack went into a studio and placed songs in a different sequence, cut some of the intros, and showed the finished product to me. I was enormously impressed.

So was Jack Sameth. But before we could come to an understanding, channel 13 renewed its series *Side by Side by . . .* , which was a program devoted to lyricists, and just happened to include Mercer as one of them. Channel 13 needed only one Mercer show.

Then *Taking My Turn* came along, and I was busy, to say the least. During this time, Johnny Hartman and I were doing a television program together. He was coughing.

"I'm not singing right," he said. "I just keep coughing. My throat feels funny. Maybe I should go see a doctor."

He asked the name of my doctor, but then left for England on a singing engagement, before seeing any physician. In England he couldn't sing. He came back to the States, found out he had throat cancer. He lived a few months longer, and then he died. I must sound heartless, but it isn't that. It's just that, well, it's expressed in *Taking My Turn*: "the older you get, the more friends you lose," and, after a while, you just get numb. That was my feeling about Johnny Hartman. At first, I couldn't believe it. And then I just got numb.

But, of course, life did go on. Geoff Parker called from Atlanta. He wanted to play the Mercer show again at Georgia State—this time for money. Loonis McGloohan called from Charlotte. He wanted to book the Mercer show into a theater, Spirit Square, for three days. We had a minitour set, but we needed a replacement for Johnny Hartman. Jack came to see *Taking My Turn* one night when Carol was substituting for Cissy.

"She's great!" he said. "Can't we use her in the Mercer show?"

And so we did. We added "A Woman's Prerogative" and some other songs from *St. Louis Woman*. Carol gave the show an energy that was like a spring tonic. I'm sure Mercer would have grinned from ear to ear, if he had heard her.

And I became the producer. I received the contracts, parceled out the paychecks, took care of the room reservations and plane tickets. Exactly what I had seen our stage manager do on *4 Girls 4*. So, now I was doing it. I'm a fairly organized woman. I enjoyed this. I was making the decisions. I was in control. I was in command. I really never had been before.

The show was such a success in Charlotte that I decided to go to Ken Olsen, at Columbia Artists, to see whether he could book it on tour.

"Oh, Margaret," he moaned, "you've come at the worst time. The business is so *slow*."

"I know, Ken," I said sympathetically, and then after twenty-five minutes, I had him asking when he could see it.

minutes, I had him asking when he could see it.

"I'll tell you tomorrow," I said. That night, I had a dream. I was asking Maurice Levine to add it on his series Lyrics and Lyricists as a bonus event.

The next day I called him up. He knew all about the show, and he agreed. We would do it on Sunday afternoon and Monday night.

It was announced, and sold out immediately. The Y had never seen such a big production. And since we had done it so often, we were well rehearsed.

The reaction was enormous. And the next week, when the reviews came out—that in itself was extraordinary for a one-time event—I found myself in a most unusual—and, now, uncomfortable—position.

Everybody wanted the show. And started to get mad when I hesitated about making a choice. That was when I turned to Alvin Deutsch, my lawyer.

He lectured me gently. "Margaret, you must be like a mother with a child. You want what's best for the child. You have friends. That has nothing to do with it. The question is: Who is going to take care of the child? You've got to *choose*."

And that's where you came in. When I was having my mini nervous breakdown.

Well, I don't want to leave you up in the air, asking, "what *happened?*"

But life is like that. I'll tell you what I can.

I chose producers for the Mercer show, but when they did not do what they had promised, I went in search of other producers.

I again had several offers. But from producers who wanted to take the show *as is*, and I know it needs work. It needs movement. It needs more theatricality for it to survive in this tough market. Now I have found a producer who agrees with me. So we have gone back to work.

I have toured with *Taking My Turn*. And now that's over.

I've been offered two new shows.

I'm doing symphony concerts all over the country. One-nighters with big bands, club dates.

The other day I got a call from *4 Girls 4*, and I'll be on the road with them for a month. It'll be fun seeing them again.

I have just released an album for Audiophile Records called *The Lady's in Love with You!*, and that's doing just fine, thank you. I've been pretty good about not quoting reviews, but these two are *new*, they're me as I am now, so forgive me. *People* magazine said·

> Margaret Whiting seems to sound better all the time. There are certainly few singers around who truly interpret popular songs as well, searching out the turns of musical and verbal phrase that highlight an emotion here, an impression there. . . .

And the *New York Times*:

> *Pop Album of the Week:* Margaret Whiting—"The Lady's in Love With You!" (Audiophile). The veteran pop singer with a voice of burnished brass, perfect diction and phrasing that respects to the letter a composer's intentions, communicates a robust emotional resilience on an album whose songs take a long retrospective view.

And now, I just found out that I'm up for an award from the New York Music Awards as the cabaret performer of the year. My two competitors are, by coincidence, Cissy Houston and her daughter Whitney.

23

One More
for the Road

I was walking down Broadway and glanced at the window of a bookstore, looking at the titles. I thought, With any luck, my book should be there in nine months. And then I thought, My life took about sixty years to live so far, and about a year to write about.

And two hours to read.

And that brought me to this last.

I'm not sure how this should go, but I'm going to put it down anyway. Call it a vision. I see it in movie terms as a great panoramic view of two streets, the two main streets of the entertainment business—a long shot from way back. And then you dolly in and focus on the little events, the private moments.

One street is called Broadway. The other is called Hollywood. (It's a combination of Hollywood Boulevard and Sunset and it isn't one street, but because this is my movie and my long shot, we'll just look at it as one street.)

Take a look at everything that happened on both those streets during my father's life, my mother's, my aunt's, and mine, and it should give some picture of not only our lives but the life of the business we were all in, the entertainment business. I'll show you what I mean.

Broadway, first. It was always first. Everything started there. Washington gave his Farewell Address on Broadway, right there at the bottom of it. Since then, Lindbergh, mayors, kings, and astronauts have had ticker-tape parades on Broadway, and marching along beside them, at one time or another, were George M. Cohan, Richard Rodgers, Moss Hart, Helen Hayes, Mike Nichols, Sarah Bernhardt.

Tin Pan Alley was on West Twenty-eighth Street, just off Broadway, and it was there the song pluggers played the piano and made hits and reputations. My father was one of those men until the success of "Till We Meet Again" during World War I placed him in the important rank of American songwriters. He came along just as the First World War exploded the old morality. Social dancing brought a craze for music, and my father was there at the right time. So, in the twenties, he trotted nervously down Tin Pan Alley, the string of successful songs like "Till We Meet Again" behind him, and a whole string of hits yet ahead for him. He walked that street, and so did Gershwin and Irving Berlin. Uncle Jerry. Harold Arlen.

Broadway. My mother, Eleanore, walked that street with Aunt Mag in tow. Like all the other vaudeville artists, they were looking for management and material. They passed under the marquee of the Palace, where Jolson played, as did my godmother, Sophie Tucker. Eleanore and her sister would be working in vaudeville with Jolson and the Marx Brothers. Aunt Mag would be recording "Hard Hearted Hannah" into a cone, for those were the days of the white "coon shouters." Aunt Mag was one of them and she recorded in a little studio off Broadway.

And then the time would come when I would be walking up Broadway, listening to the sound of my voice singing "It Might As Well Be Spring" from every record store along the way. That was in the autumn of 1945, after the V-J Day celebration that ended the Second World War jammed Times Square with servicemen and girls and children and mothers, people crying and jitterbugging on tops of cars. I passed the Paramount Theater, where teen-age girls had swooned over Frank Sinatra nine shows a day, and a bit to the west, a musical called *Oklahoma!* had opened at the St. James and quietly changed the way we thought about musical theater. Farther up Broadway was the Biltmore, where *Hair* would open and bring other changes in the way we thought about theater, and even farther ahead the Ed Sullivan Theater, where the Beatles crashed on the scene in 1964 and completely changed the way we thought about music and entertainment.

It was never a pretty street, Broadway, unless you were hearing your latest hit wafting out on the breeze. (Then, even Nightmare Alley would have sufficed.) Broadway was never pretty. It was tough. But it was alive with excitement. The marquees, the electric signs crowding each other promised happiness and drama and power. Broadway sang. Oshkosh listened. And then Oshkosh sang.

A collage of changes, from horsecars to streetcars, from streetcars to buses. And from song pluggers to swing bands, from cool jazz to rock artists, from vaudeville to radio, then radio to television, the street kept changing, but always surviving.

And so did we. Vaudeville reigned. Radio came in and put an end to vaudeville. What radio didn't do, talking pictures did. Vaudeville died.

My father went west, just as Eleanore had hoped. For a while we lived at the Hollywood Roosevelt Hotel, which was very swank then. It was during the worst depression the nation had ever seen, but for us, it was a golden time.

The other road. Hollywood Boulevard. I remember driving down Hollywood Boulevard when we first arrived in California, and I took my coat and sweater off, even though it was February and freezing, because we were in *California*.

In the thirties, all the exciting movie premieres took place on Hollywood Boulevard. Searchlights waved through the movie-starred, starry nights. It was elegant. Everyone dressed in evening clothes and went dining and dancing afterward at the Mocambo, the Trocadero, the Cocoanut Grove, with society bands and all the stars dancing close. They were glamourous, those days in the court of

Louis B. Mayer, when the collective immigrant dream of an all-singing, all-dancing, happy world was turned into a multi-billion-dollar industry. And Richard Whiting, Harry Warren, Jerome Kern, Irving Berlin—all those men were court musicians. What a free-and-easy, golf-playing, sunny existence we had. Hollywood Boulevard, where Cookie Warren and I went to the Saturday matinees, the chauffeur following discreetly behind us. Hollywood Boulevard. Hollywood and Vine. Vine Street, where the song pluggers (who had also migrated from the East) sat on the car fenders waiting for the singing stars to emerge from the Brown Derby. It was worth sitting all day on a fender if Tommy Dorsey would record one of your tunes.

Hollywood Boulevard during the war, jammed with the khaki and white uniforms of soldiers and sailors, all taking a look-see at that street of dreams, before heading for the Hollywood Canteen, on Cahuenga Boulevard off Sunset, where all those dreams came true. Dancing with Lana Turner! Washing dishes with Gene Kelly! Jitterbugging with Betty Hutton! It was a wonderful time, and we all felt very close. Strange, looking back on it now, to see how really *sweet* we were as a country. We did live those MGM lives, and dreamed their dreams.

Just north of Hollywood Boulevard stands the round skyscraper that looks like a stack of records on a jukebox. The Capitol Tower, the symbol of Capitol records, the dream that Johnny Mercer turned into a reality, the dream that started a little farther down Vine Street in the tiny office I used to visit after school, even while I was making records. And then along came "Moonlight in Vermont" and everybody knew my name, and I was part of the music business, not because I was Daddy's daughter, but because I was a record star. I was *there*. And the song pluggers got off their fenders for *me*.

And then the street changed, as Broadway had. After the war, television took over. The CBS radio studios on Sunset and Gower, where I had done so many broadcasts, were converted, like so many missionaries. And again, on Sunset and Vine, NBC's Radio City, which had opened in 1938, was now devoted to *television*. Television. CBS. NBC. They were the big names now, instead of the movie studios. "Ratings" came into the vocabulary. And vaudeville came back, in the form of Milton Berle and *The Ed Sullivan Show* and the other weekly variety shows on television.

The big bands never came back, really. But there were little clubs where their former singers sang, clubs like the Crescendo and the Interlude. The band musicians had gotten jobs on television and in the studios. Swing turned to pop, and we all caught our breath until the next change. And that came hurtling at us. Rock. Elvis. Beatles. Stones. Groups. Groupies.

Sunset Boulevard seemed home for that. Most of the business of show business moved west. There were the billboards all along Sunset advertising to the westbound traffic the newest rock sensations. They changed monthly, sometimes weekly. Along where the Sunset Strip was once the hippies' hangout, there are still remnants, a few jazz joints, and Pat Collins the Hip Hypnotist. Gleaming skyscrapers house all those many many agents, and agencies. Sometimes it seems as though there aren't enough skyscrapers in the world to house all the agents. And off Sunset, a little to the south, new empires rise up like the Emerald City in Oz.

Back on Hollywood Boulevard, there is a lot that is seedy, and that is putting it kindly. Refugees from Kearny, Nebraska, have come in to look for the stars, not knowing the stars have either disappeared or moved on, leaving no forwarding address. The only stars on Hollywood Boulevard are in cement now, in front of Grauman's Chinese Theater. *My* star, "Margaret Whiting, Star of Records, Radio, and TV," is located on the Walk of Fame right by Musso and Frank's restaurant, the one great restaurant remaining. And how convenient it is! The bums and hustlers walk over these pavements, looking for . . . what? One bookstore, the Pickwick, remains. And the rest is crummy and shoddy and down-at-the-mouth, and for years no one went near Hollywood Boulevard except for pickups. Pickup sex. Pickup booze. Pickup life.

And yet, it's changing. Grauman's Chinese is now Mann's Chinese, but it still retains its allure. The Pantages Theater has been restored. It houses legitimate theater. The Hollywood Roosevelt has been redone, remodeled, reopened.

Restored. Revived. Those are words I hear all the time now. There's an excitement in the air. People are looking back, as well as forward. Watching what was, and reexamining it. Linda Ronstadt, who loved those ballads, *our* songs, got together with the wonderful Nelson Riddle, and made the songs popular all over again for a rock generation. Streisand, after a few flings at rock, recently recorded an album of Broadway songs, which she performs brilliantly, and it has become her biggest hit in years. Now everyone's doing it. A rock musician overheard a studio session a few weeks ago. The group was playing Dietz and Schwartz's "Dancing in the Dark." "That's a real pretty tune," he observed. "I hope it makes it." Well, what did *he* know? At the same time, what do *I* know? I do know the Culture Club, but I just heard about the Roaches. And I thought the Cure was what alcoholics took. But I try to keep up. I keep listening. I keep singing new songs. I keep looking for what's good in every kind of music. So I'm still following my father's advice that way. "Listen to it all," he said. And he was right. It's fascinating.

So where are we on these streets? On these two main stems? I'm not sure. I know that for a lot of us, it's the fact that we *survived*. There's a club called Freddy's in New York, and there have been some glorious singers there this year. Kay Starr came in, and she never sounded better. Keely Smith, a most underrated jazz singer, appeared there too. We got together one night, and started to laugh. Like Peggy Lee and Rosemary Clooney. Here we were, all of us, no longer forty, and going stronger than ever. We all had lived more, learned more, and were singing better. We knew what the words meant now. Maybe we didn't at twenty. Who does? Perhaps a couple of those outrageous genius giants like Streisand and Garland. They seemed to know everything by instinct. But for the rest of us, it was a question of living, and we did. And learning, and we did that too. I'll say it now, because it's my book and I'm allowed to. I'm proud of us all, proud of me, proud of the rest of us Girl Singers who saw it through, who kept at it, who are *keeping* at it. I never felt better in my life. There are things I could have done. I could have pushed more. I perhaps could have gone farther. But it doesn't matter. I don't regret anything. I'm so very proud of my daughter, Debbie, who's grown into a beautiful woman. I have a wonderful thing going with Jack. We are one another's best friend and support. We share a great love and it's turned out to be the best relationship I ever had.

Sure, it's hard to get repairmen to make a service call, it's hard to get a venetian blind fixed, it's hard to get a package mailed with the right postage, or money from the bank without standing in line but that's life the way it is now. I still think it's wonderful and fascinating.

So, if my vision here was a Fellini film, it would end, quite possibly, with a parade of figures, hands somehow linked to one another, improbable figures together: my father, John Garfield, Louis B. Mayer, Sophie Tucker, Johnny Mercer, Judy Garland, Edward R. Murrow, Freddie Martin, Eleanore and Aunt Mag (I'm sure they would be holding hands), the Beatles (Eleanore giving them yet one more suspicious look), Mel Torme, my daughter Debbie, Jack, Cookie Warren and my sister Barbara, Johnny Meyer, and Harry Truman.

And if we had to freeze it today, what would we focus on? And whom? Madonna? Cyndi Lauper? Maybe Whitney Houston. Yes, I think, Whitney. I'll tell you why.

I watched her on television the other night, and I couldn't believe it. I used to go night after night to watch her perform with her mother, Cissy Houston, at Sweetwaters, and Whitney would stand there banging a tambourine against one hip and going "Oo-oo-oo." And Cissy would keep saying, "She's not ready yet, she's not ready yet." So she kept working with her. Debbie said, "Mother, Whitney's got such a great voice."

Clive Davis of Arista records thought so too. He took an unbelievable amount of time in selecting the right songs, the way Johnny did for me, for Whitney to sing. When the album was released, he sent her out on tour, to small places, to let her have experience in performing. She learned how to *move*. She learned how to project emotion. She learned it all, so that when the album broke, she was ready for stardom. And there she is.

It's exciting to watch this happen. To see it pass from generation to generation, to see a new generation emerging. So, freeze-frame on Whitney Houston.

At the moment I am writing this, people are decrying the state of the arts. Broadway is bombing, the record business is down, fewer movies are being produced, television ratings are ominous.

And "Baby Doc" Duvalier was kicked out of Haiti.

Coming out of a movie theater, the prime minister of Sweden was assassinated by the Red Brigade.

The election of Philippines president Marcos was challenged by his adversary, Mrs. Corazon Aquino. And she finally succeeded in becoming the new president of the Philippines.

(The downfall of two regimes, I observed, came about in part due to the shopping excesses of Mrs. Duvalier and Mrs. Marcos.)

The one thing I've learned in this business—and in this life—is: Whenever you say, nothing is going to happen—*something* happens.

I, for one, can't *wait* to see how Mrs. Aquino makes out.

And whether Barbra Streisand will star in the movie version of her life.

Discography

Capitol Records

126 That Old Black Magic/Hit the Road to Dreamland (Freddie Slack)

134 My Ideal/Without Love (Billy Butterfield)

146 Silver Wings in the Moonlight/Furlough Fling (Freddie Slack)

160 Swinging on a Star/Ain't That Just Like a Man (Freddie Slack)

182 Moonlight in Vermont/There Goes That Song Again (Billy Butterfield)

214 It Might as Well Be Spring/How Deep Is the Ocean (Paul Weston)

240 All Through the Day/In Love in Vain (Carl Kress)

247 Can't Help Lovin' Dat Man/Come Rain or Come Shine (Paul Weston)

269 When You Make Love to Me/Along With Me (Jerry Gray)

294 For You, For Me, Forevermore/Passe (Jerry Gray)

324 Guilty/Oh, But I Do! (Jerry Gray)

350 Beware My Heart/What Am I Gonna Do About You? (Frank DeVol)

383 Spring Isn't Everything/Time After Time (Frank DeVol)

410 Old Devil Moon/Ask Anyone Who Knows (Frank DeVol)

427 What Are You Doing New Year's Eve?/Don't Tell Me (Frank DeVol)

438 You Do/My Future Just Passed (Frank DeVol)

461 So Far/Lazy Countryside (Frank DeVol)

15003 God Bless America (The Pied Pipers; Paul Weston)/Freedom Train (Johnny Mercer; Benny Goodman; Peggy Lee; The Pied Pipers; Paul Weston)

15010 Pass That Peace Pipe/Let's Be Sweethearts Again (Frank DeVol, Crew Chiefs)

15024 Now Is the Hour/But Beautiful (Frank DeVol)

15038 Gypsy in My Soul/What's Good About Good-bye?

15058 Please Don't Kiss Me/April Showers (Frank DeVol)

10579 It's You or No One/Nobody But You (Frank DeVol, Crew Chiefs)

15122 A Tree in the Meadow/I'm Sorry, But I'm Glad (Frank DeVol)

15146 Look for the Silver Lining (Paul Weston)/There's Something About Midnight (Frank DeVol)

15209 Heat Wave/What Did I Do? (Frank DeVol, Crew Chiefs)

15222 Moonlight in Vermont/My Ideal (Billy Butterfield)

15278 Far Away Places/My Own True Love (Frank DeVol, Crew Chiefs)

15350 Make a Miracle/Frankie and Johnny (Duet: Jack Smith)

15364 When the Angelus Is Ringing/My Dream Is Yours

15386 Forever and Ever/Dreamer With a Penny (Frank DeVol)

15394 It's a Big, Wide, Wonderful World (Duet: Jack Smith)/Sunflower (Solo: Jack Smith; Orchestra: Frank DeVol)

15401 Comme Ci, Comme Ca/Great Guns (Frank DeVol)

15426 Story of My Life/When Is Something

57-542 A Wonderful Guy/Younger Than Springtime (Frank DeVol; The Jeff Alexander Singers)

57-596 A Wonderful Guy (Frank DeVol; The Jeff Alexander Singers)/ Some Enchanted Evening (Solo: Gordon MacRae; Paul Weston)

57-598 A Cock-Eyed Optimist (Frank DeVol)/Younger Than Spring-time (Solo: Gordon MacRae; Paul Weston) (57-596 and 57-598 are part of the album *South Pacific*/CD 162)

567 (78) Baby, It's Cold Outside/I Never Heard You Say
582 (45) (Duet: Johnny Mercer; Paul Weston)

57-590 It Happens Every Spring/Everytime I Meet You (Frank DeVol)

57-666 Let's Take an Old-fashioned Walk/Paris Wakes up and Smiles (Frank DeVol Orchestra)

57-709 Whirlwind/Dime a Dozen (Frank DeVol)

57-724 It's a Most Unusual Day/St. Louis Blues

57-748 Three Rivers/It Happened at the Festival of Roses

57-776 Sun Is Always Shining (Frank DeVol; Mellow Men)/Sorry (Frank DeVol)

57-40224 Slipping Around/Wedding Bells (Duet: Jimmy Wakely)

57-40246 I'll Never Slip Around Again/Six Times a Week and Twice On Sunday (Duet: Jimmy Wakely)

78-783 Ain't We Got Fun/Lucky Us (Duet: Bob Hope; Billy May)

800 Broken Down Merry-Go-Round/Gods Were Angry with Me (Duet: Jimmy Wakely)

809 You're an old Smoothie/He's Funny That Way (Frank DeVol)

841 I Said My Pajamas (Duet: Frank DeVol; Jud Conlon Singers)/Be Mine (Frank DeVol)

851 Solid as a Rock (Frank DeVol; Jud Conlon Singers)/Sure Thing (Frank DeVol)

874 It Might as Well Be Spring/How Deep Is the Ocean (Paul Weston)

879 Come Rain or Come Shine/Dream Peddler's Serenade (Paul Weston)

934 My Foolish Heart/Stay with the Happy People (Frank DeVol)

960 Let's Go to Church (Next Sunday Morning)/Why Do You Say Those Things (Duet: Jimmy Wakely)

1027 I Gotta Get Out of the Habit (Frank DeVol; Les Baxter Chorus)/ Razz-A-Ma-Tazz (Frank DeVol)

1041 Shawl of Galway Grey/If You Were Only Mine (Lou Busch)

1042 Home Cookin'/Blind Date (Duet: Bob Hope; Billy May; The Starlighters)

1065 Close Your Pretty Eyes/Fool's Paradise (Duet: Jimmy Wakely)

1103 I Didn't Know What Time It Was/This Can't Be Love (Frank DeVol)

1123 You're Mine You/I've Forgotten You (Frank DeVol; Les Baxter Chorus)

1132 Let's Do It Again (Joe "Fingers" Carr and The Carr-Hops)/Friendly Star (Frank DeVol)

1160 Don't Rock the Boat, Dear/I'm in Love with You (Duet: Dean Martin; Frank DeVol)

1213 I've Never Been in Love Before/The Best Thing for You

1234 A Bushel and a Peck/Beyond the Reef (Duet: Jimmy Wakely)

1255 Silver Bells/Christmas Candy (Duet: Jimmy Wakely)

1309 Once You Find Your Guy/Man Ain't A-Nothin' But a Wolf (Frank DeVol)

1343 The Moon Was Yellow/Over and Over (Frank DeVol)

1382 Easter Parade/Let's Go to Church (Duet: Jimmy Wakely)

1391 Faithful/Lonesome Gal (Frank DeVol)

1417 You Are One/Sing You Sinners

1469 We Kiss in a Shadow/Make the Man Love Me (Lou Busch)

1491 Hello, Young Lovers/Something Wonderful (Lou Busch)

1500 Till We Meet Again/When You and I Were Young Maggie Blues (Duet: Jimmy Wakely)

1555 Star of Hope/Why Am I Losing You (Duet: Jimmy Wakely)

1566 Hoppy, Topper, and Me/This Little Pig (Lou Busch)

15885 Everlasting/End of a Love Affair (Lou Busch)

1643 Slipping Around/Wedding Bells (Duet: Jimmy Wakely)

16445 It Might as Well Be Spring/How Deep Is the Ocean (Paul Weston)

1702 River Road 2-Step/Good Morning Mr. Echo (Lou Busch)

1784 And So to Sleep Again/Beer Barrel Polka (Lou Busch)

1801 More! More! More!/Bill

1816 Let's Live a Little/I Don't Want to Be Free (Duet: Jimmy Wakely)

1845 That's for Sure/If I Can Love You (Lou Busch)

1939 'Round and 'Round/Oops

1965 Give Me More, More, More of Your Kisses/Let Old Mother Nature Have Her Way (Duet: Jimmy Wakely)

1984 Foggy River/Try Me One More Time

2000 I'll Walk Alone/I Could Write a Book

2177 The Gods Were Angry with Me/Till We Meet Again (Duet: Jimmy Wakely)

2217 Outside of Heaven/Alone Together (Lou Busch)

2292 Why Don't You Believe Me?/Come Back to Me, Johnny (Lou Busch)

2331 Take Care My Love/Singing Bells (Lou Busch)

2402 Gomen-Nasai/I Learned to Love You Too Late (Duet: Jimmy Wakely)

2489 Something Wonderful Happens/Where Did He Go? (Nelson Riddle)

2528 My Heart Knows/When Love Goes Wrong (Jimmy Wakely, Buddy Cole Orchestra)

2550 Waltz to the Blues/C.O.D. (Nelson Riddle)

2599 I Just Love You/The Night Knows No Fear (Nelson Riddle)

2681 The Isle of Skye/Moonlight in Vermont (Lou Busch)

2689 The Tennessee Churchbells/There's a Silver Moon on the Golden Gate (Duet: Jimmy Wakely)

2717 I Speak to the Stars/It's Nice to Have You Home (Nelson Riddle)

2853 Joey/Ask Me (Nelson Riddle)

2869 An Affair of the Heart/How Long Has It Been? (Nelson Riddle)

2913 Can This Be Love/All I Want Is All There Is and Then Some (Nelson Riddle)

2996 My Own True Love (Tara's Theme from *Gone With the Wind*)/ My Son, My Son (Nelson Riddle)

3067 Stowaway/Allah Be Prais'd (Nelson Riddle)

3189 Man/Mama's Pearls (David Cavanaugh)

3232 Lover, Lover/I Kiss You a Million Times (Nelson Riddle)

3314 I Love a Mystery/Bidin' My Time (Frank DeVol)

3412 The Second Time in Love/Old Enough (Frank DeVol)

3473 True Love (Buddy Bregman)/Haunting Love (Frank DeVol)

3509 Hello, Young Lovers/We Kiss in a Shadow (Lou Busch) (Reissue)

3586 The Money Tree/Maybe I Love Him (Billy May)

3666 Spring in Maine/Tippy-Toe (Billy May)

3905 Silver Bells/Christmas Candy (Duet: Jimmy Wakely)

90033 Have Yourself a Merry Little Christmas/Mistletoe Kiss Polka (Frank DeVol)

4638 Who Can? You Can!/On Second Thought (Ralph Carmichael)

Singles from Album #BD-51, Margaret Whiting Sings Rodgers and Hart (Conductor: Frank DeVol)

20114 My Romance/I Didn't Know What Time It Was

20115 My Heart Stood Still/This Can't Be Love

20116 Little Girl Blue/Thou Swell

20117 My Funny Valentine/Lover

From Album #CD-49

10088 April Showers

ALBUMS

BD-10 *Gershwin*

CD-41 *Jerome Kern's Music*

CD-49 *Somebody Loves Me*

BD-51 *Margaret Whiting Sings Rodgers and Hart*

H-209 *Margaret Whiting Sings Rodgers and Hart* (LP)

H-234 *Margaret Whiting Sings* (LP)

T-410 *Love Songs by Margaret Whiting* (LP)

T-685 *Margaret Whiting Sings for the Starry-Eyed* (LP)

JM-6053 *I'll Never Slip Around Again* (Duets: Jimmy Wakely) (Hilltop Records' pressing of Capitol tracks)

EP's

EAP-1-403 *Margaret Whiting and Jimmy Wakely* (features Slipping Around)

EAP-1-410 *Love Songs by Margaret Whiting* (features It Might As Well Be Spring)

EAP-1-685
EAP-2-685 } *Margaret Whiting Sings for the Starry-Eyed*
EAP-3-685

Some collections featuring Margaret Whiting:*

MFP-1432 *Nat, Dean and Friends* (Nat "King" Cole, Helen O'Connell, and Dean Martin)

W-9028 *Merry Christmas* (Nat "King" Cole, Jimmy Wakely, and others)

H-9102 *Today's Top Hits by Today's Top Artists* (featuring Ray Anthony, Tennessee Ernie Ford, Helen O'Connell, Nat "King" Cole, and others)

H-9114 *Today's Top Hits by Today's Top Artists* (featuring Jan Garber, Nat "King" Cole, Jimmy Wakely, Bob Manning, Les Paul, Ella Mae Morse, and others)

*also featured in several volumes of Capitol's *Just for Variety* series

Albums

Capitol (additional LPs featuring Margaret Whiting)

T 1042 *Let's Go to Church* (featuring Gordon MacRae, Tennessee Ernie Ford, Jane Froman, Jimmy Wakely, Faron Young)

SLB-6952 *The Great Girl Singers* (featuring Martha Tilton, Jo Stafford, Andrews Sisters, Peggy Lee, Helen O'Connell, The King Sisters)

Dot

DLP-25113 *Margaret*

DLP-25235 *Ten Top Hits*

DLP-3072 *Goin' Places*

DLP-3176 *Margaret Whiting's Great Hits*

DLP-3337 *Just a Dream*

HLP-12143 *My Ideal* (Hamilton Records/Dot tracks)

MGM Records

E/SE 4006 *Past Midnight*

E-4243 *The Very Best of Lerner and Lowe* (also features Gene Kelly, David Rose, Mel Torme)

Verve

MG-V-4038-2 *Margaret Whiting Sings the Jerome Kern Song Book* (Russ Garcia)

MG V-2146 *Broadway, Right Now!* (Margaret Whiting and Mel Torme)

London

PS 497 *The Wheel of Hurt*

PS 510 *Maggie Isn't Margaret Anymore*

PS 527 *Pop Country*

RCA Victor

CPL 2-0362 *The Big Band Cavalcade Concert* (Margaret Whiting, Frankie Carle, Bob Crosby, Freddy Martin)

Singles

Dot Records

45-15680 I Can't Help It (If I'm Still in Love with You) (Billy Vaughn)/
That's Why I Was Born (Milton Rogers)

45-15742 Hot Spell/I'm So Lonesome I Could Cry

45-15826 I Love You Because/The Waiting Game

Verve Records

V-10230X45 Hey, Look Me Over/What's New at the Zoo? (Duet: Mel
Torme; Russell Garcia Orchestra)

London Records

10815 Somewhere There's Love/If This Is Goodbye (Arnold Goland)

101 The Wheel of Hurt/Nothing Lasts Forever (Arnold Goland)

106 The World Outside Your Arms/Just Like a Man (Arnold Goland)

108 Only Love Can Break a Heart/Where Do I Stand? (Arnold Goland)

115 I Almost Called Your Name/Let's Pretend (Arnold Goland)

119 It Keeps Right On A-Hurtin'/I Hate to See Me Go (Arnold Goland)

122 Faithfully/Am I Losing You? (Arnold Goland)

124 Can't Get You Out of My Mind/Maybe Just One More (Arnold
Goland)

126 Where Was I/Love's the Only Answer (Arnold Goland)

128 Love Has a Way/At the Edge of the Ocean (Arnold Goland)

132 (Z Theme) Love Goes On/By Now (Arnold Goland)

137 Until It's Time for You to Go/I'll Tell Him Today

Albums

Audiophile

AP-152 *Too Marvelous for Words*

AP-173 *Come a Little Closer*

DIAP-207 *The Lady's in Love with You*

RB4-033-3 *Reader's Digest*
PIRS-6025 *Great Ladies of Song*
RCA Victor

Cassette just reissued:

4XL-0404 *Margaret Whiting's Greatest Hits*
Capitol Records

Index

Index